Biological Report 30
May 1995

Ecology of Maritime Forests of the Southern Atlantic Coast:
A Community Profile

By

Vincent J. Bellis

Janet R. Keough, Project Officer
National Biological Service
Southern Science Center
700 Cajundome Blvd.
Lafayette, Louisiana 70506

U.S. Department of the Interior
National Biological Service
Washington, D.C. 20240

Contents

Figures

Tables

Preface

This is a synthesis of scientific information and literature concerning the maritime forests of the southern Atlantic Coast of the United States. Information was gathered from many sources, including published scientific literature, dissertations and theses, government agency reports and newsletters, and unpublished reports.

Maritime forests are among the rarest and least studied coastal biological communities. Even the term "maritime forest" remains ill-defined. Maritime forest8 are largely confined to barrier islands and ocean-fringing sand dune systems. Published studies pertaining specifically to maritime forest are rare; however, much information about maritime forest origin, development, and ecological function is contained in the literature dealing with barrier islands. Most information about maritime forests is descriptive in nature. Basic concepts about the causes of community zonation, the pattern of ecological succession, the origin of wildlife populations, the degree of genetic isolation among animal populations, the ecological significance of feral animal populations, and the possible barrier-island stabilizing of maritime forests remain unresolved and controversial.

On the Atlantic Coast of the United States, the maritime forest resources have been neither identified nor inventoried. Thus, there is a real danger that most maritime forest habitat not currently protected by design or by accident (inclusion within areas protected for other reasons) will be destroyed or at least functionally impaired by urban development by the end of this century.

This reports provides an understanding of the geological processes and environmental conditions needed to evaluate controversies related to maritime forest ecology and management. The information should be most useful to persons who desire, in a single source, a synopsis of the existing literature and will provide a useful source of information for persons whose duty is to interpret maritime forests to visitors.

Since some of the important literature is obscure, a reference section rather than the usual list of literature cited has been provided. The final chapter enumerates some of the information gaps and suggests some specific research needs. We hope this publication will stimulate additional support for critically needed long-term and experimental research on understanding the ecological structure and ecosystem functions of maritime forests.

This community profile was originally intended to be a part of one in a series coordinated by the U.S. Fish and Wildlife Service's National Wetlands Research Center, now the National Biological Service's Southern Science Center. Questions or comments about this community profile or others in the series should be directed to:

Director
National Biological Service
Southern Science Center
700 Cajundome Boulevard
Lafayette, Louisiana 70506

Ecology of Maritime Forests of the Southern Atlantic Coast: A Community Profile

by

Vincent J. Bellis

Department of Biology
East Carolina University
Greenville, North Carolina 278.58-4353

Janet R. Keough

Project Officer
National Biological Service
Southern Science Center
700 Cajundome Boulevard
Lafayette, Louisiana 70506

Abstract.   Maritime forests dominated by broadleaved evergreen trees and shrubs occur in a discontinuous narrow band along the barrier islands and on the adjacent mainland from North Carolina to Florida. The flora and fauna of maritime forests typically consist of a distinctive subset of the regional biota that is particularly well adapted to survive the elevated salt content, limited availability of fresh water, soil erosion and dune migration, periodic seawater inundation, and wind damage associated with oceanic storms. Maritime forests cover the more stable portions of barrier islands and coastal dune ridges. They function as refugia for wildlife, provide storage capacity for groundwater, and help stabilize the soil. Recent recognition of the relatively greater physical stability of maritime forests compared to the beachfront has resulted in intensified urban development within them. Maritime forests across the range have been increasingly impaired by clearing for roads and parking lots and fragmented by subdivision development. Further development within maritime forests should minimize impairment of their critical biological and ecological functions. Maritime forest management should be directed toward reducing forest fragmentation and toward protecting their ecological integrity.

CHAPTER 1.

General Introduction

Definitions

"Maritime forest" is a broadly inclusive term that can be used to distinguish woody vegetation growing near any of the world's oceans. These forests often exhibit canopy height limitations resulting from salt-aerosol impact and have been distinguished from other types of coastal forest on the basis of differences in growth form and the relative abundance of particular woody plant species. The concept of which forests are "maritime forests" can vary widely, depending on the relative weighting of growth form and species composition. Wells (1939) described a "salt spray climax" community along the southeastern coast and noted that the geographic limits of this community corresponded closely with those of southern live oak *(Quercus virginiana)*, often a conspicuous component of the community. Several later authorities also emphasized the importance of evergreen oaks in this forest type: evergreen oak forest (Braun 1950) and maritime live oak forest (Bourdeau and Oosting 1959; Burk 1962a). Other authorities defined the type without mention of oaks: arborous zone of the salt spray community (Boyce 1954), maritime closed dunes (Raynor and Batson 1976), and upland maritime strand forest (Wharton 1978). An early description of the coastal forests of North Carolina (Pinchot and Ashe 1897) used the term "maritime" in its general, meaning "of the sea." Pinchot and Ashe apparently accepted more than one canopy type in their concept of maritime forest because they referred to the "maritime forests" of North Carolina.

Until recently, the question of defining maritime forest only inspired arcane debates among academicians. Currently, the issue has achieved practical significance as land-use planners and managers cope with the tasks of identifying and managing the remaining maritime forests.

The North Carolina Coastal Resources Commission (CRC) recently defined maritime forests (Appendix A) as "those woodlands that have developed under the influence of salt spray on barrier islands and estuarine shorelines." The CRC further differentiated maritime forests from inland forests by their adaptations to high wind velocities, salt-aerosol impact, and sandy soils characteristic of the coastal environment. Concomitantly, the North Carolina Natural Heritage Program developed a classification system (Schafale and Weakley 1990) for biological communities of the coastal zone that recognizes several related, yet distinguishable, communities within the limits of forests with maritime forest characteristics.

The following descriptive outlines are presented as an overview of the physiographic locations and general vegetation of maritime forest communities. The community types were defined on the basis of their physical and floristic expression along the North Carolina coast; the descriptions should serve, with appropriate modification, as a basis for distinguishing among maritime forests of the southern Atlantic coast of the United States (modified from Schafale and Weakley 1990).

Maritime Shrub Community

Location

Stabilized sand dunes, dune swales, and sand flats protected from saltwater flooding and most extreme salt spray.

Hydrology

Poorly to excessively drained sands. May have a high water table. Subject to heavy salt spray.

Vegetation

Dense growths of shrubs, most frequently *Myrica cerifera, Ilex vomitoria, Baccharis halimifolia, Juniperus virginiana, Zanthoxylum clava-herculis,* and stunted *Quercus virginiana.* Other species include *Toxicodendron (Rhus) radicans, Smilax* spp., *Parthenocissus quinquefolia, Vitis* spp., and *Callicarpa americana.*

Associations

May grade into maritime evergreen forest. May contain interdune ponds. Grades into or sharply borders on, dune grass on less protected or more actively moving dunes. Grades into or borders on dry or wet maritime grassland in areas that receive overwash. May grade into salt shrub in lower places subject to brackish or saltwater intrusions.

Distinguishing Features

Distinguished from maritime wet and dry grassland and dune grass by the natural dominance of shrub-sized woody vegetation and from maritime evergreen forest by its more exposed environment and lower stature. Boundary defined (by Schafale and Weakley 1990) at full canopy height of 5 m. Distinguished from salt shrub by its occurrence on upland sites only rarely and catastrophically subject to saltwater intrusion and by vegetation composition.

synonym

Maritime thicket.

Maritime Evergreen Forest

Location

Old, stabilized dunes and flats protected from saltwater flooding and the most extreme salt spray.

Hydrology

Terrestrial, xeric to mesic, well to excessively drained, subject to moderate to light salt spray.

Vegetation

Low to moderately high tree canopy, often stunted or pruned into streamlined shapes by salt spray, Dominated by combinations of *Quercus virginiana*, *Pinus taeda*, and *Q. hemisphnerica*, with a few other species. Typical understory species *Persea borbonia* (*sensu stricto*), *Carpinus caroliniana*, *Juniperus virginiana*, *Cornus florida*, *Osmanthus americanus*, *Ilex opaca*, *Prunus caroliniana*, and *Zanthoxylum clava-herculis*. Shrubs include *Ilex vomitoria*, *Myrica cerifera*, *Sabal minor*, and *Callicarpa americana*. Vines such as *Toxicodendron* (*Rhus*) *radicans*, *Vitis rotundifolia*, *Smilax* spp., *Parthenocissus quinquefolia*, *Bignonia* (*Anisostichus*) *capreolata*, *Berchenrin scandens*, *Ampelopsis nrborea*, and *Gelsemium sempervirens* are often important. The herb layer is sparse and low in diversity, with species such as *Mitchella repens*, *Asplenium platyneuron*, *Chasmanthium* (*Uniola*) *laxum*, *Piptochaetium* (*Stipa*) *avenacea*, *Galium pilosum*, *Dicanthelium* (*Panicum*) *commutatum*, *Elephantopus nudatus*, and *Passiflora lutea*.

Associations

Frequently grades into maritime shrub at more exposed edges. May border on dune grass or maritime grassland at the edge of actively moving sand dunes or overwash deposits. May grade into maritime swamp forest, maritime shrub swamp, or interdune pond in wet swalcs.

Distinguishing Features

Distinguished from maritime deciduous forest by the occurrence of *Quercus virginiana* and *Q. hemisphuerica* as the dominant and often only canopy hardwoods. *Pinus taeda* may occur in both types; its abundance is determined by natural and artificial disturbance. A southern variant of this forest type occurs in the Smith Island complex on the southern coast of North Carolina. This southern Variant includes *Sabal palmetto* as an important canopy dominant and becomes conspicuous further south in South Carolina and Georgia. Maritime evergreen forest is distinguished from maritime shrub by a tree canopy higher than 5 m. It is separated from maritime swamp forest and maritime shrub swamp by the dominance of the same suite of canopy species that are found in maritime evergreen forest. It is distinguished from coastal fringe evergreen forest by its occurrence on barrier islands or the ocean side of Peninsulas.

Synonym

Maritime forest.

Maritime Deciduous Forest

Locations

Most protected parts of old, stabilized dunes and beach ridges on widest barrier islands.

Hydrology

Terrestrial, dry to mesic, with little salt spray.

Vegetation

Forest dominated by mixtures of *Pinus taeda* and various hardwoods, particularly Quercus *falcata*, *Fagus grandifolia*, *Liquidambar styraciflua*, *Q. nigra*, *Carya glabra*, and *C. pallida*. Understory trees include *Carpinus caroliniana*, *Ilex opaca*, *Cornus jlorida*, *Vaccinium arboreum*, *Ostrya virginiana*, *Juniperus virginiana*, *Sassafras albidum*, and *Hamamelis virginiana*. Shrubs and vines include *Gaylussacia frondosa*, *Arundinaria gigantea*, *Callicarpa americana*, *Myrica cerifera*, *Rhus copallina*, *Vaccinium stamineum*, *Vitis rotundifolia*, *Toxicodendron* (*Rhus*) *radicans*, *Parthenocissus quinquefolia*, *Smilax bona-nox*, and *Gelsemium sempervirens*. The herb layer includes *Mitchella repens*, *Pteridium aquilinum*, *Prenanthes serpentaria*, *Asterpatens*, *Solidago* spp., *Panicum* sp., *Schizachyrium* (*Andropogon*) *scoparium*, *Desmodium* spp,, *Cnidoscolus stimulosus*, and *Galium hispidulum*.

Associations

Grades into maritime swamp forest, maritime shrub swamp, and interdune ponds in wet swales. May grade into maritime evergreen forest seaward.

Distinguishing Features

Sometimes regarded as similar to mesic forests inland and sometimes regarded as only one extreme of the maritime forest category. While both statements are true to some extent, this community includes many species not normally associated with the maritime environment, in a topographic and climatic environment not found inland. In general, differentiation of species along a topographic moisture gradient seems to be poorly expressed. Species occur here in associations not generally found inland. This may be a result of the more frequent disturbance, the continuous input of nutrients by salt spray, or the more moderate temperature.

Synonym

Maritime mesophytic forest.

Coastal Fringe Evergreen Forest

Locations

Flats and low hills near the mainland coast.

Hydrology

Terrestrial, mesic.

Vegetation

Forest dominated by various mixtures of *Quercus hemisphaerica*, *Q. virginiana*, and *Pinus taeda*. Other canopy trees include *Quercus falcata, Carya glabra, Q. nigra,* and *Pinus palustris. The* understory may include *Osmanthus americana, Persea borbonia* (sensu stricto), *Magnolia virginiana, Ilex opaca, Juniperus virginiana,* and *Sassafras albidum. The* most typical shrub is *Ilex vomitoria.* Other shrubs include *Myrica cerifera, Hamamelis virginiana, Sabal minor,* and species of the understory. Vines such as *Vitis rotundifolia, Smilax bona-nox, Gelsemium sempervirens,* and *Campsis radicans are* sometimes numerous. The herb layer is generally sparse and low in diversity; *Mitchella repens* and *Asplenium platyneuron* are most typical.

Associations

Frequently grades to coastal fringe sandhill on higher, drier sites. Usually grades into salt marsh or brackish marsh.

Distinguishing Features

Most easily distinguished from maritime evergreen forests by the mainland location. Floristically, somewhat to much more diverse than maritime evergreen forests. Distinguished from coastal fringe sandhills by a closed forest canopy structure and predominance of the canopy species listed under vegetation over the sandhill species. Distinguished from other mainland forest communities by the significant occurrence of species typically confined to maritime areas, such as *Quercus virginiana, Osmanthus americanus,* and *Ilex vomitoria.*

Synonym

Maritime forest.

Coastal Fringe Sandhill

Locations

Sandy areas such as relict beach-ridge systems, generally within a few kilometers of the coast. Less commonly on dry, sandy fluvial deposits, as in river floodplains.

Hydrology

Terrestrial, xeric because of excessive drainage.

Vegetation

Open to sparse canopy of *Pinus palustris,* sometimes with *P. taeda. Quercus virginiana may* form occasional to frequent clumps. Open to sparse understory dominated by *Quercus geminata, Q. laevis,* and *Q. hemisphaerica.* Other understory species may include *Sassafras albidum, Nyssa sylvatica, Q. incana, Q. margarettae,* and *Vaccinium arboreum.* Shrubs such as *Gaylussacia dumosa, Ilex glabra, Myrica cerifera, Ilex vomitoria,* and *Osmanthus americanus* may occur in sparse to dense patches. The herb layer varies with woody cover, with *Aristida stricta* usually the

dominant species. Other common herbs include *Rhynchospora* sp., *Schizachyrium (Andropogon) scoparium, Stipulicida setacea, Euphorbia ipecacuanhae, Stylisma (Bonamia) patens,* and *Cnidoscolus stimulosus.* Macrolichens such as *Cladonia evansii* and *Cladonia* spp., and sandhill mosses such as *Dicranum condensatum are* prominent and often dominate.

Associations

Grades into xeric sandhill scrub on the deepest, driest sands. Grades into maritime forest, pond pine woodland, or streamside pocosin in wetter places.

Distinguishing Features

Distinguished from pine-scrub oak sandhills and xeric sandhill scrub by the occurrence of maritime-associated species such as *Quercus geminata, Q. hemisphaerica, Q. virginiana, Ilex vomitoria,* and *Cladonia evansii;* appear to be confined to locations near the coast. Distinguished from wet pine flatwoods and mesic pine flatwoods by their structure, which includes a significant scrub oak component and less shrub and herb layer. They often have abundant lichens and bare sand.

synonyms

Sandhill, coastal scrub forest, pine-scrub oak sandhill.

Maritime Swamp Forest

Locations

Wet areas in well-protected swales, edges of relict dunes, and edges of freshwater embayments.

Hydrology

Palustrine, seasonally or intermittently flooded or saturated, to intermittently exposed.

Vegetation

Forest dominated by various wetland trees such as *Nyssa biflora, Acer rubrum, Liquidambar styraciflua, Fraxinus americana, Taxodium distichum, Pinus taeda, Quercus nigra,* and *Q. michauxii.* Understory trees and shrubs may include *Carpinus caroliniana, Persea borbonia, Myrica cerifera, Cornus foemina, Magnolia virginiana, Vaccinium fuscatum (atrococcum),* and *V. corymbosum. Arundinaria gigantea* may be common. Common vines include *Berchemia scandens, Toxicodendron (Rhus) radicans,* and *Vitis rotundifolia.* The usually sparse herb layer may contain *Woodwardia virginica, W. areolata, Osmunda cinnamomea, O. regalis var. spectabilis, Boehmeria cylindrica, Saururus cernuus, Mitchella repens,* and *Carex* spp.

Associations

Grades into maritime forest or maritime mesophytic forest, occurring as inclusions within them or between them and marsh.

Distinguishing Features

Distinguished by occurrence in nontidal maritime wetlands and its dominance by wetland trees other than *Persea palustris*.

Synonym

Swamp forest.

Maritime Shrub Swamp

Locations

Wet dune swales and depressions on barrier islands.

Hydrology

Palustrine, seasonally flooded or saturated to intermittently exposed.

Vegetation

Open to dense canopy of shrubs or small trees. *Persea borbonia* is the most typical dominant, although some areas are dominated by *Cornus foemina*. Occasional larger trees such as *Pinus taeda* or *Acer rubrum* may be present. Vines, particularly *Smilax* spp., *Toxicodendron (Rhus) radicans*, and *Berchemia scandens*, often form dense tangles above or among the shrubs. The sparse herb layer may contain *Osmunda cinnamomea*, *O. regalis* var. *spectabilis*, *Woodwardia virginica*, *Onoclea sensibilis*, or *Thelypteris palustris* var. *pubescens*. Clumps of *Sphagnum* may be common.

Associations

Usually surrounded by maritime evergreen forest or maritime deciduous forest. Occasionally may border on dune grass, marsh, or interdunal pond communities.

Distinguishing Features

Distinguished by its occurrence in maritime nontidal wetlands and its dominance by wetland shrubs or small trees.

Synonyms

Maritime swamp forest, bay forest.

Interdune Pond

Locations

Depressions in active or relict dune areas on barrier islands.

Hydrology

Permanently flooded to intermittently exposed. (Sometimes described as water table windows connected to the local groundwater system [Kling 1986].)

Vegetation

Varies with depth of water. Deep-water areas may have various floating or submerged aquatic plants, including *Azolla caroliniana*, *Ceratophyllum muricatum (echinatum)*, *Limnobium spongia*, *Riccia fluitans*, *Ricciocarpus natans*, *Spirodela polyrrhiza*, *Wolfiella gladiata (floridana)*, *Utricularia gibba (biflora)*, *Lemna gibba*, and *Hattonia inflata*. Shallow-water and intermittently exposed areas have various freshwater marsh species, such as *Leersia oryzoides*, *Eleocharis baldwinii*, *Typha angustifolia*, *Sacciolepis striata*, *Setaria magna*, *Hydrocotyle ranunculoides*, *Bidens frondosa*, *Triadenun (Hypericum) walteri*, *Lycopus rubellus*, *Boehmeria cylindrica*, *Thelypteris palustris* var. *pubescens*, *Zizaniopsis miliacea*, *Cladium mariscus* ssp. *jamaicense*, *Typha latifolia*, *Fimbristylis castanea*, *Juncus* spp., and *Polygonum* spp. Some pond margins have a border of shrubs and trees such as *Salix nigra*, *Acer rubrum*, *Nyssa biflora*, *Rosa palustris*, *Cephalanthus occidentalis*, and *Decodon verticillatus*. Some have been invaded by the aggressive weed *Phragmites australis (communis)*.

Associations

Small areas, surrounded by dune grass, maritime wet or dry grassland, maritime shrub swamp, maritime swamp forest, maritime evergreen forest, or maritime deciduous forest.

Distinguishing Features

Distinguished from maritime wet grasslands by having standing water all or much of the year and by vegetation; may be distinguished from the inland small depression ponds by their location on barrier islands. Distinguished from tidal freshwater marsh by the lack of fluctuation in water levels.

Synonyms

Dune marsh, dune swale, sedge.

Geographical Distribution

Maritime forests occur all along the Atlantic Coast of the United States. The distribution is not continuous. Forest cover is interrupted by bays and inlets, by narrow barrier island segments too unstable to support forest growth, and, increasingly, by urban development. Adjacent maritime forests are often floristically similar to one another and show strong floristic affinity with nearby mainland forests. On a finer scale, subtle floristic differences have been noted with respect to the relative abundance of plant species in nearby forests or on adjacent islands. The cumulative effect of these subtle floristic changes becomes evident when the maritime forest flora of Cape Cod, Massachusetts, is compared with that of Cape Canaveral, Florida. The extreme locations are quite different floristically, although the shifts in species composition are transitional and without sharp discontinuities.

Godfrey (1976a:8) described the floristic gradient along barrier islands of the Atlantic Coast of the United States (Fig. 1.1): as

The region from Maine to New Hampshire provides a meeting ground for typically southern species and those of the boreal north. In southeastern Maine, spruce and fir trees mingle on sand dunes with pitch pines and oaks. In general, the Maine barriers are part of the northern hardwoods region; those of northern Massachusetts and New Hampshire belong

to the Appalachian oak forest region. In southeastern Massachusetts, Rhode Island, New York, and New Jersey, the barrier island forest vegetation fits into the northeastern oak-pitch pine region. The transitional zone from the Delmarva Peninsula to North Carolina can be considered part of the southeastern oak-pine forest, but northern beach grass (*Ammophila breviligulata*) and deciduous oaks remain dominant.

From North Carolina to northern Florida and the gulf coast, the barrier island vegetation is part of the southeastern evergreen oak-pine subunit of the oak-hickory and southeastern pine forest. The presence of sea oats (*Uniola paniculata*) and live oak (*Quercus virginiana*) distinguishes this vegetation from that found inland. In south Florida, the flora of the Caribbean plays an important role in the vegetation, while on the gulf coast there is a rich coastal grassland.

State	Number of islands	Total acreage
Alabama	5	28,200
Connecticut	14	2,362
Delaware	2	10,100
Florida	80	467,710
Georgia	15	165,600
Louisiana	18	41,120
Maine	9	2,640
Maryland	2	14,300
Massachusetts	27	37,600
Mississippi		9,500
New Hampshire		1,100
New Jersey		48,000
New York		30,310
North Carolina		146,400
Rhode Island	6	3,660
South Carolina	35	144,150
Texas	16	383,500
Virginia	11	68,900
18 states	295	1,605,152

Fig. 1.1. Composite location map of barrier islands of the Atlantic coast of United States (U.S. Fish and Wildlife Service 1990).

Godfrey recognized three major barrier island sections that could be distinguished geographically and floristically as follows: (1) northern section (Maine to New Jersey), (2) transition or central section (Delmarva Peninsula), and (3) southern section (North Carolina to Florida). This report primarily addresses the southern section of the reef islands on the southeastern coast of the United States.

Godfrey further subdivided the southern section into four subsections based primarily on geomorphology. According to this subdivision, the Outer Banks of North Carolina extend from near the northern boundary of the state with Virginia south to Beaufort Inlet. The Outer Banks are readily exposed to oceanic storms and exhibit relatively high rates of barrier island retreat (Fig. 1.1). West and south of Beaufort Inlet to Cape Romain, South Carolina, the barrier islands are closer to the mainland, are generally more protected from oceanic storms, and support more stable dunes and more extensive maritime forest cover. The Georgia Embayment, south of Cape Romain, is characterized by low wave energies except during hurricanes. Here, the Sea Islands occupy the most protected section of the south Atlantic Coast. These islands typically consist of Holocene beaches attached to older Pleistocene beach ridges, and the oldest portions have remained stable long enough to develop fertile soils that support vigorous maritime forest cover. The northern Atlantic Coast of Florida above Jacksonville appears to represent an extension of the Sea Island system. Between Jacksonville and Cape Canaveral, maritime forests are scattered along a narrow barrier island system. Tropical species, including wild coffee (*Psychotria nervosa*), bloodberry (*Rivina humilis*), and naked wood (*Myrcianthus fragrans*), begin to appear as shrubs and small trees at Canaveral National Seashore. These and other tropical species increase in abundance, height, and species diversity farther south (A.F. Johnson, Florida Natural Areas Inventory, personal communication). South of Cape Canaveral, quartz sand beaches are replaced by increasing concentrations of carbonate sands, and the sand ridges are replaced by limestone. The barrier islands and beaches of Florida have become so completely modified by urban development and introduced exotic species such as Australian pine (*Casuarina equisetifolia*) that their predevelopment characteristics cannot be determined. In the Florida Keys, south of Miami, the maritime forest containing Virginia live oak (*Quercus virginiana*) is completely replaced by tropical evergreen forest and mangrove swamps.

Barrier Island Origins

Maritime forests of the southeastern United States develop almost exclusively on barrier islands or coastal sand ridges. Is this distribution pattern simply a fortuitous circumstance of geography, or are there certain characteristics associated with barrier island microclimates, hydrology, soils, and other factors contributing to development of that particular forest cover termed "maritime forest"? It is beyond the scope of this report to review the history of geological controversies concerning the origin of barrier islands; however, to appreciate the discussions of plant succession, faunal distribution, and community stability within maritime forests, a basic understanding is necessary.

A barrier island is a narrow strip of deposited sand located some distance offshore from the mainland. Barrier islands form along seacoasts throughout the world wherever there is an adequate supply of sand-size sediments, a low, sloping coastal plain, and a wave-dominated energy regime with tidal ranges of less than 3 m (S. R. Riggs, East Carolina University, personal communication; Bascom 1980). Barrier islands and maritime forests on them are geologically ephemeral features. Barrier islands are formed and maintained by changing sea level in three possible ways. First, when sea level remains relatively stable for some time, barriers may prograde seaward with a series of parallel beach ridges if there is a net surplus of sand, or they may migrate landward by shoreface erosion, overwash, and inlet migration processes if there is a net deficiency of sand. Second, when sea level is rising relative to land, landward migration processes dominate but at significantly increased rates. Third, when sea level is falling relative to land, the barrier island progrades seaward, leaving a series of parallel beach ridges, ultimately stranding the former barriers as a series of sand ridges above and behind a new barrier island system. Thus, the net retreat or advance of the shore is dependent on the availability of sand, as well as on changes in sea level.

Three different explanations are plausible for the origin of the southeastern barrier islands. Otvos (1970) presented evidence suggesting some Gulf of Mexico Coast barriers formed by emergence of submarine bars (Fig. 1.2). Hoyt (1967) suggested that most Atlantic Coast barrier islands originated by submergence of relict dune ridges (Fig. 1.3), whereas Fisher (1968) thought that they formed by progradation of sandspits entrained by headlands (Fig. 1.4). It became evident to Pierce and Colquhoun (1970) that these different explanations may not be mutually exclusive. Schwartz (1970) attempted to synthesize the explanations into a single conceptual model; thus the engulfed ridge of Hoyt became a "primary" barrier island, while Fisher's breached spit and Otvos's emergent bar became "secondary" barrier islands.

The barrier islands of the southeastern United States are now thought to represent complex features in which primary barrier islands are modified by numerous processes to produce complex secondary barriers. Pierce and Colquhoun

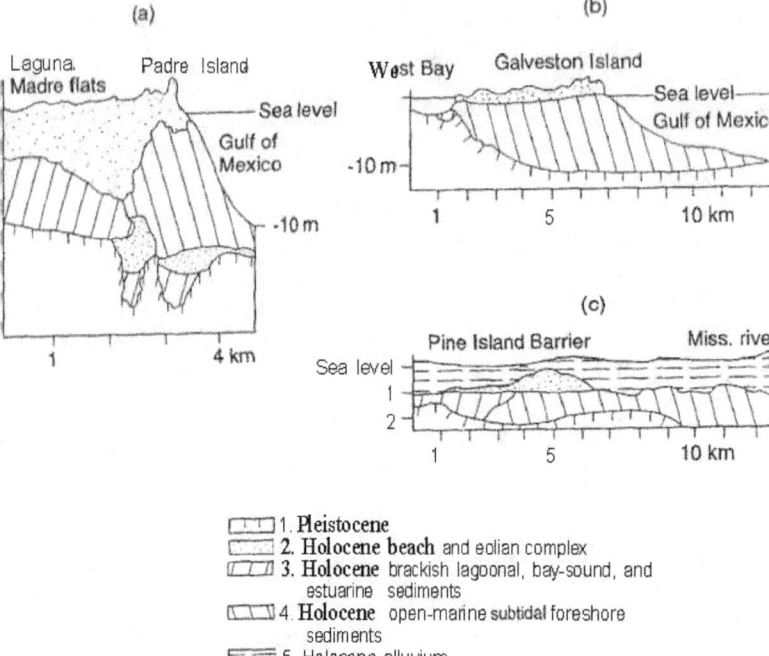

Fig. 1.2. Cross-sections of Gulf coast barrier islands. (a) = Padre Island; (b) = Galveston Island; and (c) = Pine Island (from Otvos 1970; used with permission of Geological Society of America).

☐ 1. Pleistocene
☐ 2. Holocene beach and eolian complex
☐ 3. Holocene brackish lagoonal, bay-sound, and
     estuarine sediments
☐ 4. Holocene open-marine subtidal foreshore
     sediments
≡ 5. Holocene alluvium

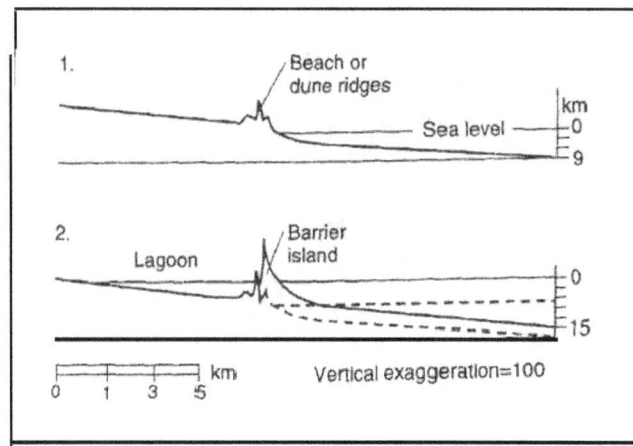

Fig. 1.3. Formation of barrier islands by submergence. 1. Beach or dune ridge forms adjacent to shoreline. 2. Submergence floods area landward of ridge to form barrier island and lagoon (from Schwartz 1971 after Hoyt 1967; used with permission of Geological Society of America).

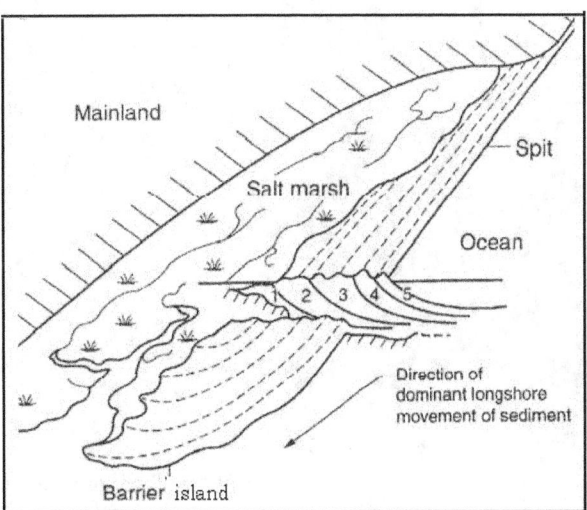

Fig. 1.4. Development of barrier islands (indicated by *dashed lines*) through breaching of complex spits (from Schwartz 1971 after Fisher 1968; used with permission of Geological Society of America). *Numbers* 1-5 indicate a series of prograded beaches.

(1970) consider the Outer Banks of North Carolina to have started as a primary barrier along a topographic high zone formed by an older barrier island during a temporary standstill associated with a previous Pleistocene sea level high. As the sea level rose during the last 5,000 years, the modern shoreline intercepted the older barrier and inundated the low-lying land behind, detaching it from the mainland. The present configuration of the North Carolina Outer Banks evolved by the modification and migration of this primary barrier and associated headlands and by formation of secondary barriers by spit progradation across shallow open bays on the Continental Shelf. Only about 40% of the present barrier consists of a modified primary barrier, and the remainder is of secondary origin (Fig. 1.5).

The Sea Islands of Georgia were described as compound barriers of relatively recent (4,000–5,000 years) Holocene barriers welded onto a core of older Pleistocene ridges (Fig. 1.6)(Johnson et al. 1974). Different-age portions of barrier islands can be distinguished on the basis of their soils. For example, Sea Island has poorly developed soil because of insufficient time for formation; on the other hand, St. Simon's Island has more mature soil to a depth of more than 2 m in places (Johnson et al. 1974).

South toward St. Augustine, Florida, Amelia and Little Talbot Islands are similar to the Sea Islands of Georgia. The modern sands of Little Talbot Island are welded onto the older Pleistocene core of Big Talbot Island.

The "drumstick" shape of the Sea Islands was interpreted by Hayes (1979) as a response to the relatively great tidal amplitude in the Georgia Embayment. Interaction of waves on the major ebb-tide deltas (formed by strong tidal currents through the inlets) leads to longshore drift and formation of curved beach ridges at the tips of the islands.

Florida has the longest coastline in the coterminous United States. The Atlantic coast north of Miami consists of sandy beaches fronting a chain of barrier islands (Figs. 1.7 and 1.8). The sands of the beaches north of Cape Canaveral were derived by southerly longshore sediment transport of quartz sands originally weathered from Piedmont rocks in Georgia and the Carolinas (Giles and Pilkey as cited in Johnson and Barbour, 1990). Like the barrier islands to the north, the Florida barrier islands seem to occupy locations determined by geological events of the Pleistocene (Johnston and Barbour 1990). From St. Augustine to Boca Raton, the modern barriers are perched on an underlying coquina ridge known as the Anastasia Formation. South of Boca Raton, the beach sediments are composed of a mixture of quartz sand and fragmented molluscan shell hash. The Pleistocene Anastasia Formation grades southward into Pleistocene oolites, a series of limestone units that occur at Miami and southward and form the substrate of the keys. Along the Florida Keys, the southern evergreen maritime forest is replaced by mangrove islets and palm-pine scrub.

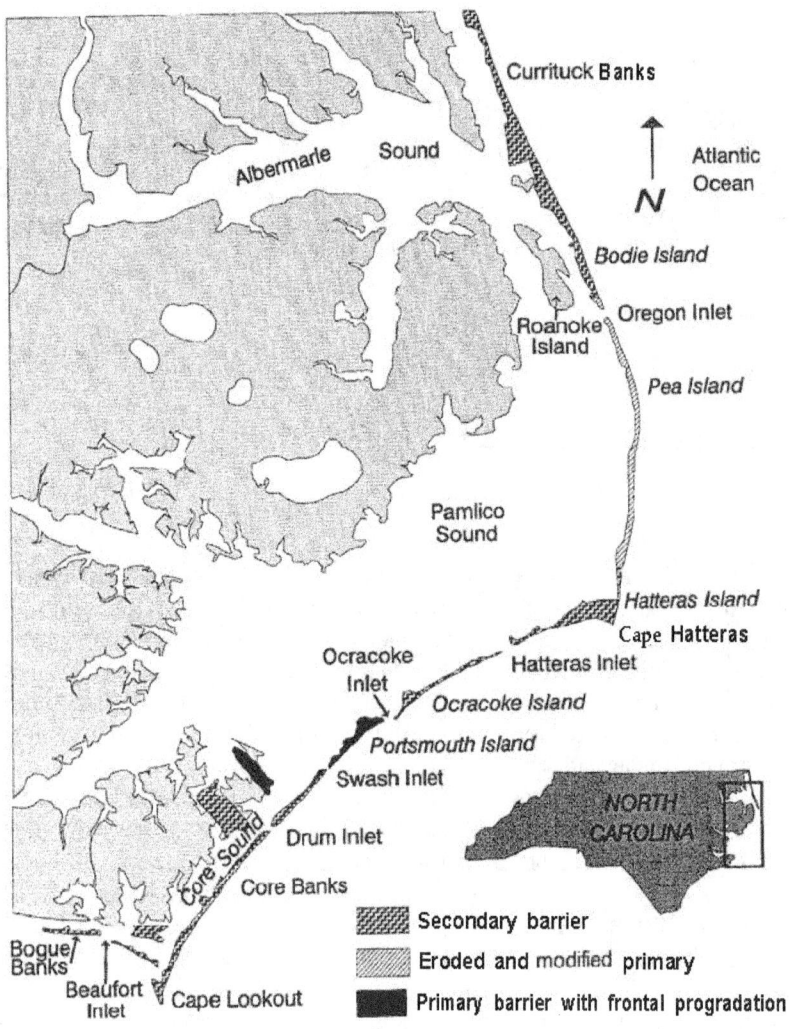

Fig. 1.5. Types of barrier islands forming the Outer Banks of North Carolina (from Pierce and Colquhoun 1970).

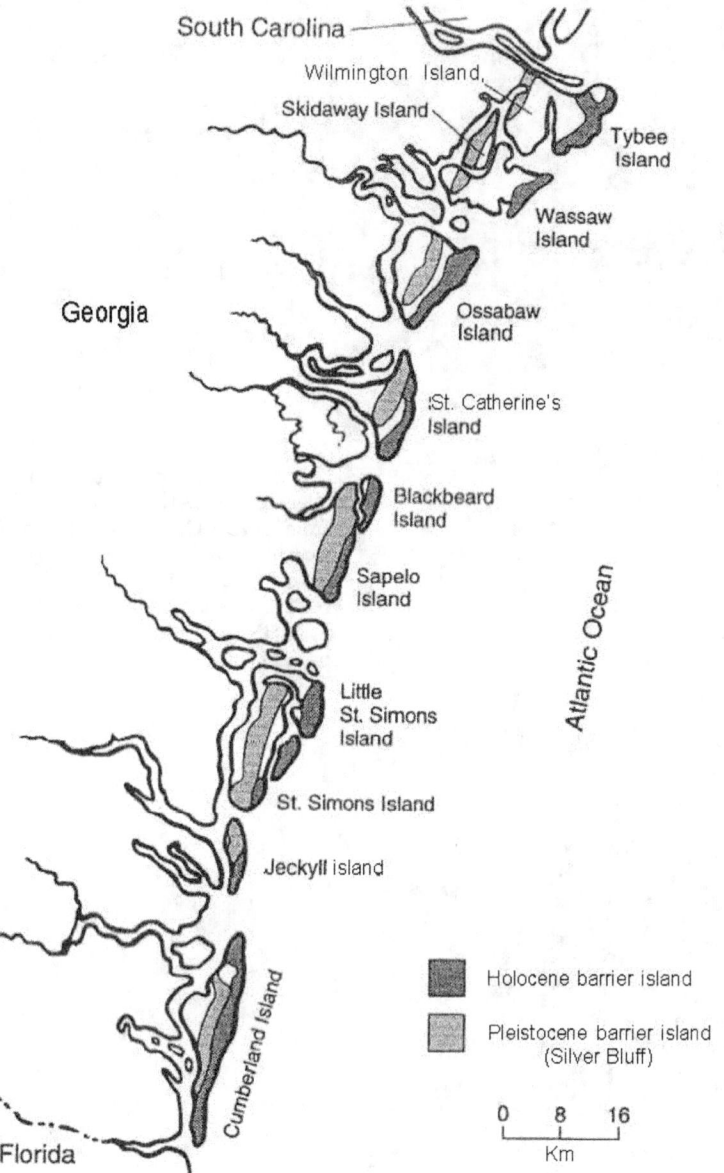

Fig. 1.6. Geologic age of the barrier islands (Sea Islands) of Georgia (modified from Johnson et al. 1974 after Hoyt 1968).

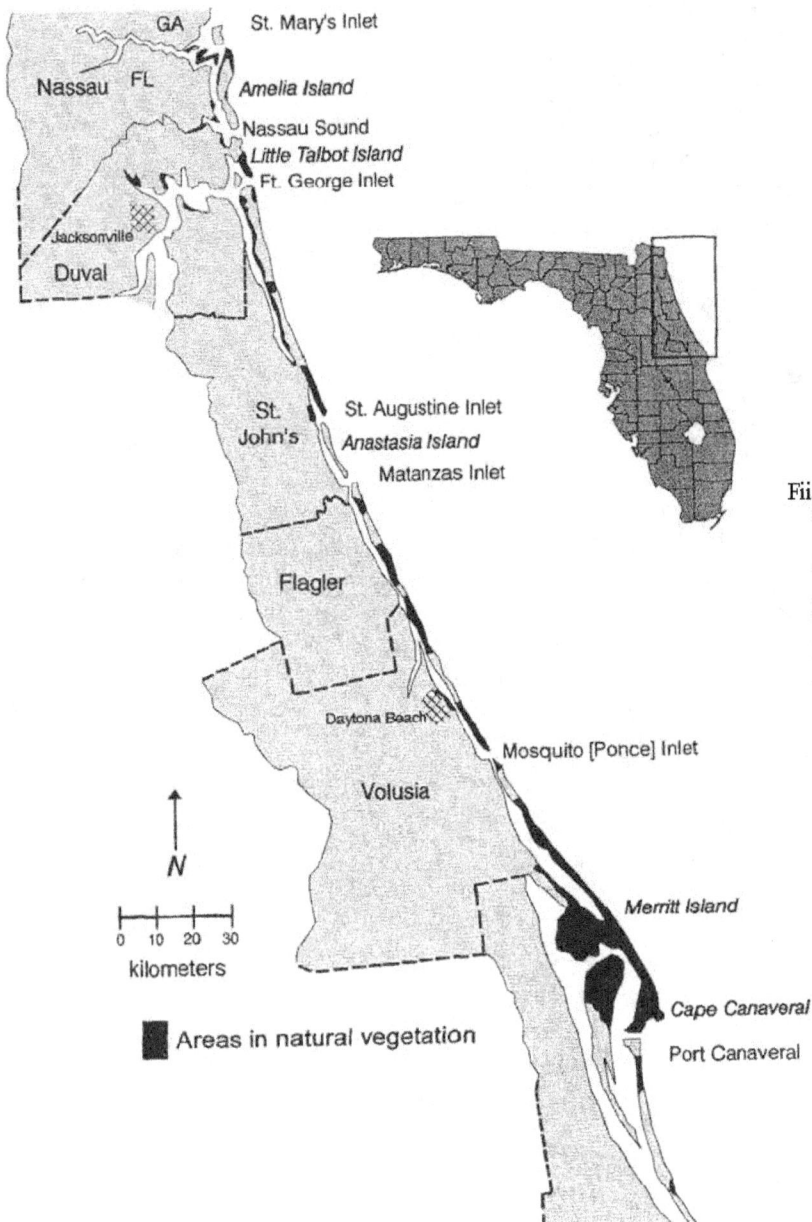

St. Mary's Inlet
Amelia Island
Nassau Sound
Little Talbot Island
Ft. George Inlet

St. Augustine Inlet
Anastasia Island
Matanzas Inlet

Mosquito [Ponce] Inlet

Merritt Island

Cape Canaveral
Port Canaveral

GA
FL
Nassau
Jacksonville
Duval
St. John's
Flagler
Daytona Beach
Volusia

N

0   10   20   30
kilometers

Areas in natural vegetation

Fii. 1.7. Areas of natural vegetation on barrier islands of the Atlantic coast of Florida from Duval County south to Volusia County (from Johnson and Barbour 1990). Several of these are state parks (SP), state recreation areas (SRA), national monuments (NM), national seashores (NS), and national wildlife refuges (NWR).

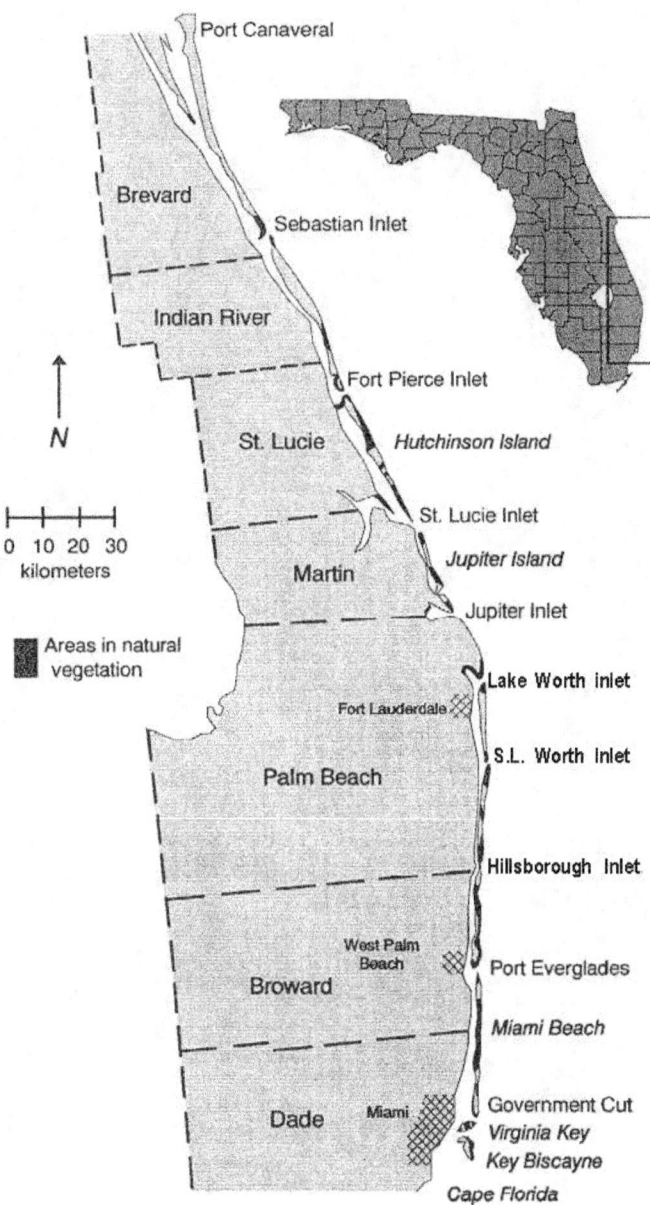

Fig. 1.8. Areas of natural vegetation on barrier islands of the Atlantic coast of Florida from Brevard County south to Dade County (from Johnson and Barbour 1900). See Fig. 1.7 for site label.

CHAPTER 2.

The Maritime Environment

Introduction

It is widely recognized that the biological communities almost exclusive to barrier islands owe their characteristic structure to some factor or combination of factors related to their maritime environment. Special environmental conditions associated with barrier-island environments typically include exposure to potentially toxic levels of salt; exposure to strong winds, shoreline erosion, and ocean overwash during storms; low levels of plant nutrients in the soil; low and unpredictable supply of freshwater; and unstable soil substrate that is subject to wind or water erosion. Along the southeastern coast of the United States, the proximity of the barrier islands to the warmer waters of the Gulf Stream results in a northerly shift in the frost line and winter temperatures that are somewhat higher than inland at a given latitude. The proximity of the barrier islands to the sea tends to dampen seasonal temperature extremes. Barrier islands also tend to be geologically unstable. Inlets open and fill, and entire islands slowly migrate before the advancing sea. Fire frequency may not be directly related to conditions of the maritime environment but can exert a significant impact on island biota.

Climate

On the barrier islands, geological processes determine the types of habitat available, whereas climate sets broad limits on such critical environmental conditions as temperature extremes, solar energy input and day length, storm exposure, and availability of fresh water.

The barrier islands of the Atlantic Coast between Virginia and the Florida Keys extend almost 1,600 km along a roughly north-south axis. The climate ranges from temperate to subtropical; most of the area is best described as warm temperate (Eastern U.S. road map).

South of Cape Hatteras, the maritime climate is influenced by the warmer water of the Gulf Stream, whereas north of the Cape, the nearshore zone is influenced to a greater extent by colder water moving south from the North Atlantic Ocean with the longshore Virginia Current. Biologists have long recognized this natural boundary in their distinction between "Virginian" and "Carolinian" biotas. Northeastern North Carolina represents a transition or tension zone between these two biotas. Many species of plants, as well as marine and terrestrial animals, reach their northernmost or southernmost range limit here and may exist as pairs competing for the same habitat. The presence of this transition zone may account for the greater diversity among plants and vertebrate animals along the northern barrier islands of North Carolina compared than in other locations along the southern barrier island system (Otte et al. 1984).

Another biotic effect of climate is a greater northerly range of southern and subtropical species along the barrier island chain than at comparable latitudes inland. The effect has been noted for maritime forests in New York (Greller 1977) and Florida (Greller 1980). In Florida, Greller (1980) mapped the distribution of three major upland broad-leaved forest types (Fig. 2.1). These were identified as tropical forest (tropical), temperate broad-leaved evergreen forest (evergreen), and southern mixed hardwood (hardwood). The tropical forest was dominated by evergreen and drought-deciduous tropical taxa

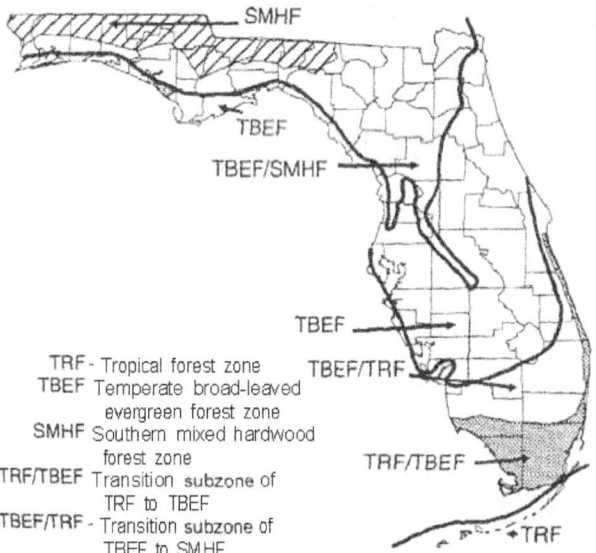

TRF - Tropical forest zone
TBEF Temperate broad-leaved evergreen forest zone
SMHF Southern mixed hardwood forest zone
TRF/TBEF - Transition subzone of TRF to TBEF
TBEF/TRF - Transition subzone of TBEF to SMHF

Fig. 2.1. Zones and subzones of broad-leaved forest in Florida.

(gumbo limbo *[Bursera simaruba]*, wild tamarind *[Lysiloma latisiliqua]*, mastic *[Mastichodendron foetidissimum]*, and stoppers *[Eugenia spp.]*), and was associated with a hot to very warm, subhumid to humid climate. The evergreen forest, dominated by live oak *(Quercus virginiana)* and palmetto palm *(Sabal palmetto)*, occurred under warm to very warm, subhumid to humid climatic conditions, The hardwood forest was dominated by southern magnolia *(Magnolia grandiflora)*, American beech *(Fagus grandifolia)*, pignut hickory *(Carya glabra)*, flowering dogwood *(Cornus florida)*, American holly *(Ilex opaca)*, and other taxa commonly found in the coastal plain forests of the Southeast. The hardwood forest occurred in association with a warm temperate and humid climate.

The boundaries between these climate regimes and associated forest types correspond best to the average daily minimum temperature of the coldest month (T_{min}). The boundaries defined by Greller (1977, 1980) (Fig. 2.2) were tropical ($T_{min} = 12°$ C), evergreen ($T_{min} = 10.5°$ C), and hardwood ($T_{min} = 5.5"$ C). The range limits of several indicator tree species in each of these forest types closely followed the appropriate isotherms (Fig. 2.3). Furthermore, the T_{min} isotherm boundaries bend sharply to the north immediately along the east coast of Florida. Each successive forest type extends much farther to the north along the east coast than along the west coast of Florida. This trend of southern plant species reaching a more northerly limit immediately along the coast than they do inland, appears to

extend northward at least as far as Cape Hatteras, North Carolina.

A comparison of climatological records for selected coastal locations along the southeastern Atlantic Coast (Table 2.1) indicates the range in climate regimes for maritime forests between Virginia and south Florida. Mean percentage (of maximum possible) sunshine and mean annual relative humidity vary little across the latitudinal gradient between Norfolk, Virginia, and Miami, Florida. Mean annual percentage (of maximum possible) sunshine is within ±3% of 65%, and mean relative humidity is within ±4% of 83% at all six locations (Ruffner and Blair 1977, USDC-NOAA 1974).

Mean annual precipitation ranges from 1,135 mm/year at Norfolk to 1,5 19 mm/year at Miami. The intervening locations precipitation of 1,334 ± 45 mm/year. Maximum precipitation occurs in July or August at all locations except in Miami where it occurs in June (Ruffner and Blair 1977, USDC-NOAA 1974).

Latitudinal differences of 6.1 to 8.4 km/s in mean annual wind velocity are probably insignificant; however, the recorded maximum wind velocity of record was highest at Jacksonville, Florida (87.5 km/s), but lowest at nearby Savannah, Georgia (47.3 km/s). Prevailing winds are from the west from Savannah northward, from the northwest in north Florida, and from the east at Miami (Ruffner and Blair 1977, USDC-NOAA 1974).

Temperature variables form the most conspicuous gradient along the latitudinal axis between Norfolk and

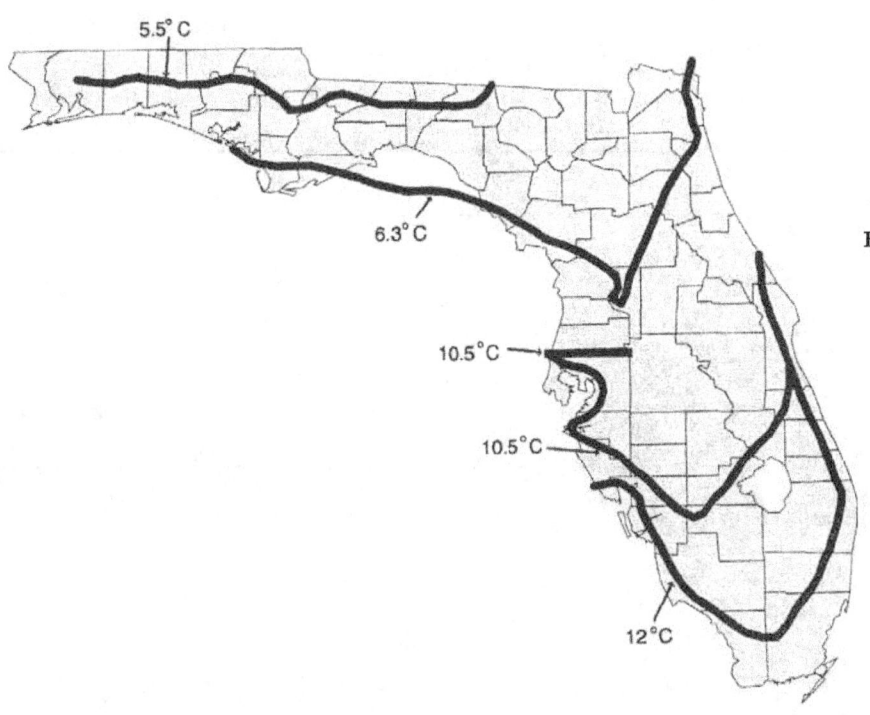

Fig. 2.2. Isotherms of 5.5°C, 10.5°C, and 12°C mean daily minimum temperature of the coldest month (T_{min}) in Florida (from Greller 1980; used with permission of Torrey Botanical Club).

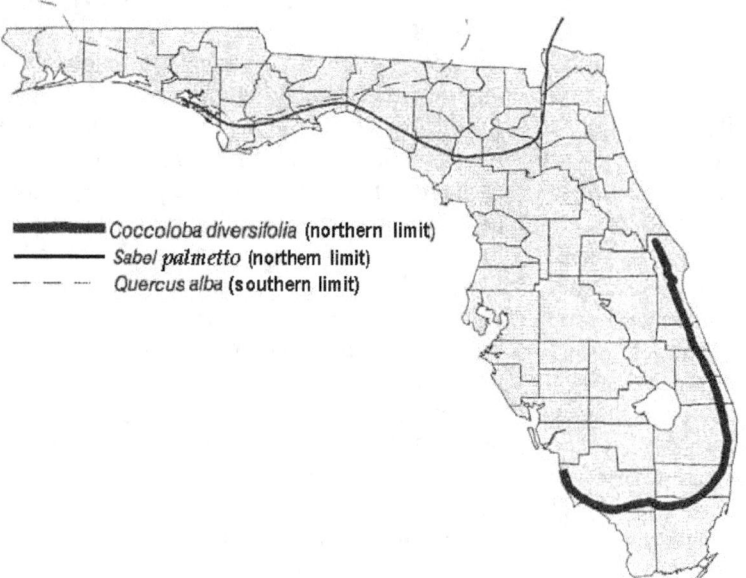

Coccoloba diversifolia (northern limit)
Sabel palmetto (northern limit)
Quercus alba (southern limit)

Fig. 2.3. Limits of the distribution of a tropical taxon (*Coccoloba diversifolia*), a temperate zone evergreen species (*Sabal palmetto*), and a temperate zone deciduous hardwood (*Quercus alba*) in Florida (from Greller 1980; used with permission of Torrey Botanical Club).

Miami. The mean annual temperature is 15.4" C at Norfolk and 24.0" C at Miami. Frost-free days range from 256/year at Norfolk to 313/year at Savannah to 365/year at Miami (Raffner and Blair 1977, USDA-NOAA 1974).

Given the ranges in climate variables noted previously, it seems reasonable to assume that growing season, length of exposure to freezing temperatures, and hurricane exposure may constitute the major climatic factors corresponding to variations in maritime forest biota. North of Cape Hatteras, the shoreline tends to face east and northeast, whereas south of that location the shore faces east, south, or southeast. Storm effects tend to be greatest when storm winds are onshore. Winter storm winds tend to come from the west and north, whereas summer winds come from the west and south. Along the Virginia and northern North Carolina coasts, storm damage often results from northeasters during spring months, while coastal residents south of Cape Hatteras tend to be more concerned by the threat of hurricanes from the southeast in late summer or autumn.

Table 2.1. Climatological data for selected Atlantic Coast locations of the southeastern United States (Ruffner and Blair 1977 and USDC-NOAA 1974).

Location	Temperature (°C) $\bar{x}$ Annual	$\bar{x}$ (Jan.)	$\bar{x}$ (July)	FFD[a]	Sunshine[b]	Precipitation (mm) Annual	Month of maximum	Humidity[d]	Direction[e]	Wind Velocity[f]	Maximum[g]
Norfolk, Va.	15.4	5.0	26.1	256	62	1,135	July	79	SW	7.6	55.8
Buxton, N.C.	16.8	8.3	25.6	296	63	1,384	Aug.	83	S	8.4	51.8
Charleston, S.C.	19.2	10.0	21.2	294	66	1,323	July	86	SW	6.3	51.0
Savannah, Ga.	19.1	11.1	27.2	291	63	1,308	Aug.	85	SW	6.1	47.3
Jacksonville, Fla.	20.8	13.3	28.3	313	62	1,295	July	85	NW	8.2	87.5
Miami, Fla.	24.0	19.5	27.8	365	67	1,519	June	81	E	6.6	53.3

[a] Freeze-free days.
[b] Annual possible percentage of sunshine.
[c] Month of maximum precipitation.
[d] Relative humidity (percent at 0100 local time annual mean).
[e] Direction of prevailing wind.
[f] Mean annual velocity (km/s).
[g] Maximum velocity (km/s), highest recorded.

Hurricanes form from tropical cyclones in the Atlantic, Caribbean, or Gulf of Mexico (Simpson and Lawrence 1974). Off the East Coast of the United States, hurricanes tend to follow the warmer, less dense air above the Gulf Stream. Since the Gulf Stream approaches closest to shore along the east coast of Florida and again off Cape Hatteras, North Carolina, these two areas serve as focal points for hurricane landfall (Fig. 2.4).

The effects of a major hurricane on forest trees were observed following Hurricane Camille, which struck the Gulf of Mexico Coast in 1969, and were described by Touliatos and Roth (197 1:288). Most of the direct damage to trees from hurricanes is caused by high-velocity wind. Camille came ashore with winds of over 89 m/s and a record storm surge as high as 6.7 m. Wind effects were evident for more than 160 km inland. Poorly anchored trees were uprooted, and well-anchored trees were stripped of their leaves. Secondary effects included salt-aerosol damage to foliage and flooding of root systems by brackish water.

Touliatos and Roth (197 1) concluded that a tree's ability to withstand hurricane winds was dependent on the strength of the wind, the size and shape of the crown, the extent and depth of the root system, the antecedent soil moisture content, and the shape of the bole. They assessed the degree and type of damage among 20 commonly occurring coastal native and ornamental trees. In terms of resistance to breakage, uprooting, salt damage, and subsequent susceptibility to insect attack and disease, live oak (*Quercus virginiana*) and palm (*Sabal palmetto*) consistently exceeded all other species. Live oak was described as having "exceedingly strong and resilient" wood (Fig. 2.5). "Palm trees," they noted, "offer little surface to the wind because they have almost no laterally extended crown. This characteristic makes them a fairly wind-resistant tree, despite their close and small root structure" (Touliatos and Roth 1971:288). Common shallow-rooted trees, including dogwood (*Cornus florida*), water oak (*Quercus nigru*), sweet bay (*Magnolia virginiana*), and red maple (*Acer rubrum*), were among the least resistant to hurricane damage.

Hurricane Camille's effects on forest canopy described by Touliatos and Roth were confirmed by the author of this report for Hurricane Hugo, which struck Charleston, South Carolina, in September 1989. I had visited the area in August to compare current vegetative cover on the Isle of Palms with the described vegetation (Coker 1905). Since 1905, the Isle of Palms has undergone intensive urban development, but much of the forest canopy had been left intact. Prior to the storm, many residential streets and lawns were deeply shaded by live oaks. Tall cabbage palms and loblolly pines were also abundant canopy trees. In November, after the storm, shrub vegetation that had been present in the interdune area between the beach and the first line of homes had been washed away or buried under sand. Almost all large pines were broken off about a meter above the ground.

Falling pine trees were a major cause of roof damage in Hurricane Hugo; roof damage then led to increased water damage to the inside of the houses. The storm surge of up to 5.5 m flooded the lower floors of most homes and resulted in irreparable damage to possessions

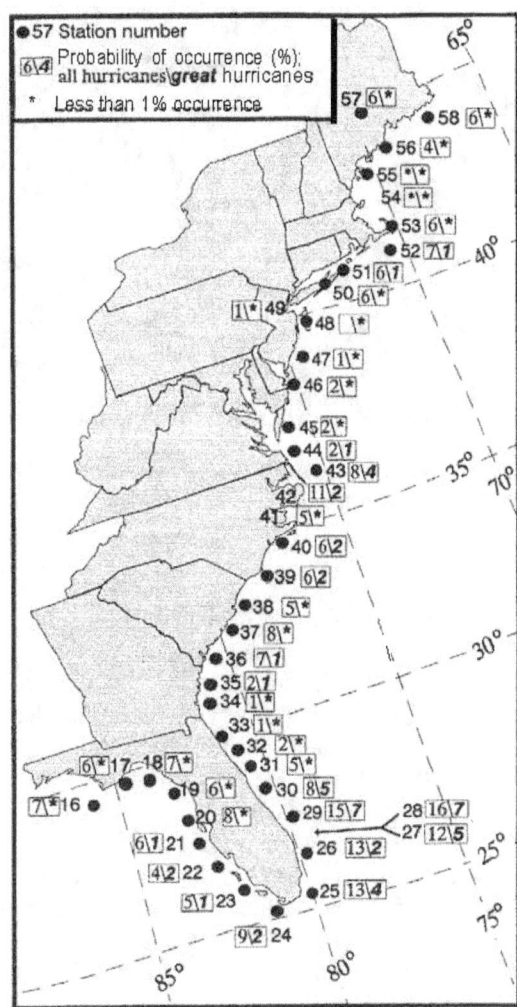

Fii. 2.4. Hurricane probability at numbered stations along the Atlantic and gulf coasts of the United States. The probability (expressed in percent) that a hurricane (winds exceeding 30 meters per second or 73 miles per hour) or a great hurricane (winds exceeding 56 meters per second or 125 miles per hour) will occur in any 1 year in an 80-km segment of coastline. (Modified from Simpson and Lawrence 1971 as cited in U.S. Department of Interior 1978.)

Fig. 2.5. This live oak *(Quercus virginiana)* near Monck's Corner, South Carolina, was defoliated by the winds of Hurricane Hugo in September 1989. The photo, taken in May 1990, shows new growth originating along the surviving branches (photo by author).

on the ground level. Some pines were simply uprooted and tipped over, resulting in structural damage to foundations and service lines. In contrast to the pines (Fig. 2.6), palms and live oaks remained. The surviving oaks were stripped of their leaves and leafy branches, and the palms stripped of most of their mature fronds. The nearly closed evergreen forest canopy of August now resembled more that of late autumn in a deciduous forest. These observations about the different survival of live oak and palm following damage by Hurricane Hugo were confirmed for the uninhabited Bulls Island, South Carolina (J. Nelson, University of South Carolina, personal communication).

I visited the Isle of Palms again in May 1990. Half a year after Hurricane Hugo struck, rebuilding was well under way, but some cleanup was still in progress. A contractor, who removed and burned fallen and damaged trees, estimated that 1.5 million cubic yards of wood and branch debris had been removed from the Isle of Palms and Sullivans Island (an area encompassing 1,024 ha of forested land), and he noted that most of the debris was

from pine trees. The typically greater frequency of live oak and palm within the canopy of southern barrier island forests may be related, at least partly, to the greater ability of these two species to survive storm damage.

Maritime forests and their sandy substrate are ultimately dependent for their origin and maintenance on changes in sea level. Sea level appears to respond to long-period oscillations in climate. The present barrier island system is thought to have assumed approximately its current location and configuration about 5,000 years ago, concomitant with a marked decline in the rate of sea-level rise from about 0.3 m/century to 0.1 m/century (Fig. 2.7).

At present, many scientists believe that the rate of sea-level rise may soon increase relatively rapidly to a level equal to or exceeding that existed before to the origin of the present barrier island system. Any significant increase in the rate of sea-level rise has obvious implications for maritime forests. If rising sea level hastens the process of barrier island migration, will maritime forests be able to keep pace? In more practical

Fig. 2.6. Loblolly pine *(Pinus taeda)* forest in Francis Marion National Forest, South Carolina, showing damage caused by Hurricane Hugo in September 1989 (photo by author).

terms, barrier island managers are already recommending that the lowest portions of barrier island segments, which are subject to overwash and flooding, be identified and that further development in such locations be discouraged (Cantral 1988). Because maritime forests typically occupy the highest, most stable portions of barrier islands, one result of such a policy may be to increase development on the few remaining maritime forests.

Oceanic Salts

The growth-inhibiting effect of salt has been thought to be a major ecological factor governing floristic zonation on barrier islands. Wells and Shunk (1938) reported that the dominant woody plants fronting the ocean (wax-myrtle [*Myrica cerifera*], yaupon [*Ilex vomitoria*], and live oak [*Quercus virginiana*]) were all more salt tolerant

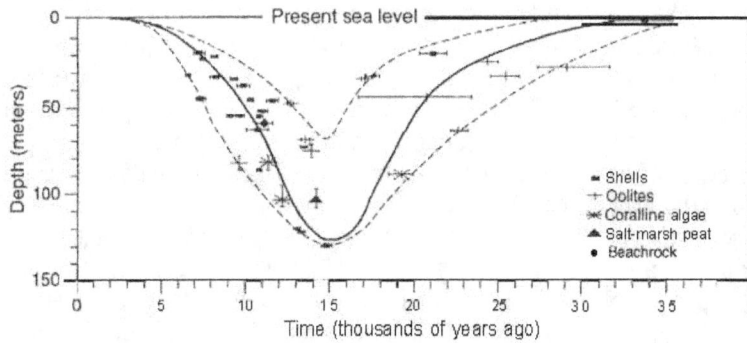

Fig. 2.7. Depths and ages of sea level indicators from the Atlantic Continental Shelf of the United States. The *solid line* is the inferred sea level curve for the past 35,000 years; the *dashed line* indicates range in sea level estimates inferred from the fossil record (adapted from Milliman and Emery 1968; used with permission of Science).

than loblolly pine (*Pinus taeda*), a tree that usually occurs in greater abundance at some distance behind the beach. Wells (1939) subsequently described a "salt-spray-climax community" dominated by live oak (*Q. virginiana*) on Smith Island, North Carolina. He believed that live oak dominated the canopy in the Smith Island maritime forest because its salt tolerance gave the slower-growing live oak a competitive edge over faster-growing but less salt-tolerant trees.

The term "salt spray" has been extensively used to describe the salt aerosol that is blown over barrier islands from the sea by onshore winds. Unless used in a direct quote, the term "salt aerosol" will be used throughout this report to identify this material.

The salt-aerosol explanation of vegetative-cover zonation was tested experimentally by Oosting and Billings (1942). They evaluated the correlation between plant zonation and the environmental parameters of soil moisture, soil salinity, soil temperature, air temperature, evaporation rate, salt-aerosol input, and relative humidity. Of these parameters, only salt-aerosol input correlated with the plant zonation pattern.

Convincing evidence about the toxic effects of salt aerosols on vegetation was provided by Boyce (1951a, 1951b; 1954). He experimentally investigated the origin, atmospheric transport mechanism, salt-deposition pattern into the vegetation, and mode of entry into plant tissues of ocean-derived salt aerosol. He also studied the translocation and physiological effects of salt after it had entered the plants.

Boyce (1954) showed that maximum salt-aerosol impact on vegetation occurs under conditions of strong onshore wind. Salt spray, propelled into the air after the plunge of a breaking wave, becomes an aerosol entrained in the wind. The entrained aerosol flows with the wind and is deposited according to wind patterns determined by the shape and texture of the underlying surface. Salt is deposited when aerosol droplets fall on surfaces; salt-aerosol concentration is greatest close to the ocean or land surface. Vegetation along the windward edge of the maritime forest intercepts most of the salt. Unhardened developing branches derived from terminal buds may grow into the space above the canopy, where they are killed by salt desiccation. Terminal buds nearest the ocean rarely complete their development. Death of the terminal bud or branch produces a hormonal change in shrubs and trees, which results in growth stimulation to previously repressed lateral buds. Continued loss of terminal growth, together with development of lateral buds, produces the "espalier" or wind-sculpted appearance in the maritime forest canopy. Close to the ocean, the maritime forest canopy is kept low and of uniform height by the effects of salt aerosol. As salt is lost by impact

with surfaces, its concentration in the atmosphere decreases. Farther back from the beach, the maritime forest canopy gradually assumes the more uneven surface of a mainland forest as individual tree height becomes more an expression of the genetic potential of the species rather than a growth response to an inhibitory environmental factor. Greatest salt damage to plants typically occurs during the spring or early summer, just as new buds are breaking.

Plant leaves may become necrotic and die if subjected to excessive salt exposure. Wind-driven aerosols tend to concentrate along the edges of leaves. Small, simple, smooth-edged leaves having a thick mesophyll, tough epidermis, and thick cutin seem to withstand salt-aerosol impact better than larger, thinner lobed or compound leaves. Trees and shrubs with small, salt-resistant leaves dominate the maritime forest canopy nearest the sea. Less salt-tolerant hickories, sweetgum, maples, and lobe-leaved oaks generally increase in relative abundance with increasing distance from the beach (Boyce 1954).

Salt ions appear to enter the leaves through cracks in the epidermis caused by vigorous bending and brushing together of twigs during high-wind conditions. Boyce (1954) has shown that in many types of leaves, excess salt is translocated to the leaf tip. The resulting V-shaped yellowed or necrotic area with the apex of the V originating at the leaf midrib, constitutes a diagnostic characteristic of damage from salt. Salt may accumulate in a leaf until it is killed; the dead salt-laden leaves then fall from the tree. As a result, only portions of the affected plants rather than the entire plant are killed.

Proffitt (1977) measured salt inputs at various locations and elevations within the maritime forest on Bogue Banks, North Carolina (Fig. 2.8) but found no consistent seasonal pattern in salt deposition (Fig. 2.9). Proffitt used the field data from his study to develop regression equations for predicting the atmospheric mineral inputs at any location where the topography is known. These equations were as follows: for chloride, $y = 21.9x - 5.48$; for calcium, $y = 0.40x + 0.98$; and for magnesium, $y = 1.11x - 0.26$; where y represents the atmospheric inputs in grams per square meter per year and x is the topographic index for the site (Fig. 2.10). Proffitt (1977) demonstrated an inverse relation between maritime forest canopy height and chloride input (Fig. 2.8). The correlation between measured canopy height above mean sea level and measured chloride inputs during one year at six locations across the barrier island yielded a correlation coefficient of -0.87 ($P = 0.05$).

Seneca and Broome (1981) found reasonable agreement between measured salt input into the forest canopy and values predicted using the Proffitt equations at another site on Bogue Banks (Fig. 2.11). Proffitt also reported a relationship between canopy-species community structure and the effects of salt-aerosol. Species diversity and species evenness were lowest in the area of maximum salt impact.

Exposure to salt aerosol is a major agent that regulates both the height and species composition of the maritime forest canopy. Both of these effects attenuate rapidly as salt impact diminishes away from the seaward edge. This feature

of maritime forest structure also suggests that the forest type termed "maritime forest" originates as a result of progressive loss of canopy species from an existing, more diverse forest with a floristic composition similar to that on the adjacent mainland. If this scenario is correct, then mixed-hardwood-pine barrier island forests are continuously transformed into maritime forest as rising sea level and beach erosion cause the zone of salt-aerosol impact to shift toward the mainland.

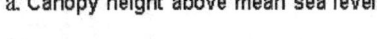

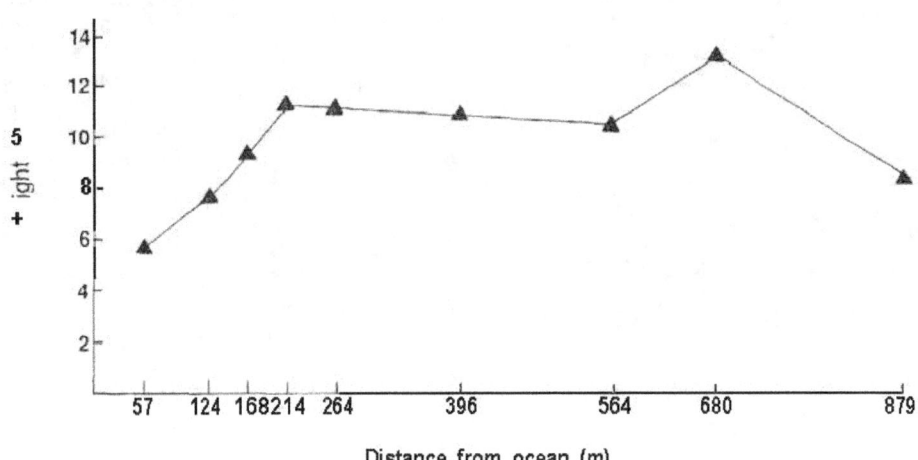

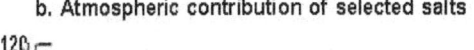

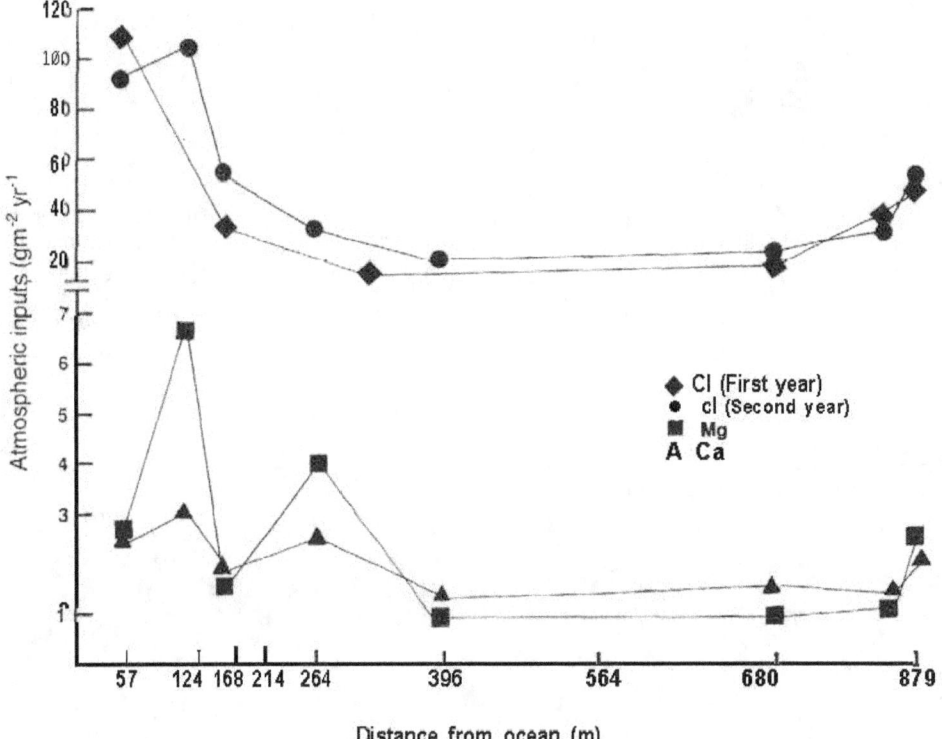

Fig. 2.8. Canopy height and atmospheric contribution of selected salts of the maritime forest canopy at various distances from the ocean, Bogue Banks, North Carolina (from Proffitt 1977).

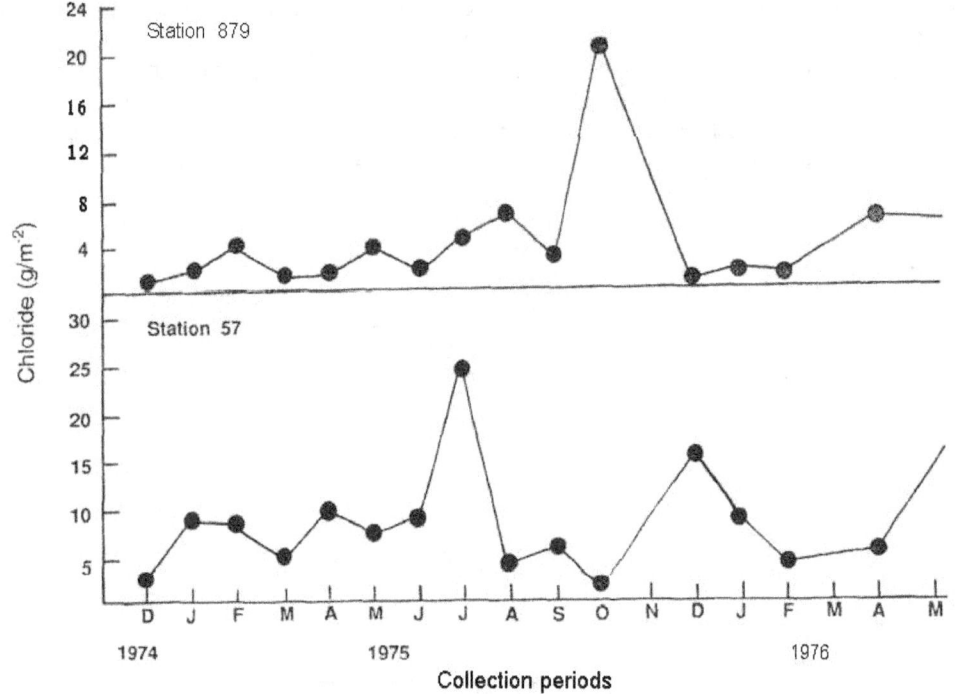

Fig. 2.9. Chronological pattern of chloride deposition into the maritime forest canopy at two locations on Bogue Banks, North Carolina (from Proffitt 1977).

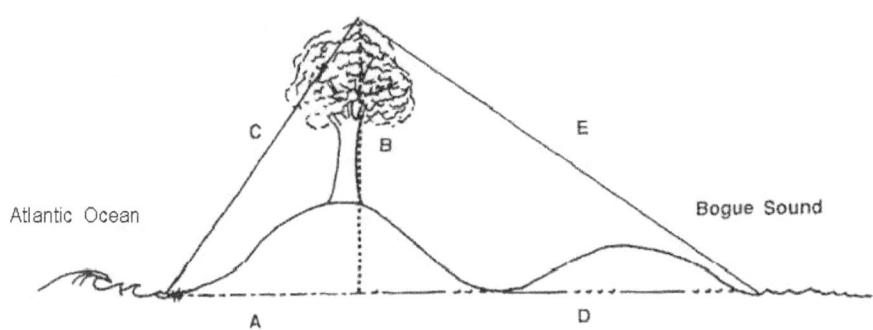

Fii. 2.10. Reference points for calculations of mineral inputs from salt aerosols at Bogue Banks, North Carolina (from Proffitt 1977).

Topography index at a station = CIA + 0.078 BID
A= Distance of the station from the ocean (m)
B= Elevation of gage above mean sea level (m) x 100
D= Distance of the station from the sound (m)

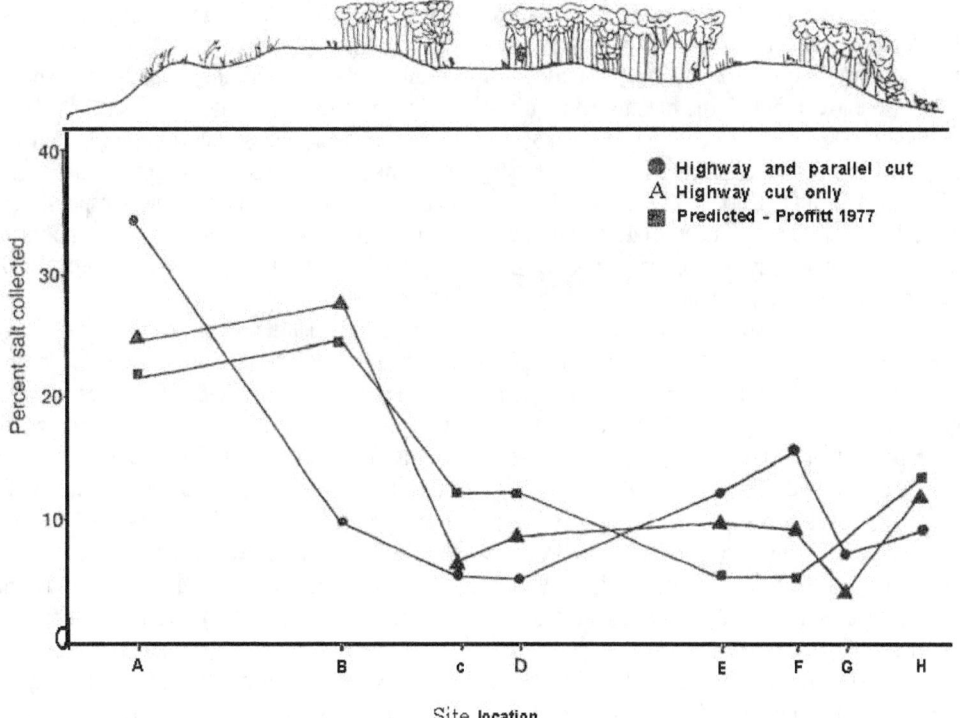

Fig. 2.11. Percent of salt spray collected at the foredune (A), ocean side of forest (B), leeward edge of the barrier forest (C), ocean side of the central barrier forest (D), leeward edge of central barrier forest (E), ocean side of the barrier forest near sound (F), interior of forest (G), and sound side of barrier forest (H) for various representative transects (from Seneca and Broome 1981).

Soil Formation and Mineral Cycling

Soils of maritime forests are typically one of two general types. Forested dune ridges consist of sandy soil, whereas interdune swale wetlands may contain accumulations of peat. Maritime forest soils tend to be highly permeable, acidic, deficient in plant nutrients, and poorly developed because of their secondary origin from well-leached ocean sediments, geologically recent origin, and relatively high regional precipitation.

An orderly process of soil formation and stabilization on maritime dunes was described by Chapman (1976). Newly formed sand dunes progress through four stages as they develop from "embryo dunes" to "yellow dunes," then "gray dunes," and finally "mature vegetated dunes."

Embryo dunes are formed when sand is freshly deposited on an accreting beach, when migrating dunes reform following destabilization, or when fresh sand is swept from the beach to form a berm along the leading edge of a maritime forest on an eroding beach. Initially, the embryo dune is devoid of vegetation, its soil is undeveloped, and no soil profile is apparent. Given sufficient time, however, sea oats and other grasses and herbaceous plants may

become established. This vegetative cover helps retain nutrients, soil moisture, and dune stability. After a vegetative cover develops, the dune is called a yellow dune. Yellow dunes also lack a distinctive soil profile.

Koske and Polson (1984) found that the phosphate concentration in yellow dune soils on Rhode Island was typically two orders of magnitude lower than in agricultural soils. Under the condition of low phosphorus availability, a phosphate deficit zone develops around the roots of grasses and other plants. Root hairs are apparently unable to bridge this gap unaided; however, plants of American beachgrass (*Ammophila breviligulata*) infected with the zygomycetan mycorrhizal fungus *Gigaspora* sp. are able to grow very well. Laboratory studies demonstrated that this and other vesicular-arbuscular mycorrhizae assist in phosphorus uptake and appear necessary for significant growth of dune grasses. Fungal mycelia also serve to bind sand grains together and help retain soil moisture.

American beachgrass (*Ammophila breviligulata*), waxmyrtle (*Myrica cerifera*), and beach pea (*Lathyrus japonicus*) are common plants in the yellow dune zone; all are associated with nitrogen-fixing bacteria (Godfrey 1976a). Nitrogen fixation by endosymbiotic bacteria is probably a major source of nitrogen on barrier islands. Haines (1976) reported that the amount of nitrogen delivered annually to the Georgia coast by rainfall was about 0.3 g/m^2, an amount well below the calculated requirements of coastal plants.

Development of a soil microflora enhances nitrogen and phosphorus availability (Koske and Polson 1984). As these essential plant nutrients accumulate in the dune ecosystem, growth by woody species is promoted and organic matter begins to accumulate in the soil, giving it a gray color. This is the "gray stage" in dune development. Shrubs and dwarf trees dominate the vegetative cover of gray dunes (Chapman 1976). If they remain stable long enough, gray dunes may mature into maritime forest. Art et al. (1974) reported that on Fire Island, New York, forest can form on siliceous sands within 200-300 years.

As vegetative cover increases on mature forested dunes, a soil profile develops as organic acids are leached downward. The uppermost soil horizon is the litter or duff layer and consists primarily of dead leaves, twigs, and other plant materials. Beneath the litter, the soil is ashy white because most of the humic substances have been leached into the sand to a depth of several centimeters, where they accumulate to form a tan or orange layer. Because moving sands have buried soils repeatedly, often a series of soil horizons can be seen in the exposed face of eroding dunes, demonstrating the instability of some barrier islands (Koske and Polson 1984).

Although the mycorrhizae and endosymbiotic nitrogen-fixing bacteria of the soil microflora play an important role in the process of dune stabilization by stimulating vegetative cover (Koske and Polson 1984), comparable studies of the microflora of mature maritime forest soils are lacking. The mycorrhizae (*Gigaspora* sp.) that promote phosphate uptake in beach grass do seem to have specific host requirements and are associated with several tree species, including oaks (Koske and Polson 1984). Waxmyrtle with its nitrogen-fixing bacteria is a common component of maritime forests. It is therefore highly probable that these microflora play an important role in the cycling of phosphorus and nitrogen in mature maritime forest soils, as well as during soil development.

The pattern of mineral cycling on barrier islands is quite different from the pattern in forests that cover rocky soils (Art et al. 1974). In most mainland forests, minerals lost in runoff are replaced by weathering and decomposition of the soil's parent rock. Mineral-deficient quartz sand is the primary parent material of barrier island soils. Maritime forest soils have low water-holding capacity and low cation-exchange capacity. Soluble minerals released into the soil are transported quickly downward into the ground water unless intercepted by organic matter, fungal mycelia, or plant rootlets near the soil surface. Most maritime

forest plants have their roots concentrated in the upper 30 cm of the soil (Art et al. 1974). At any given time, most of the minerals in a maritime forest are contained in the form of living or dead biomass. Continued survival of the ecosystem may depend on the ability of the microflora inhabiting the rhizosphere to sort rapidly and retain such critically important plant nutrients as phosphorus and nitrogen, while simultaneously allowing potentially toxic levels of chloride to pass into the ground water for dilution and dispersal.

If barrier island soils are inherently deficient in minerals, then where did the minerals now contained in the biomass come from? Possible sources include excrement from migratory birds, transfer from estuarine sources by animals that graze in the salt marsh but seek shelter (and defecate) on high portions of the island, wind transport of ocean-derived detritus (dry sea wrack) into the dune system, and atmospheric inputs.

Art et al. (1974) attempted to measure the meteorological contribution of cations to the maritime Sunken Forest on Fire Island, New York. Although the Fire Island maritime forest is composed predominantly of deciduous species of trees and is therefore floristically quite different from typical maritime forests of the Southeast, there are enough similarities in soil origin and growth form of the forest to consider this work the best model for understanding cation cycling in a maritime forest. Art et al. (1974:61) concluded that cation sources other than meteorological were insignificant and that the Fire Island ecosystem was "nearing a steady state [in which] meteorological inputs balance losses to groundwater." This pattern of nutrient cycling was similar to that inferred for some tropical moist forests. Both forest types have highly weathered soils, low mineral input from weathering, and large proportions of their cations held in living biomass. Both depend on rapid circulation of nutrients between soil and biomass.

Interactions between meteorological inputs of nutrients and primary production apparently are instrumental in the development and maintenance of the forest cover on the Fire Island dunes. Vegetation is the major interceptor of meteorological nutrient inputs to the ecosystem. Living vegetation, litter, and humus constitute the major sink for nutrients. Thus, a potential positive feedback system develops in which increases in vegetative biomass result in greater capture and retention of minerals from the atmosphere, thereby producing still greater biomass. The growth-stimulating potential of increased nutrients is countered by the growth-retarding effects of toxic salt aerosols. Maritime forest-growth response at any given location or time would seem to result from the ambient tension between these two contrasting effects of salt aerosols.

The forest canopy on Fire Island is dominated by several deciduous species, such as sassafras (Sassafras *albidum*) and shadbush (*Amelanchier canadensis*), *as well* as the evergreen American holly (*Ilex opaca*) *(Art* et al. *1974). The* deciduous species lose all their leaves over a short period in the fall; mineral recycling then begins and continues in spring. In contrast, the canopy of southern maritime forests tends to be dominated by evergreen species. The Fire Island climate might be described as mild and temperate, while that of the Southeast coast is hot and humid. The warmer, wetter southern climate provides an extended season during which rapid decomposition and mineral cycling can occur. Monk (1966a) noted that evergreen species tend to lose their leaves continuously rather than seasonally. The litter from ever-green trees tends to be tough, waxy, and aromatic and thus moderately to strongly resistant to decomposition through insect milling followed by fungal decay. This vegetative adaptation so commonly found in the southern maritime forest may help to ensure a continuous, albeit low, supply of mineral nutrients.

Two general systems of mineral uptake in relation to tree growth form were described by Hillestad et al. (1975). Live oaks have a shallow, spreading root system about equal in diameter to that of the crown. The crown serves as a high-surface-area collector of meteorologically de-rived nutrients that are diverted by rainfall directly into a dense, shallow root zone. Art et al. (1974) reported that the salt-aerosol-sculpted canopy at Fire Island exhibited an extremely large ratio (9.5: 1) of branch-to-canopy surface area. In contrast to live oak, pines have sparse, shallow root systems but deep taproots. This growth form leads to a large root surface area in contact with a large section of the soil profile, allowing pines to scavenge nutrients that percolate through the groundwater. Pine canopies tend to be more sensitive to salt-aerosol damage than those of oaks. Because oaks are more resistant to salt damage, they can better exploit minerals carried with the salt aerosol, whereas pines are better adapted to exploit soil nutrients at sites protected from salt aerosol. Both life forms and their associated nutrient-capture systems reduce nutrient losses over the entire forest gradient.

Cation retention is affected by soil-water acidity (God-frey 1976a). Maritime forest soils provided with calcium or magnesium tend to be less acid and probably retain mineral nutrients longer than soils in which calcium and magnesium cations are in lower concentration. Important sources of calcium and magnesium for maritime forests are the carbonates (aragonite) from mollusk shell frag-ments and other biogenic carbonates carried by the wind from the beach. Available cations increase in a southerly direction along the Atlantic coast as the proportion of limestone-derived carbonates in beach sand increases (Godfrey 1976a).

The second major soil type in maritime forests is peat or sandy peat (Brown 1983; Bumey and Bumey 1987).

Feat soils accumulate in interdune swales when the swales arc intercepted by the freshwater table or flooded by brackish water from the estuary. Swale ponds are initially temporary bodies of water. Freshwater ponds become seasonal and finally permanent as rising sea level pushes the freshwater lens higher. Eventually, any trees in the swale may be killed by flooding. Organic matter (leaves, branches, stumps) tends to collect in these low, wet depres-sions between forested dunes. Pond sediments are often very anaerobic and charged with hydrogen sulfide, result-ing in reduced oxidative decomposition. Pond sediments typically consist of unconsolidated, coarse woody debris and leaves at the surface. Humification of this material produces a fine-grained, sticky black mud. Beneath this are coarse wood fragments and an indurated surface that represents remains of a soil profile predating pond forma-tion. Beneath this layer, the soil consists of fairly clean sand. Cores drawn from the peat and sandy peat sediments of freshwater ponds have yielded pollen and microfossil evidence from which pond origins and recent vegetative events in the surrounding maritime forest can be recon-structed (Brown 1983; Bumey and Bumey 1987).

Hydrology

The hydrological regime on barrier islands is distinctive (Fig. 2.12) (Art et al. 1974). Precipitation provides the only natural source of fresh water. Typically, the barrier is underlain by permeable sediment containing salt water. Under these conditions, fresh water tends to float as a lens over the underlying salt water. Under ideal geological conditions, the freshwater lens can be modeled by using the Ghyben-Herzberg lens principle (Ward 1975). This predicts that for every meter of free water table above mean sea level, there will be 40 m of fresh water in the lens above the saltwater aquifer. The freshwater lens can be quite deep below elevated ridges on the barrier but short-ens abruptly to zero depth at the island and saltwater interface (Fig. 2.13).

The sea islands of Georgia receive an average annual precipitation of 1,308 mm (Table 2.1), an amount that appears to be typical for barrier islands of the Southeast. Floyd (1979) estimated that a major portion of the average annual precipitation of 1,143 mm at Nags Head, North Carolina, was lost through evaporation, runoff, and dis-charge of ground water to the ocean or bay by lateral movement. Only 25% of the precipitation was available for percolation into the zone of saturation where it could become part of the groundwater supply.

Water in the freshwater lens is usually very low in dissolved salts, considering the periodic pulses of salt aerosol delivered to the vegetative cover (Proffitt 1977). Apparently, excess salt is rapidly diluted by precipitation

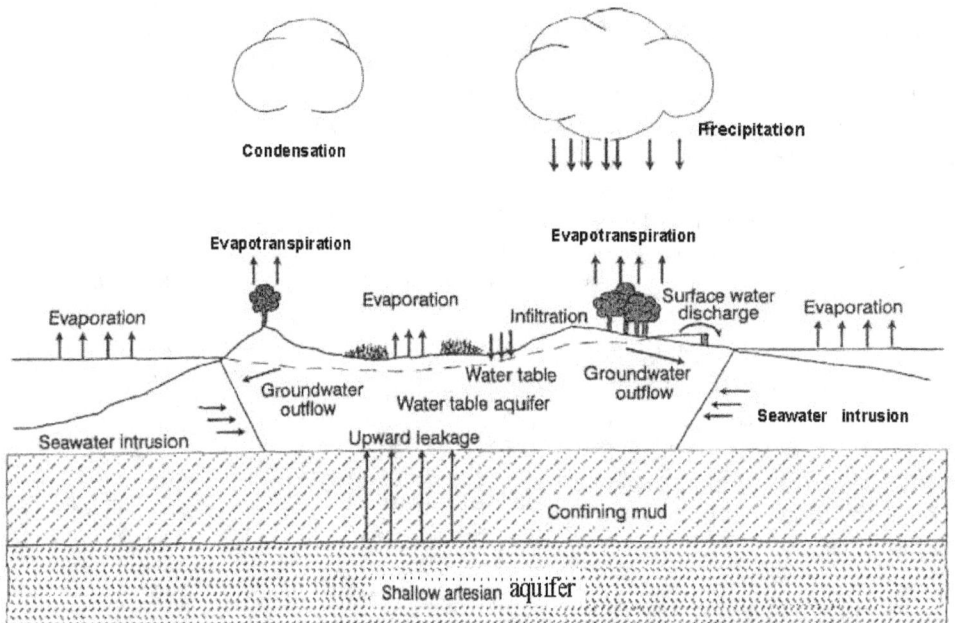

Fig. 2.12. Hydrologic cycle of a typical Holocene **barrier island (from Missimer 1976; used with permission of** *Science*).

and flushed from the system. Precipitation entering the soil near the interior of the watershed is rapidly drawn downward to the bottom of the freshwater lens. Counter-flow along the contact with salt water brings excess fresh water back to the surface, where it seeps into the bay or ocean (Fig. 2.13).

Rapid dispersal of salt below the root zone was demonstrated by Proffitt (1977). He buried 2.3 kg of rock salt just below the litter layer on a forested slope on Bogue Banks, North Carolina, and measured chloride concentrations in the soil a& various depths and distances from the salt burial site for a period of 3 months. Soil salt content in the root zone (O-30 cm deep) at the source remained about two orders of magnitude above the background level. Lateral salt transport near the surface was minimal, since chloride concentrations were never found above background in the root zone at monitor stations 0.6 m from the salt burial site. After 47 days, the chloride concentration had returned to near background in the root zone at the salt burial site, and movement of chloride was mainly downward, concentrations exceeding background by one order of magnitude at greater depths.

Evapotranspiration rates are unknown for maritime forest. Is surface moisture lost more rapidly from unvegetated sandy soils or from forested dunes? How effective are the various canopy surface patterns in absorbing and holding precipitation? What are the cumulative effects of destroying maritime forest while simultaneously pumping water from the freshwater lens to serve the needs of barrier island development? Given the high permeability and low cation-exchange capacity of barrier island soils, what is

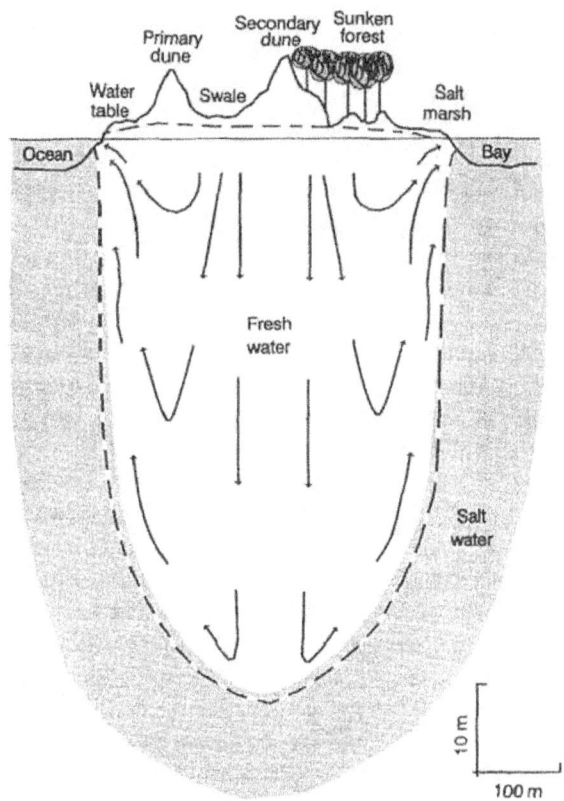

Fig. 2.13. Idealized diagrammatic cross section of a barrier island, showing water-flow pattern in the freshwater lens (from Art et al. 1974).

their potential for becoming contaminated by septic tank seepage? What effect does septic tank seepage or disposal of wastewater by spraying have on soil microflora and mineral cycling?

On most developed barrier islands, the remaining maritime forest is the primary watershed and source of public water supply. At what point does transfer, by pumping of groundwater to the surface, speed up saltwater intrusion? Excess pumping and the cutting of canals and marinas along the freshwater lens and saltwater margin may lead to loss of hydrostatic head in the freshwater lens and thus result in saltwater intrusion at the groundwater surface (Winner 1975; Ward 1975).

The potential interrelation between surface groundwater and maritime forest cover on barrier islands appear to be numerous, but information about them is scarce. Further research on the role of vegetation in influencing the hydrology of barrier islands is needed.

Wetlands

Several types of wetland habitat may be associated with maritime forest. Wetlands are usually associated with topographically low areas between dunes and form when the groundwater table rises and intercepts low-lying soils. Temporary rain pools formed in this manner may develop into semipermanent freshwater ponds. Shallow ponds support growths of willow (*Salix* spp.), gums (*Nyssa sylvatica* and *Liquidambar styraciflua*), ash (*Fraxinus americana*), or other wetland trees and thus resemble the deciduous hardwood swamps found on the mainland. Deeper ponds support submersed vegetation. These kinds of freshwater wetland are often called maritime forest swamps or swale ponds. Both types are a "water table window" (Bensink and Burton 1975).

Ponds of brackish water are formed when the ends of swale ponds are captured by an expanding salt marsh, along closed ocean inlets, or by tidal flooding (Bensick and Burton 1975). Long, narrow brackish ponds of the first type may grade into narrow "finger salt marshes" toward their lower ends. Larger, more open brackish ponds are often called "salt ponds." Odum and Harvey (1988) classified these pond types, using the wetland classification system of Cowardin et al. (1979), as palustrine emergent, palustrine shrub/shrub, palustrine forested, estuarine emergent, and estuarine shrub/shrub.

Bumey and Bumey (1984) reported palynological evidence illustrating the pattern of development of freshwater ponds at Nags Head Woods, North Carolina. Radiocarbon dating of the oldest organic sediments in ponds indicated a recent origin of less than 400 years ago. The pollen percentages at all levels exhibited a near-constant background of the same species of flowering trees and shrubs

that inhabit the area now. Pollen from bottomland trees and shrubs increased steadily, whereas pine pollen declined from bottom to top in sediment cores. This palynological pattern is consistent with the hypothesis that the hydric forests that now occupy dune swales developed quite recently from upland forest in response to a rising water table. During the initial stage in wetland development, waterlogged soil was colonized by fast-growing herbaceous plants such as Mexican tea (*Chenopodium ambrosioides*) and false nettle (*Boehmeriu cylindrica*). These wetland plants were replaced by freshwater aquatics such as species of *Typha, Nymphaea, Myriophyllum,* Lemnaceae, *Utricularia,* and *Potamogeton.*

Water quality of maritime forest ponds is variable, even among ponds near one another (Kling 1986). Variability in water-quality characteristics among ponds is probably related to the fact that at any given location the various ponds are usually in differing stages of development. Ponds vary in hydroperiod, solar exposure, and degree of exposure to direct inputs of atmospheric salts. Based on a comparison of ion ratios, Kling (1986) concluded that the water in the Nags Head Woods ponds more closely resembled that of the local groundwater than diluted seawater or typical river water in the region. A. Cole (North Carolina State University, personal communication) confirmed low salinity and absence of water chemistry variability of freshwater ponds of similar age and origin in the Buxton Woods, North Carolina.

Freshwater ponds in maritime forest were described by Odum and Harvey (1988) as generally having slightly higher ionic concentrations than typical inland freshwater ponds (Table 2.2). Interdunal ponds tend to be circumneutral in pH and poorly buffered. When dense populations of aquatic vegetation deplete the water of bicarbonate through intensive photosynthesis on bright days, pH can increase to about 9.0; when decaying vegetation releases organic acids into the water, pH can decline to about 4.5. Fresh ponds typically do not exhibit excessive amounts of nitrogen or phosphorus and are not normally described as eutrophic. Anaerobic conditions may exist in the peaty sediments of the ponds throughout the year and may extend to the pond bottom during warm weather.

Freshwater ponds often provide the only dependable source of water for animals on barrier islands. The associated freshwater wetlands also expand habitat diversity. Major groups of animals such as frogs, salamanders, water snakes, turtles, aquatic birds, and aquatic mammals are largely excluded from barrier islands without freshwater ponds. When such ponds are present, however, many of these animals provide a varied and more dependable food source for nonaquatic inhabitants. Hillestad et al. (1975) described an oscillating pattern of predator-prey relationships related to perturbations in the wetland communities

Table 2.2. Mean values of physical-chemical parameters for five freshwater ponds in the Nags Head Woods, North Carolina (modified from Kling 1986).

Parameter[a]	Mean	Range
pH	6.8	6.2-7.2
Conductivity(μS/c m)	207.6	112.0-381 .0
HCO_3-	46.6	13.8-81.4
Cl^-	26.3	21.4-38.0
SO_4--	3.6	**0.02-6.3**
Na^+	18.0	12.0-35.3
Ca^{++}	10.9	**2.9-19.5**
Mg^{++}	4.3	**2.40-7.44**
K^+	1.7	1.1-3.3
NO_3--N(μg/L)	3.9	**0.0-8.0**
NH_4+-N(μg/L)	13.7	**9.2-18.5**
H_2PO_4--P(μg/L)	31.4	5.1-80.6
DOC	5.5	3.6-8.3
Secchi(cm)	54.0	40.0-70.0
O_2	6.6	2.5-8.3

[a] Milligrams per liter unless indicated otherwise.

on Cumberland Island, Georgia. When the water table is high, certain prey species such as frogs, insects, and mosquito **fish** are provided with ample food and breeding habitat and thus, predation pressure tends to be relatively low. When the water table falls and water levels are low, the prey animals concentrate in shallow water, and the habitat advantage shifts in favor of predators such as snakes, herons, and alligators. Prey species are again favored when the water level falls below the bottom of the ponds. Then, predators are reduced in number or temporarily eliminated, while prey species find refuge in alligator holes or crayfish burrows or under damp vegetation. The abundance of prey populations quickly increases with the return of higher water levels.

Some observers (Mayes and List 1988) indicatedconcern over possible ecosystem-damaging effects of periodic drought conditions on maritime fresh ponds, whereas others (Hillestad et al. 1975) suggested that water-table oscillations may be necessary to maintain these pulse-stabilized aquatic systems. Without perturbations such as drought and tire, shallow-water wetlands would rapidly till with organic matter and develop toward a shrub or swamp forest. When the shallow bottom is exposed to the atmosphere and solar drying, aerobic decomposition is accelerated, releasing nutrients that can later support wet-season productivity.

The biota of freshwater ponds in Nags Head Woods, North Carolina, was inventoried by a multidisciplinary team of researchers. Their surveys were carried out during a drought phase in the local climate and served to assess the ability of the pond biota to survive drought.

The algal flora of the Nags Head Woods ponds was dominated by desmids, euglenoids, and periphytic diatoms

(Bellis 1988). Seventy-two algal taxa representing the seven major algal groups normally present in fresh water were reported from rather few collections. The ecological significance of the algae in these ponds is as yet poorly understood; however, several nitrogen-fixing cyanobacteria such as *Nostoc commune* and *Anabaena azollae,* an endosymbiont of the mosquito fern (*Azolla caroliniana*), were among the most frequent algae in several ponds.

Periphytic diatoms in the ponds included *Pinnularia braunii, P. latevittata var. domingensis,Gomphonema gracile,* and *Eunotia curvata.* These taxa were described by Patrick and Reimer (1966) as indicators of waters with low dissolved mineral content and relatively low pH. A variety of euglenoid taxa (*Euglena, Trachelomonas, Phacus) occurred* abundantly among the often-anaerobic organic debris.

The algal flora of the Nags Head Woods freshwater ponds was dominated by motile unicells (Bellis 1988). Algae exhibiting this morphology typically form very resistant cysts or spores when environmental freshwater ponds consisted of taxa that commonly occur in similar environments on the mainland and seemed adapted for survival during episodic droughts.

Vascular plants in the Nags Head Woods ponds consisted of 40 aquatic or emergent taxa and 3 wetland shrub taxa (Davison 1988a). Other vascular taxa associated with pond margins included 22 taxa of ferns, herbs, shrubs, and trees.

Pond water levels were extremely low during thevascularplant survey (Davison 1988a). Differences in species composition and diversity among ponds strongly correlated with differences in pond size and depth gradient. Despite individual differences among ponds, certain general patterns were evident. Where pond margins were exposed to sunlight, they were invaded by opportunistic seedlings. In several ponds, the open water surface was completely replaced by a vegetated "quaking bog." Wetland species growing on exposed pond bottoms and along pond margins shaded by forest canopy included false nettle (*Boehmeria cylindrica*) and lizard's tail (*Saururus cernuus*). Vascular plant opportunists in fully exposed areas were dominated by graminoids (*Leersia oryzoides, Eleocharis baldwinii*), *Polygonum* spp., and pennywort (*Hydrocotyle ranuncutoides*). Deeper portions of the ponds were reduced to small pools of open water during the drought; they were completely covered by floating aquatics, dominated by duckweeds (*Spirodefla polyrhiza, Lemna* spp., *Wolffia columbiana*), mosquito fern (*Azolla caroliniana*), and frog's bit (*Limnobium spongia*).

Prolonged lowering of the water level permitted establishment of saplings of loblolly pine (*Pinus taeda*), redbay (*Persea borbonia*), Carolina willow (*Safix caroliniana*), black gum (*Nyssa sylvatica*), and red maple (*Acer rubrum*) (Davison 1988a). The latter three species can survive seasonal flooding and may become established around the pond margins after the water table returns to normal.

The microinvertebrate fauna of the Nags Head Woods ponds was surveyed by MacPherson (1988), who reported 70 taxa from a few collections limited to a single season (spring). Taxonomic richness was greatest among Diptera (18 taxa), Coleoptera (15 taxa), and Odonata (11 taxa). Amphipods, isopods, and a clam (*Sphaerium*) represented the most abundant microinvertebrates present. Most of the microinvertebrates were associated with mats of floating or emergent vegetation, a habitat also dominated by dragonflies and beetles. Benthic microinvertebrates were less abundant and included clams, leeches, and worms. Surveys of aquatic and wetland vertebrates in the Nags Head Woods ponds included fish (Schwartz 1983, 1988), amphibians and reptiles (Braswell 1988), birds (Cooper 1988), and mammals (Webster 1988).

Schwartz (1983, 1988) proposed multiple possible origins of fish that now inhabit ponds along the northern Outer Banks of North Carolina. Marine fish may be transported into ponds from the ocean or from the estuary during overwash events. Freshwater fish remain on the islands in ponds formed from relict river channels, or they may gain access by overwash transport from estuaries that became much less saline in recent times. The fish with a saltwater affinity are generally absent from ponds in the Nags Head Woods; this may be related to the apparent lack of recent washover.

Schwartz conducted intensive fish surveys on the Nags Head Woods ponds in 1983 and again in 1987. Five fish species were found in each survey; however, only three of the species in the second survey were the same as those reported in the first survey. Fish reported in both surveys were mosquito fish (*Gambusia holbrooki*), bluegill (*Lepomis macrochirus*), and largemouth bass (*Micropterus salmoides*). Species reported in only one of the surveys were golden shiner (*Notemigonus crysoleucas*), black crappie (*Pomoxis nigromaculatus*), rainwater fish (*Lucania parva*), and pumpkin seed (*Lepomis gibbosus*). Schwartz suggested that the species missing in the second survey (rainwater fish and pumpkin seed) may have been extirpated through predation by the largemouth bass or other carnivores. He believed the new residents were recent accidental introductions.

A survey of amphibians and reptiles of the Nags Head Woods by Braswell (1988) indicated that availability of freshwater habitat resulted in greater herpetofaunal diversity. The herpetofauna associated with the Nags Head Woods ponds appeared to be the most diverse of any barrier island of the Atlantic Coast. Of the 41 species reported, 23 species were directly dependent on the freshwater pond habitat.

Freshwater ponds enhance habitat quality for some vertebrates as well. A listing of breeding birds near Nags Head Woods (Cooper 1988) showed the greatest species richness in the pine-dominated forest. Greatest abundance of birds, however, was found in a gum swamp (interdunal forested swale) along the margins of a series of fresh ponds.

Webster (1988) reported that mammalian diversity was greater on Currituck-Boclie Island (including the Nags Head Woods) than on any other barrier island in North Carolina or adjoining states. Mammalian diversity was somewhat less in the Nags Head Woods itself than in the larger area. Webster (1988) attributed this reduced mammalian richness to a more limited range of habitats in the Nags Head Woods. The freshwater ponds were frequented by muskrats, raccoons, otters, deer, and bats (Webster 1988).

Fire

Anthropogenic and natural fires have been reported on barrier islands from early in the European colonial period until the present. Since the land-clearing and hunting practices of the aboriginal inhabitants of the islands involved the use of fire, it is probably safe to assume that barrier island biotic communities have been influenced by fires caused by humans throughout much of their presumed approximately 5,000-year existence.

In recent history, residents of barrier islands have used fire to improve grazing land, remove unwanted vegetation, maintain open vistas, create wildlife habitat, and eliminate unwanted insects and snakes. The use of fire for these and related purposes is deeply ingrained in the southern agricultural tradition (Davison 1983; Turner 1985; Bratton 1985, 1986a; Turner and Bratton 1987; Bratton and Davison 1987).

Natural fires initiated by dry lightning do not occur with uniform frequency along the southeastern coast but seem to have a gradient of increasing frequency from north to south (author's observation). Summer thunderstorms occur almost daily along the coasts of Georgia and Florida and dry lightning is common. Staff at national wildlife refuges at Canaveral and Merritt Island, Florida, recorded some of the highest lightning frequencies in the United States. In contrast, Cape Hatteras National Seashore experiences fewer summer thunderstorms and virtually no lightning-initiated fires(Bratton 1986a).

In forested areas, fire intensity varies with the litter deposition pattern (Williamson and Black 1981). Early seral plants such as pines and shrubs may be inferior long-term competitors; however, these plants exhibit fire tolerance and even fire facilitation, characteristics that may give them a short-term advantage in environments where fires occur fairly frequently. Williamson and Black (1981) measured the air temperature at various distances above the litter layer in burning forests of several types and discovered that fires in pine forests consistently produced a higher temperature at any given level above the ground than fires in a live oak forest. In the seedling zone and up as high as 0.5 m above the soil, the temperature in a live oak stand averaged about 175" C, whereas the temperature in the pine forest at the same level averaged about 290" C. Williamson and Black (1981) concluded that maximum temperatures of fires were high enough under pines to eliminate the otherwise competitively superior oaks in areas near mature pines.

Davison (1983) noted repeated fires on a portion of Cumberland Island, Georgia; she suggested that this pine-dominated woodland is maintained by fires of natural origin. The nutrient-poor soils of the site prevent the oaks from growing fast enough to form a dominant canopy before the conjunction of the climatic conditions and fuel accumulation result in fire. The significance of fire as a disturbance that maintains vegetative cover on Cumberland Island has since been questioned by McPherson (1988:1), who concluded from studies of the shrub-forest and marsh-forest boundaries that "succession to oak-palmetto (*Quercus* spp. and *Serenoa repens*) forest is controlled by soil moisture." Fire played only a minor role in community dynamics.

Davison (1983) reported that recovery of maritime forest on Cumberland Island, Georgia, during the year after an intense fire in 1981 did not involve a change in species composition. No new species appeared after the fire and none was lost. Only the apparent age distribution of individuals was altered by the fire.

Oak forests and pine forests differ in the way in which they carry a fire (Davison 1986; Davison and Bratton 1986; author's observations). Closed-canopy maritime oak forests tend to have a dense evergreen canopy with sparse understory and herbaceous vegetation. Shading also promotes moisture retention in the litter layer. Under these conditions, fires tend to be smoldering ground fires; crown fires are rare. Fires often originate outside the oak forest and enter it from adjacent marsh or pine forest.

Pine-dominated forests are usually drier and provide a better quality fuel that allows intense and fast-moving fires. Along the coasts of Georgia and Florida, a dense understory of palmetto beneath short, scattered pines promotes intense crown fires.

Canopy trees of the maritime forest appear to be well adapted to fire. Live oak is protected from fire by its thick, ridged bark, while cabbage palm is protected by its sheathing leaf bases. The terminal bud of cabbage palm is surrounded by woody, flame-resistant leaf petioles. Aboveground portions of understory trees and shrubs such as dwarf palmetto (*Sabal minor*), waxmyrtle (*Myrica cerifera*), American holly (*Ilex opaca*), sparkleberry (*Vaccinium arboreum*), and redbay (*Persea borbonia*) are *less* resistant to fire, but all have underground or surface structures from which burned individuals regenerate sprouts. Loss of aboveground portions of these plants through fire stimulates hormonal release of latent buds. Rapid regrowth and recovery follow as the sprouts use nutrients stored in underground roots and rhizomes in an open environment temporarily freed from intense competition for solar energy. Thus, it is clear that fire has been an important factor in organizing forest cover patterns on barrier islands since long before the present.

CHAPTER 3.

Flora of Maritime Forests

Introduction

Extensive information about the vascular flora of the Atlantic Coast barrier islands has been amassed since the beginning of this century. Typically, this information was presented as taxonomic lists of species in particular sites. Woody trees, shrubs, and vines ate usually dominant. Understory shrubs and herbs are sparse in the shade provided by the dense evergreen canopy characteristic of most maritime forests. Many floristic studies also described vegetation zonation, and some authorities attempted to relate the several distinctive vegetative cover zones into a successional sequence. Quantitative studies of plant community structure and function are extremely rare and simply not available for most barrier island and coastal dune forests.

Latitudinal Gradient in Floristic Composition

The maritime forests of the south Atlantic Coast of the United States do not seem to represent a single well-defined plant community that can be described by characteristic taxa. The available floristic data suggest that maritime forests actually consist of a northern and a southern forest assemblage that overlap to produce a diversity maximum at about 35" N latitude along the North Carolina coast (author's observation). Evidence in support of this concept was derived by the author by expanding and modifying a list of the range limits of common barrier island plant species along the Atlantic Coast (Art 1971). Floristic lists were included in the analysis that were not available to Art in 1971, especially for southern barrier islands. The resulting data (Fig. 3.1) summarize floristic lists from 40 different reports covering 32 barrier-island forest locations between 25" N (southern Florida) and 42" N latitude (Cape Cod, Massachusetts). This summary contains no weighting for relative abundance of the local flora. Fifty taxa of commonly encountered barrier-island forest trees and shrubs are listed. The species are arranged in order of their first southerly occurrence along a south-to-north line.

Of the 50 taxa listed, only red maple (*Acer rubrum*) occurs throughout the range of the survey. Some taxa listed toward the top of Table 3.1 (live oak [Quercus *virginiana*], palmetto palm [*Sabal palmetto*], laurel oak [*Quercus laurifolia* = *Quercus hemisphaerica*], redbay [*Persea borbonia*], etc.) seem to represent a southern assemblage. Taxa listed near the bottom (white oak [*Quercus alba*], bayberry [*Myrica pennsylvanica*], pitch pine [*Pinus rigida*], beach plum [*Prunus maritima*], etc.) seem to represent a northern assemblage. Finally, there is a large assemblage of plants distributed widely along the central Atlantic Coast. This group includes water oak (*Quercus nigra*), loblolly pine (*Pinus taeda*), yaupon (*Ilex vomitoria*), American beauty-berry (*Callicarpa americana*), toothache tree (*Zanthoxylum clava-herculis*), and sweetgum (*Liquidambar styraciflua*).

Figure 3.2 is a plot showing the number of taxa (of the 50 listed) occurring at 1-degree intervals of latitude. The pattern is one of maximum species diversity near the middle (35" N) of the geographic region. A dendrogram based on Jaccard's Index of Similarity (Fig. 3.3) also supports the concept of overlapping plant assemblages. The pattern is one of greatest similarity among locations between Georgia (31" N) and North Carolina (36° N). A second cluster of similar vegetative locations extends northward from Virginia (37° N to 42° N). The third cluster (25" N to 30° N) consists entirely of Florida records, and is least similar to all other locations.

The maritime forests of the southeastern Atlantic states (Virginia to Florida) consist of a discontinuous chain of forests that is seldom more than 1.5 km wide but nearly 1,600 km long. This narrow island chain extends generally along a north-south axis from a subtropic to a temperate climate. Much of the gradual variation in floristic composition along the major axis can be accounted for as representing a differential response of individual species to the climatic gradient.

Zonation

On a local scale, the floristic expression of a maritime forest appears to be influenced by another smaller scale gradient, the proximity to direct ocean influence. Although relative exposure to salt is generally considered the major factor controlling zonation, the actual process may be more complex and involve interactions between water supply, nutrient cycling, sand blasting, sand migration, storm exposure, and other factors.

The earliest botanical descriptions of barrier islands (Johnson 1900; Kearney 1900; Coker 1905) consisted primarily of botanical inventories that were made during brief visits to particular islands. These early botanists were intrigued by the conspicuous zonation of vegetative communities. The following description of the Isle of Palms, South Carolina, by Coker (1905: 136) is typical:

The island is about four and one-half miles long and one mile across at its broadest part. The time at my disposal being limited, I did not attempt to study the entire island, but confined myself to the western half. Within this small area, however, there is as great a diversity of ecological conditions as is generally found over a much more extended region, From the few struggling and half-buried halophytes of the beach one may pass over the dunes with their palms, then across a narrow marshy strip and into a dense forest of oaks and pines, with trees over forty feet in height—and all within a distance of three hundred yards.

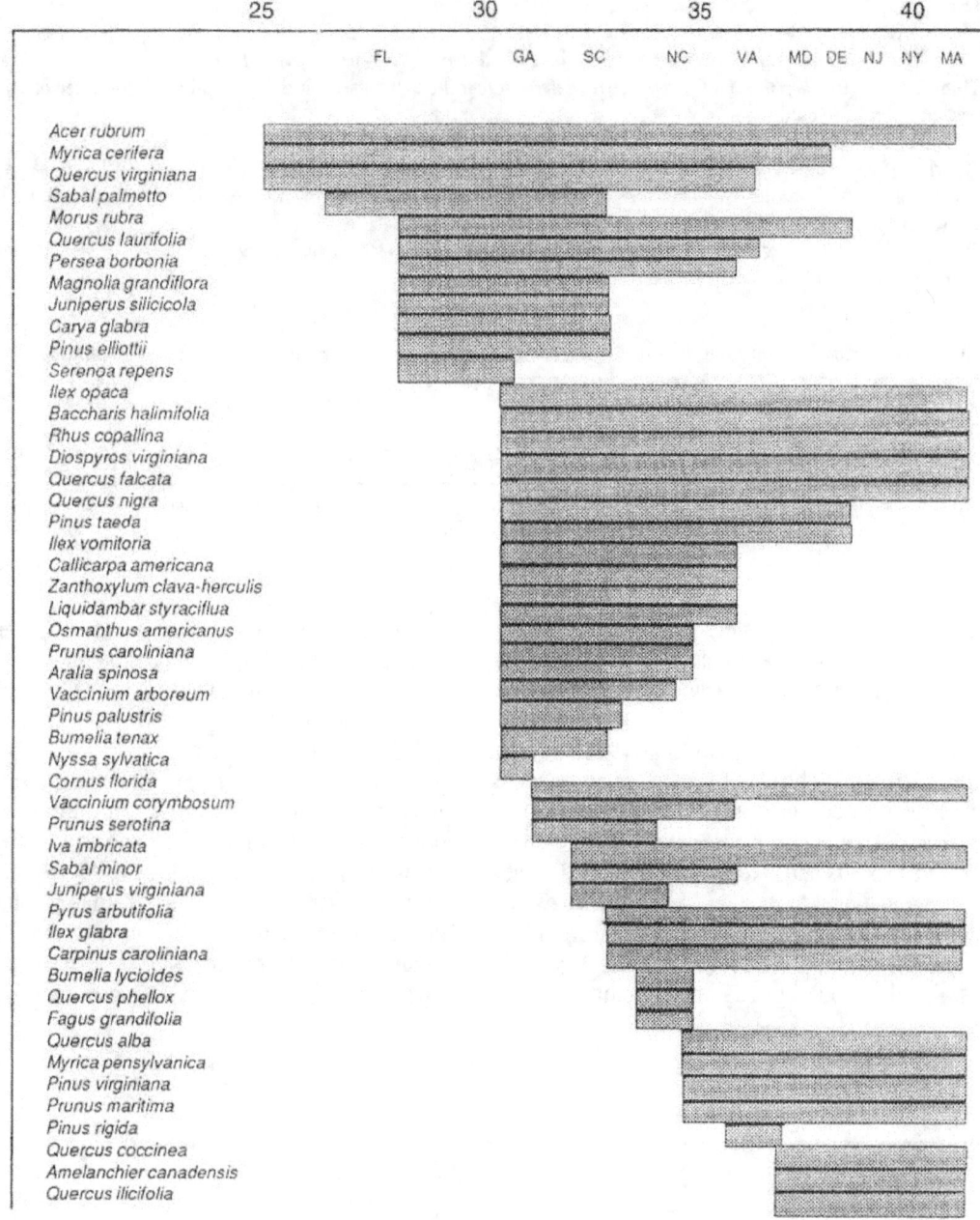

Fig. 3.1. Latitudinal range limits of 50 species of trees and shrubs reported in literature as forest constituents at 32 barrier island forest locations between Miami, Florida, and Cape Cod, Massachusetts. The list does not include mainland records. The *lines* indicate the northernmost and southernmost location reports for each taxon but should not be interpreted as indicating that the taxon occurs at every location along the line.

Table 3.1. Characteristic plant communities of the barrier islands of the southeastern United States (Oosting 1954).[a]

I. Sand Strand Vegetation

  1. Treeless (open)
    a. Inner Beach-Croton *punctatus*, *Cenchrus tribuloides*, (*Cakile edentula*, *Spartina patens*, *Physalis maritima*)
    b. Outer Beach—*Salsola kali*, *Euphorbia polygonifolia* (*Fimbristylis castanea*, *Spartina patens*)
    c. Dune Beach—*Uniola paniculata* (*Strophostyles helvola*, *Oenothera humifusa*, and any of others from inner or outer beach)
  2. Trees and Shrubs (closed)
    a. Thicket-Alex *vomitoria* (*Myrica cerifera*, *Juniperus virginiana*)
    b. Thicket Woodland—*Persea borbonia* (and forma *pubescens*) (*Juniperus virginiana*, many lianas including *Ampelopsis arborea*, *Parthenocissus quinquefolia*, *Vitis* spp., *Smilax* spp., *Toxicodendron radicans*, numerous ericaceous shrubs, especially *Vaccinium arboreum*)
    c. Woodland-Quercus *virginiana* (*Carpinus caroliniana*, *Ilex opaca*, *Morus rubra*, *Quercus laurifolia*, *Bumelia lycioides*, *Zanthoxylum clava-herculis*, *Osmanthus americanus*)

II. Marsh Vegetation

  1. Salt *Marsh-Spartina alterntflora*, *Salicornia virginica*, (*Suaeda linearis*, *Borrichia frutescens*, *Spergularia marina*, *Limonium carolinianum*, *Distichlis spicata*, *Kosteletzkya virginica*)
  2. Creek Marsh-Juncus *roemerianus*
  3. Dune Marsh-various species
  4. Tidal Flat—*Scirpus americanus*, *Paspalum distichum* (*Fimbristylis castanea*, *Spartina patens*)

[a]List is of plant communities. Community dominants are listed first. Taxon names in parentheses indicate common associates.

Coker (1905) completed his observations with detailed descriptions of vegetative cover types, identified as upper beach, dune, fresh marsh, forest, hammock, salt flat, and salt marsh.

Almost half a century later, Oosting (1954) summarized the information about the vegetative cover along maritime strands in the southeastern United States. Oosting revised the earlier list of vegetative cover associations for Ocracoke Island, North Carolina by Kearney (1900), by expanding it to include "those species repeatedly found elsewhere along the Atlantic coast from New England to Florida in similar zones" (Oosting 1954:230). This list (Table 3.1) assigned names to characteristic

plant communities on barrier islands. Different names have been assigned to these communities, (see Chapter 1) but most would probably agree with the species groupings presented by Oosting (1954).

Although the relative abundance of particular plant species may vary from site to site on the barrier islands along the Atlantic Coast, the same fundamental life zones occur in essentially the same arrangement at each site. From ocean to estuary, these zones are ocean beach, dunes, maritime forest, and salt marsh. Shackleford Banks, North Carolina, is a specific example of this zonation pattern on forested and unforested portions (Fig. 3.4). Godfrey (1976b) produced a generalized

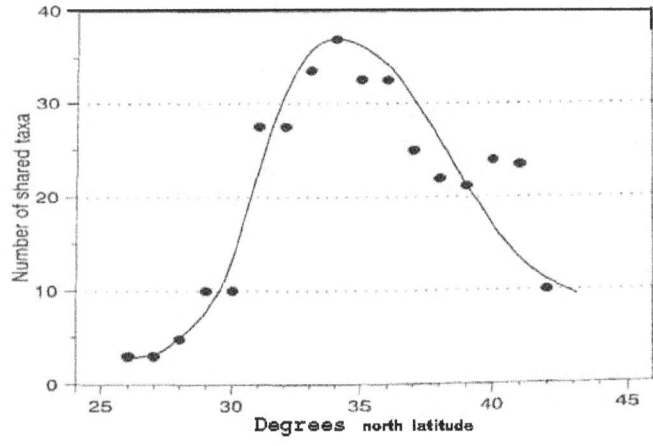

Fig. 3.2. Number of taxa (of the 50 shown in Fig. 3.1) occurring at 1-degree latitude intervals from 25°N to 45°N.

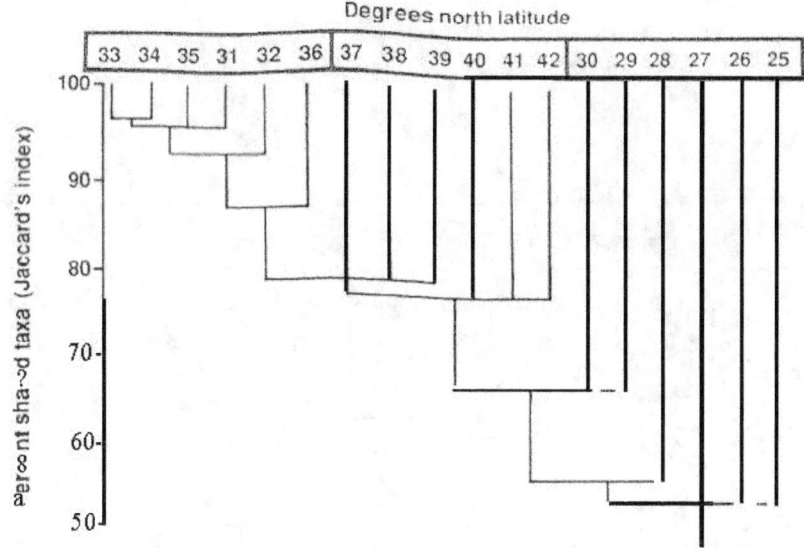

Fig. 3.3. Taxonomic similarity (Jaccard's Index) for assemblages of maritime forest trees and shrubs.

transect diagram of the physiographic and ecological zones of a typical barrier island (Fig. 3.5). In the same study, Godfrey also observed that the proportion of a typical barrier island covered by forest increases between New England and the Sea Islands of Georgia (Fig. 3.6). He attributed this increase to geologic differences in barrier island origin and processes. The southern barrier islands (sea islands) are more stable because they consist of drowned relict portions of mainland ridges or resulted from accretion along stable shorelines. The more northerly barriers seem to be affected to a greater extent by the destabilizing effects of ocean washover and dune migration. The characteristic taxa in a given zone along a northeastern barrier are typically replaced by a visually similar but floristically dissimilar assemblage along a southeastern barrier (Fig. 3.7).

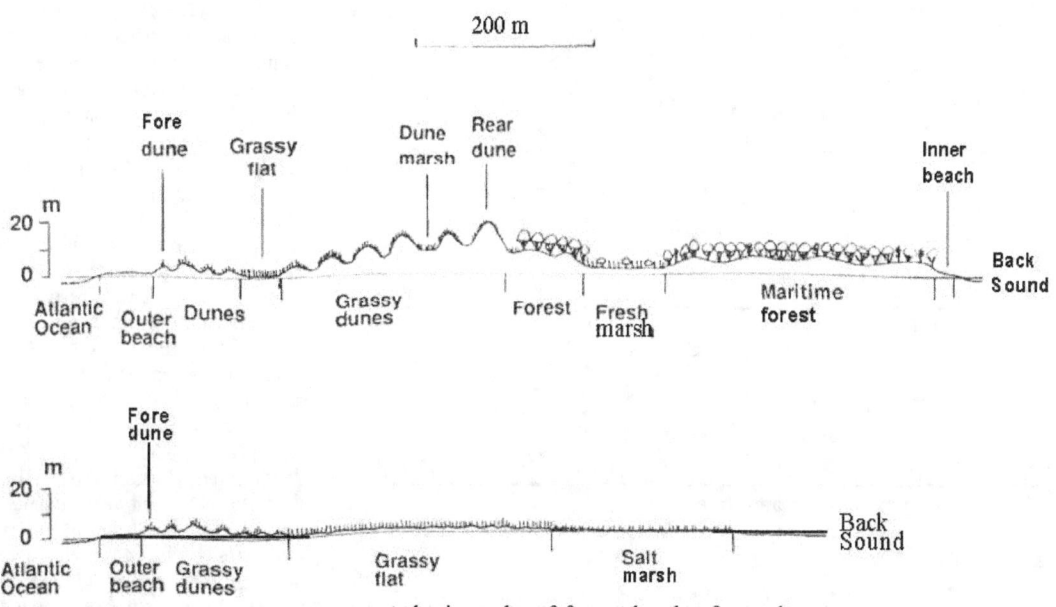

Fig. 3.4. Transect diagrams showing generalized physiography of forested and unforested portions of Shackleford Banks, North Carolina (From Au 1969).

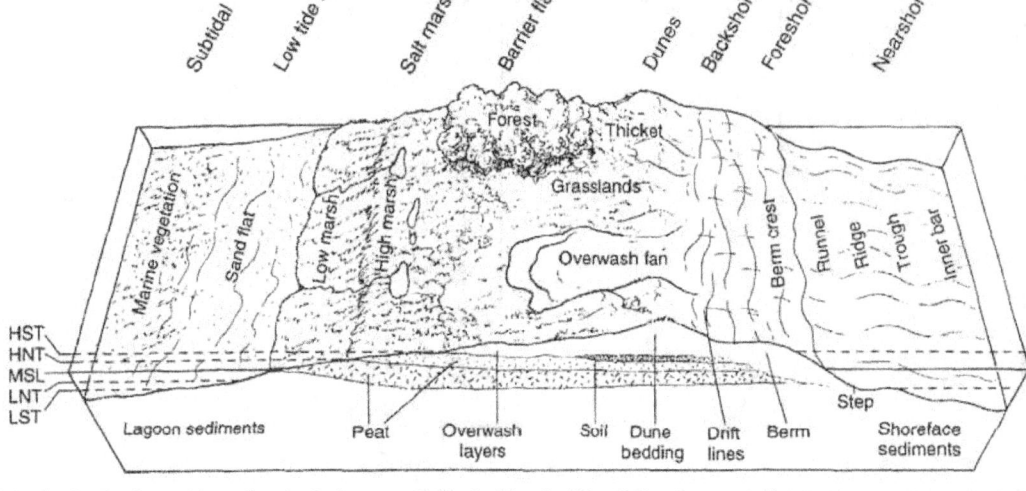

Fig. 3.5. The basic physiographic and ecological zones of a typical barrier island (the diagram indicates the zonation on typical barrier beaches, and does not imply that every barrier resembles the drawing).

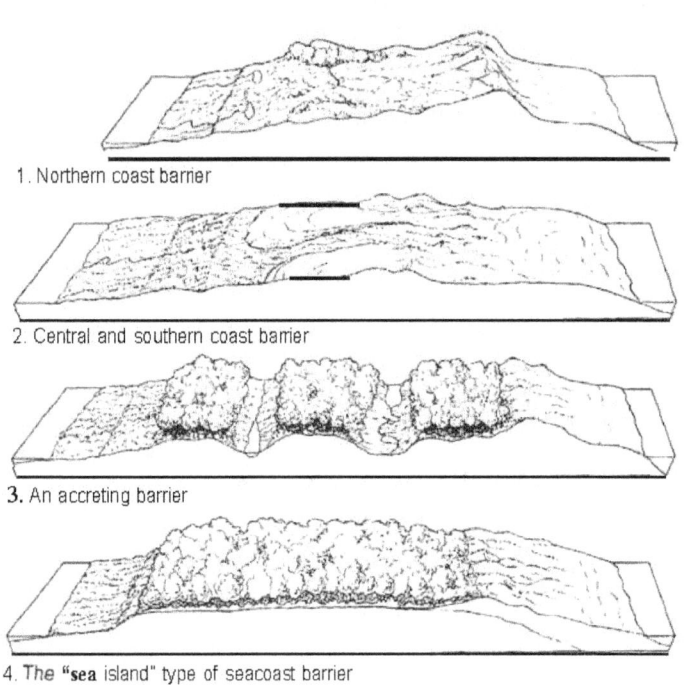

1. Northern coast barrier

2. Central and southern coast barrier

3. An accreting barrier

4. The "sea island" type of seacoast barrier

Fig. 3.6. Typical barrier island profiles found along the east coast of the United States. 1) A northern coast barrier where dune building is more significant than overwash. Well-developed dune lines exist close to the beach, and are often scarped if the beach is retreating. The barrier is made up of dunes on top of earlier overwash deposits. Where enough protection exists, it is vegetated by dune grasses, shrubs, and woodlands. 2) A central and southern coast overwash barrier. Regular overwashes create a broad, generally sloping barrier that is made up primarily of overwash strata and terraces with dunes scattered on top. The barriers are basically flat, covered with grasslands and scattered thickets toward the backside, and extensive salt marshes behind. 3) An accreting barrier, or one that is relatively stable, having been built originally as dunes formed on a growing beach. The uplands are forest and the interdune lowlands are pond, marsh, or swamp. Woodlands occur just behind the main barrier dune and are "pruned" by salt spray. 4) The "Sea Island" type of southeastern coastal barrier. These are drowned sections of the mainland, with a modern beach attached. The vegetation is dominated by forest, usually right up to the main dune ridge. Such barriers are common where sea energy is low, and tide range wide (from Godfrey 197613).

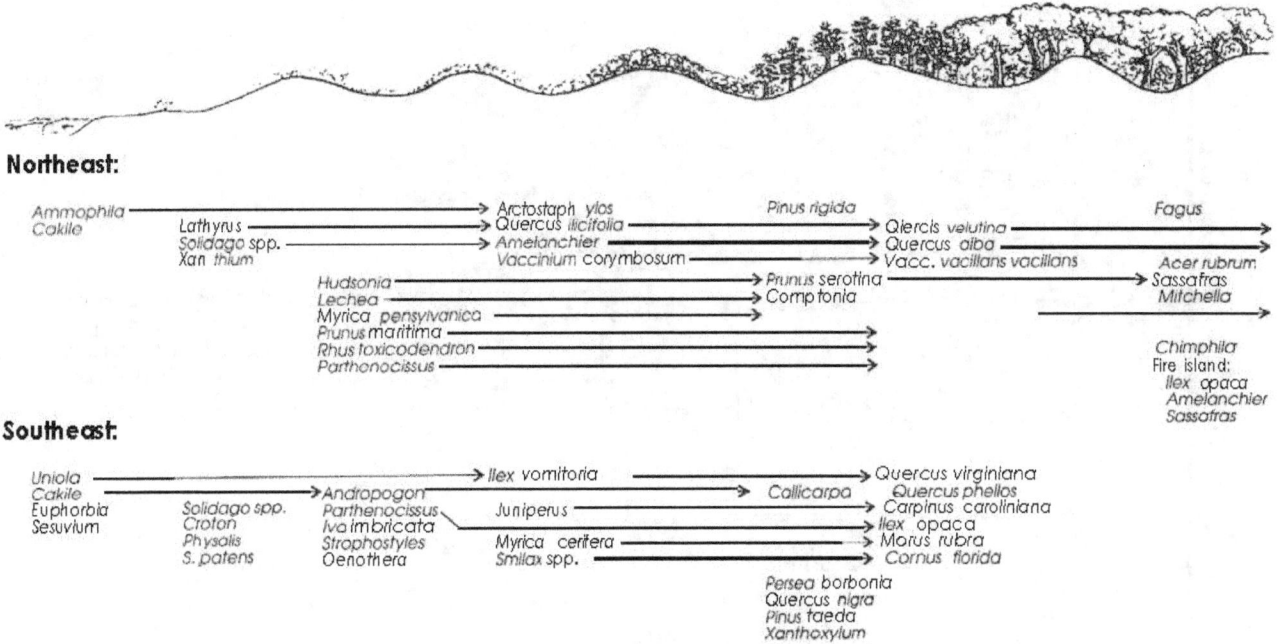

Northeast:

Ammophila
Cakile

Lathyrus
Solidago spp.
Xanthium

Arctostaphylos
Quercus ilicifolia
Amelanchier
Vaccinium corymbosum

Pinus rigida

Quercus velutina
Quercus alba
Vacc. vacillans vacillans

Fagus

Hudsonia
Lechea
Myrica pensylvanica
Prunus maritima
Rhus toxicodendron
Parthonocissus

Prunus serotina
Comptonia

Acer rubrum
Sassafras
Mitchella

Chimphila
Fire island:
Ilex opaca
Amelanchier
Sassafras

Southeast:

Uniola
Cakile
Euphorbia
Sesuvium

Solidago spp.
Croton
Physalis
S. patens

Andropogon
Parthenocissus
Iva imbricata
Strophostyles
Oenothera

Ilex vomitoria

Juniperus

Myrica cerifera
Smilax spp.

Callicarpa

Quercus virginiana
Quercus phellos
Carpinus caroliniana
Ilex opaca
Morus rubra
Cornus florida

Persea borbonia
Quercus nigra
Pinus taeda
Xanthoxylum

Fig. 3.7. Generalized zonation of maritime vegetation: a comparison between a northeastern and a southeastern barrier island (from Godfrey 1976b).

Succession

Several botanists proposed successional schemes for plant communities on barrier islands predicated on a convergence toward a maritime forest community (Figs. 3.8 to 3.11). Most of these succession models lack supporting evidence, however, and must be considered speculative. Few of these authorities defined what they meant by the term "succession," but it is clear from the context there was order in the progression of changes in plant communities (Hillestad et al. 1975). Two explanations have been offered for the pattern of plant succession on barrier islands. Wells (1928) and more recently Chapman (1976), believed barrier island plant succession was internally driven and each stage succession, from unvegetated dune to mature forest, progressively stabilizing the soil and preparing the way for the next stage (Figs. 3.12 and 3.13). This viewpoint (called autogenic succession) considers vegetative cover the fundamental agent of soil accumulation and topographic control on barrier islands.

Others (Oosting 1954; Martin 1959; Au 1969; Art 1971) questioned this explanation of succession and instead, proposed that topographic differences result from geological processes and that the zones of vegetation communities develop independently of one another in the various environments produced by varied topography. Wells (1942:537) recognized the importance of environment and wrote that each vegetation zone has

been "stabilized by different salt intensities [such that] the grass, the shrubs, and the live oak forest communities are all climax on a stable coastline."

Perhaps a key to understanding this difference in interpretation is found in Wells's (1942) use of the term "stable coastline." Coastlines are notoriously unstable. Wells (1942) arrived at his initial conclusion about autogenic succession because in 1928 he thought that the North Carolina coastline was accreting. He was describing a primary successional pattern for freshly deposited sand. Chapman (1976) was also clearly describing primary succession when he stated that the three requisites enabling formation of maritime dunes are a source of sand, a wind to move it, and plant colonization to stabilize it. As one dune stabilizes its plant community, another successively begins to form in front of it (Chapman 1976).

Both successional concepts can be accommodated if one accepts the idea that most beaches are unstable. On a worldwide basis, many beaches are retreating in the face of rising sea level. Other beaches are accreting because of continental uplift or as a result of temporary processes such as proximity to ocean inlets, beach replenishment, or construction of dikes (e.g., Netherlands) (Chapman 1976).

Observers of accreting beaches or migrating dunes may be describing primary succession leading ultimately to stabilized forest. Observers of eroding beaches may be viewing remnants of forest undergoing species attrition and severe habitat modification as a result of increased exposure to

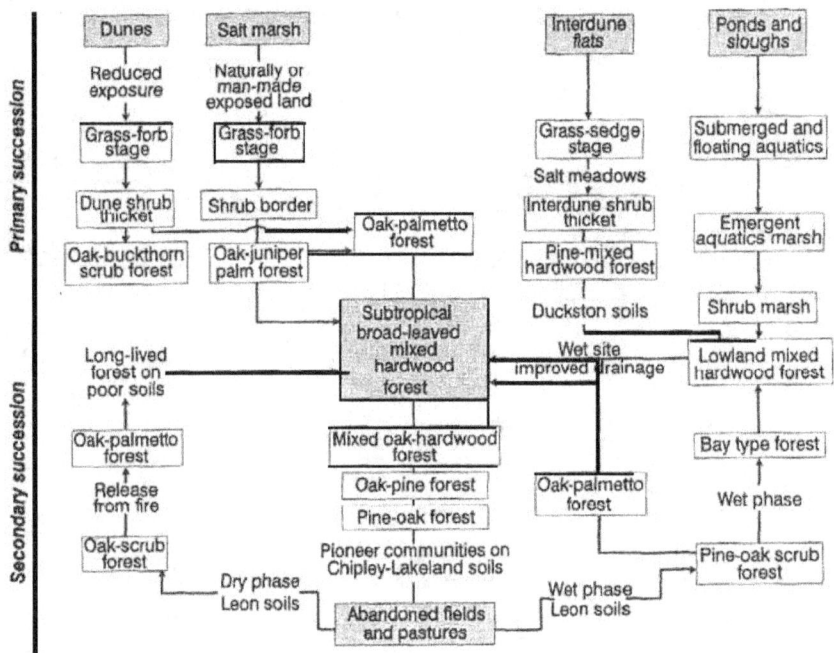

Fig. 3.8. Successional relationships between plant communities on Cumberland Island, Georgia (from Hillestad et al. 1976, after Bozeman 1975).

wind damage, salt aerosol, and sand burial. On eroding beaches, the grassy dunes and shrub thicket can be viewed as representing the result of gradual attrition of species from a mature community. In this way plant communities of similar structure may be produced by two different processes (Chapman 1976).

In the absence of evidence in support of the complete successional progression from sand dunes to maritime forest on barrier islands of the southeastern United States, a few researchers attempted to account for plant community diver-

sity and zonation simply in terms of response to disturbance. Turner and Bratton (1987:99) reported that on Cumberland Island, Georgia, the heterogeneity of the landscape produced differing degrees of response to each type of disturbance (fire, grazing by feral animals, or storms). The boundaries between components of the landscape may be changed as a result of disturbance. These investigations suggested that antagonism among disturbances may function as a stabilizing force in the landscape, concluded that "[it] is unclear...to what extent the community boundaries are a function of

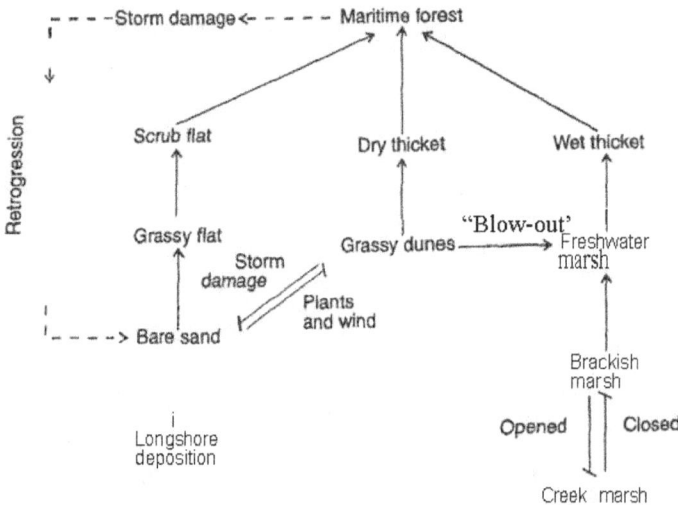

Fig. 3.9. Schematic representation of successional stages in vegetative cover on Shackleford Banks, a North Carolina barrier island (from Au 1969).

Cyclic process

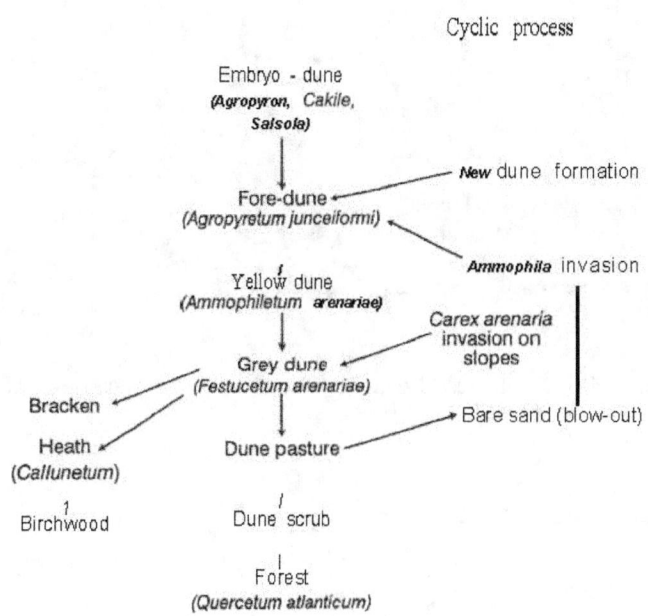

Fig. 3.10. Successional stages in the development of coastal dunes in Great Britain (from Chapman 1976; used with permission of Pergamon Press).

Successional trends

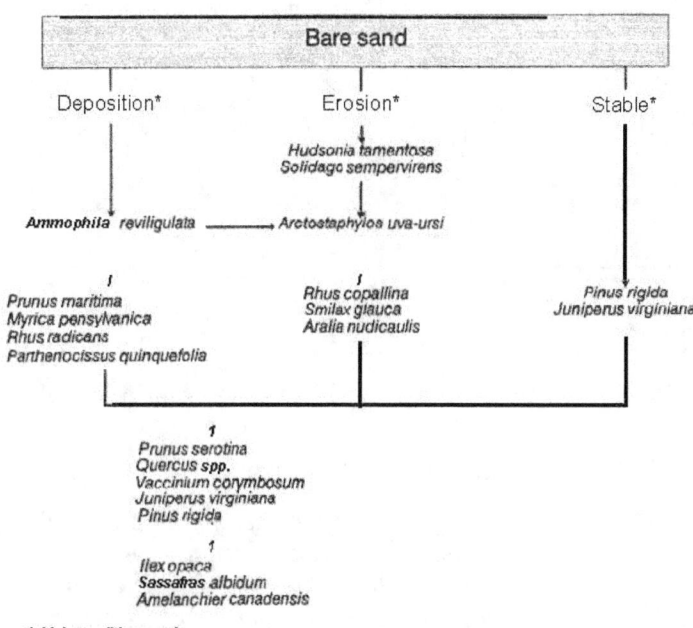

Fig. 3.11. Trends in plant community succession within the Fiie Island, New York, Sunken Forest (from Art 197 1).

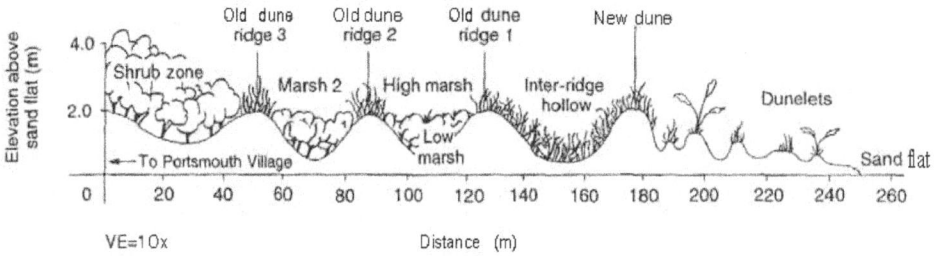

Fig. 3.12. Generalized transect across a system of parallel dune ridges at Portsmouth, North Carolina, showing vegetation suc-cession that accompanied development of the dune system between 1945 and 1975 (from Burk et al. 1981).

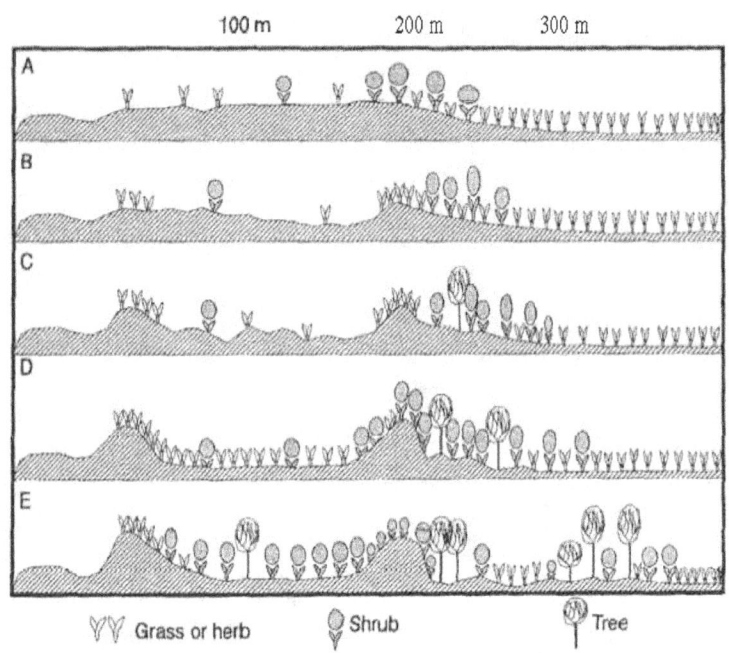

Fig. 3.13. Hypothetical profile development and succession of vegetation zones on an accreting barrier island. The ocean berm is at left, the sound or mainland side of the barrier at right in each diagram (from Martin 1959; used with permission of the Ecological Society of America).

environmental conditions and to what extent they are determined by disturbance dynamics."

McPherson (1988: 1) addressed this issue by studying boundary dynamics along the scrub-forest and the marsh-forest interface areas on Cumberland Island, Georgia. Results of this study

> . . . indicated that areal extent of scrub and marsh patches varied independently of disturbance. Scrub/forest boundaries were relatively dynamic compared to marsh/forest boundaries. Marsh and scrub [patch] sizes were correlated with long-term precipitation patterns. Overstory vegetation change resulted primarily from differences in the stature of live oak (*Quercus virginiana*). Vegetation change in the shrub layer reflected differences in grazing

pressure from large herbivores. Soil chemical characteristics did not vary along transects.

McPherson (1988: 1) concluded that

> . . . [the] data suggest that marsh/forest and scrub/forest boundaries are controlled by fluctuations in water table depth, and succession of scrub to oak-palmetto (*Quercus* spp. and *Serenoa repens*) forest is controlled by soil moisture. Disturbance (by fire or by the grazing of herbivores) plays a minor role in community dynamics. . .

Although biologists generally agree about the distinctions in growth form and species composition used to differentiate among the several major vegetation types on barrier islands and coastal sand ridges, they differ somewhat about the causes. direction. and rate of possible transformation among types. The relative contributions of such possibly influential factors as climate, soil characteristics, role of pioneer species, and habitat disturbance in establishing or transforming dune plant communities has not been determined. The relative contributions of these environmental factors may also vary according to geological conditions existing at a particular location. The rate of vegetation change may be highest on accreting or eroding dunes and may appear to be lower on more stable dunes. Although (he vegetation cover on an accreting dune and on an eroding dune may be similar, the direction of change is different (Chapman 1976).

The patterns of vegetation interaction and response conditions imposed by the environment and the effects of disturbance seem to be complex, and not enough is currently known to support a comprehensive concept of plant community succession on coastal dunes. Thus, the term "community succession" should be used cautiously until more quantitative information is available about community interactions.

Origin of the Maritime Forest

Geologic evidence suggests that the post-Pleistocene rate of sea-level rise slowed markedly about 5,000 years ago (Milliman and Emery 1968). Presumably, our present barrier islands formed at that time as the rising sea surrounded relict beach ridges left stranded on the coastal plain. Since becoming barrier islands, some ridges have grown larger by accretion of additional sediments, whereas others have destabilized and reformed farther up on the sea floor, or have been destroyed and their sediments welded onto more stable shorelines. presumably also, our **present maritime** forests achieved something of their present form and species composition during this period of adjustment to relative geological stability (author's observation).

Maritime forest may have developed as a result of primary succession from propagules of plants dispersed by water, wind, or animals from mainland coastal forests (Bellis, personal observation). Once established, the maritime forest community could be self-sustaining as long as the special environmental conditions that Produced it continued to exist. The latitudinal gradient of the Present maritime forest flora might, therefore, indicate that this community is influenced as much by climatic gradients as by the oceanic environment and bears a greater floristic affinity to the adjacent mainland than to more distant maritime forests (Bellis, Personal observation).

It seems equally possible, though, that maritime forests developed by modification of the forests already covering newly stranded ancient beach ridges that now form the more stable core of many barrier islands. There are other older

beachridges, or escarpments, that are as yet unaffected by risingsealevel. The natural **forest** cover at such sites in North Carolina appears to be mixed pine-hardwood with an understory including hollies, waxmyrtle, redbay, and red cedar (*Juniperus virginiana*). similar to the mature forests on barrier islands (Bellis, personal observation).

The following is a scenario in which a maritime forest may develop by modification of an older stand as the relict ridge becomes surrounded by salt water (Bellis, personal observation). Tall, broad-leaved deciduous elements and pines of the ridge forest could be lost as a result Of salt toxicity and storm damage. Gradual reduction of the original canopy releases the mostly evergreen understory of small-**leaved oaks, hollies,** waxmyrtle, redbay, and red cedar. These former understory species expand to fill the light gaps produced by loss oftheoriginal canopy. The new canopy is composed of short-statured (formerly understory) species, which now form the dense mosaic of small trees (hat is **recognized** as maritime forest.

Once formed, species of the maritime forest emigrate onto Holocene deposits in a series of stages recognized as secondary succession. At particularly well-protected sites such as the **mainland** side of seaward-accreting barrier is-**lands, the maritime forest** reverts to its original stature and species composition and is indistinguishable from nearby mainland forest (Bellis, personal observation).

Alternatively, on barrier islands with rapid erosion, salt-aerosol damage and storms may damage or kill large individual trees, allowing survival of only compact shrub growth forms. Ultimately, even these are destroyed by burial beneath drifting sand, by loss of roots, or through salt toxicity. At this point slow-growing trees and shrubs are replaced by faster growing grasses that are more tolerant of unstable soil conditions. In this example, the apparent sequence of succession is from maritime forest to grassy dunes.

Under all scenarios, individual forests are expected to more closely resemble the nearby mainland forests than other distant, maritime forests. The maritime forests of the southeastern United States do not represent a single distinctive. floristic Unit separate from the coastal plain forest, but rather exist in as much variety as the mainland forests of the region.

Fungi and Lichens

Nonvascular plants are frequently omitted from general inventories of barrier island flora and fauna. A list of bolete basidiomycetes from (he Nags Head Woods, North Carolina (Wolfe, 1984, Table 3.2), suggests that the fungal flora of maritime forests can be quite varied. The bolete taxa listed in Table 3.2 also appear to occur commonly in other woodland settings on (he mainland

(Wolfe 1984). The basidiomycetes are ecologically significant because they represent the major agents of decay and remineralization within the detrital layer in the maritime forest.

Some fungi, such as the zygomycete *Gigaspora* sp., form symbiotic mycorrhizal associations with the roots

Table 3.2. Bolete fungi in the Nags Head Woods, North Carolina (C. B. Wolfe, Pennsylvania State University; personal communication in 1984).

Species	Source
Boletus aurisporus	Peck
B. griseus	Frost and Peck
B. pallidus	Frost
B. subvelutipes	Peek
Gyporus castanus	(Bull. ex Fr.) Quel.
Leccinum griseum	(Quel.) Singer
Pulveroboletus sp.	
Strobilomyces floccopus	(Vahl ex. Fr.) Kar.
Suillus cothematus	
ssp. *hiemalis*	Singer
Tylopilus fumosipes	(Peck) Smith anyd Thiers
T. plumbeoviolaceus	(Snell and Dick) Singer
T. rubobrunneus	Mazzer and Smith
Phylloporus rhodoxanthus	
ssp. *americanus*	singer
P. rhodoxanthus	
ssp. *foliiporus*	(Murrill) Singer
Collybia sp.	
Xanthoconium stamineum	(Murrill) Singer

of vascular plants. These associations are essential for efficient uptake of phosphorus in dune soils (Koske and Polson 1984).

Many taxa of lichens occur in the maritime forests as arboreal epiphytes. Crustose forms often completely surround the trunks of American holly (*Ilex opaca*) with a mosaic of pink, white, gray, and green patches. Foliose lichens such as *Parmelia perforata* and fruticose forms such as old man's beard (*Usnea* sp.) are often conspicuous on branches in the canopy. Although the ecological role of lichens in the maritime forest has not been studied, lichens, because of their relatively great surface area, may function in mineral-ion sorting and uptake from ocean-derived aerosols. Foliose and fruticose lichens extending from branches in the canopy may wick excess salts away from sensitive buds, thus conferring a survival advantage to lichen-covered branches. Still other lichens may contain nitrogen-fixing endosymbiotic cyanobacteria and thus constitute a significant source of this often-limiting plant nutrient. The tree-inhabiting microflora may be as functionally important as those of the soil in terms of mineral cycling in a maritime forest. The abundance of epiphytic lichens on trees in the maritime forest represents one of several characteristics shared with tropical forests. Both forest types occur on nutrient-poor soils, tend to consist of broad-leaved evergreen trees, and depend to a great extent on foliar uptake and epiphytes as a means of expanding the surface available to trap low concentrations of minerals from the atmosphere. Large mats of fruticose lichens (*Cladonia* spp.) often cover expanses of dune soil in the maritime forest wherever light gaps occur in the forest canopy.

CHAPTER 4.

Fauna of Maritime Forests

Introduction

Comprehensive inventories of fauna for most barrier islands are lacking, and faunal studies specifically of maritime forests are especially rare. The available information frequently covers only selected groups of vertebrate animals such as reptiles and amphibians, birds, or mammals. Invertebrate animals are usually not included. The few inventories that are available often take the form of a checklist of animals for an entire island with little information about their preferred habitat.

Invertebrate Fauna

Insects and spiders are conspicuous components of maritime forests. From their abundance and diversity, it seems logical to assume that such animals perform important ecological functions in mineral cycling and energy flow that affect population dynamics in other groups of organisms. Certainly insects and spiders are essential components of other forest communities where their ecological role has been defined.

Although a few arthropods, such as mosquitos, sandflies, deerflies, chiggers, and ticks, are generally well known to anyone who has ever visited a maritime forest, the majority of invertebrates inhabiting this community and the ecological or behavioral adaptations they may have made to the oceanic environment or island isolation remain unreported. Information about maritime forest invertebrates other than snails, spiders, and insects is apparently absent (Bellis, personal observation).

Snails and Slugs (Pulmonate Gastropods)

Gastropods have occasionally been collected from barrier islands, but information on this group is incomplete and scattered. Hillestad et al. (1975) conducted a year-long survey of pulmonate gastropods of Cumberland Island, Georgia, as part of a comprehensive ecological evaluation of the then recently established Cumberland Island National Seashore. These investigators listed 10 gastropod species, most of which were collected in habitats created by human activity. Five snails were found in litter under an exotic plant (*Cycas* sp.): *Polygyra pustula*, *Zonitoides arboreus*, *Helicina orbiculata*, *Hawaiia minuscula*, and *Pupoides modicus*. Gastropods collected from interdune flats were *Succinea campestris* and *Lymnaea humilis*. Snails inhabiting well-drained pastures and lawns covered with centipede grass (*Eremochloa ophiuroides*) were *Euglandina rosea*, *Succinea campestris*, and *Tridopsis hopetonensis*. *Polygyra sep-*

temvolva and *Succinea campestris* were found in a slash pine (*Pinus elliottii*) plantation. With the exception of the slash pine, no forested habitat was included among the sample locations, and it is unknown whether these snails and slugs occur also in natural communities.

Spiders

Spiders inhabiting the maritime forests on four barrier islands near Charleston, South Carolina, were inventoried by Caddy (1981, Table 4.1). Spiders were observed to be active throughout the warm season (February to October). Species of orb-weaving spiders (Araneidae) reached maturity at different times during this period. The largest number of mature individuals was observed during early summer, although most species actually matured during late summer. Most of these spiders are also distributed in forest habitats on the mainland throughout the region (Gaddy 1981).

Gaddy's (1981) census included 22 taxa of orb-weaving spiders, 3 species of spiders that live in nests or webs of other spiders (*Argyrodes* spp.), large male black widow spiders (*Lutrodectus mactans*), and the fishing spider (*Dolomedes* sp.). Black widow females seemingly prefer to live among the debris in sand dunes dominated by sea oats and seldom venture into the forest. Contrary to a previous suggestion that a saltwater barrier might account for the absence of the fishing spider (*Dolomedes*) from most of the barrier islands of the southeastern United States (Carico 1973), Gaddy (1981) found *D. triton* in a freshwater wetland less than 50 m from the beach.

Twenty-three species of orb- or nest-spinning spiders were recovered from pitfall traps set for insects on Cumberland Island, Georgia, by Hillestad et al. (1975). Although this total number of species is similar to that reported by Caddy (1981), for barrier islands in South Carolina (22 species), not one species or even genus was common to both locations. The Cumberland Island study encompassed all habitats on the island, not just the maritime forest. Nonetheless, absolute absence of taxonomic overlap seems remarkable. Families of spiders reported for Cumberland Island in order of decreasing number of taxa per family included wolf or ground spiders (Lycosidae), 13; hunting spiders (Gnaphosidae), 5; jumping spiders (Salticidae), 2; and one taxon each of white-eyed spider (Amaurobiidae), crab spider (Thomisidae), and uloborid (Uloboridae) (Hillestad et al. 1975).

The availability of freshwater habitat (swale ponds) in maritime forests seemingly increases habitat diversity for spiders as for plants and other animals. Availability of aquatic habitat is invariably associated with greater biodiversity in a maritime forest.

Table 4.I. Frequency (number of adults per transect) of orb weaving spiders on several South Carolina barrier islands (Gaddy 1981).

Species	Feb.	Mar.-Apr.	May-Jun.	Jul.-Aug.	Sep.–Oct.
Araneus pegnia	0.3	0.5			
Araneus miniatus		0.5			
Araneus bicentenarius		3.5	3.0	-	-
Cyclosa sp.		0.2	0.5		
Acanthepeira spp.		7.1	20.5	2.0	
Mangora placida		7.9		0.2	
Eustala anastera		0.5		0.2	
Leucouge venusta		0.8	5.5	4.7	1.0
Mangora maculata	-	-	1.0		
Mecynogea lemniscata	-	-	0.5		
Micrathena gracilis			1.0	0.7	
Micrathena sagittata			0.5	1.2	
Mangora gibberosa		-	0.5	0.3	
Neoscona arabesca			18.5	6.5	2.0
Agriope trifasciata		-	2.0	4.5	2.0
Araneus pratensis				0.3	
Gasterocantha cancriformis				0.7	
Gea heptagon	-	-		0.2	
Acacesia hamata				0.2	
Nephila clavipes				13.7	31.5
Argiope aurantia	-	-		0.2	0.1
Neoscona domiciliorum	-	-		0.3	2.0
Totals	0.3	21.0	53.5	35.9	38.6

Insects

Insects of the forest floor

Perhaps the most comprehensive inventory to date of insects inhabiting a barrier island was by Hillestad et al. (1975) for Cumberland Island, Georgia. This inventory, conducted in summer, included each of eight plant communities, ranging from interdune grass flats to various stages in forest succession. The latest stage in forest succession was represented by a subtropical broad-leaved mixed hardwood forest with live oak, laurel oak, redbay, American holly, cabbage palm, and other trees of maritime forests of the southeastern United States. Because insects were collected in pitfall traps, the data are biased in favor of forest-floor and crawling species over forest canopy and flying species.

Results of the inventory on Cumberland Island (Hillestad at al. 1975) in the mixed oak-hardwood forest type indicated that dominant forest-floor insects were, in decreasing order of numbers of individuals and relative abundance: June beetles, rove beetles, roaches, ants, flies, crickets, carrion beetles, blister beetles, and ground beetles (Table 4.2). Essentially the same order of abundance was observed among the other, presumably less

successionally advanced, forest cover types on Cumberland Island; June beetles thoroughly dominated the collections, frequently accounting for 50–85% of all individuals collected (Hillestad et al. 1975).

Wasps

Wasps of the Nags Head Woods, North Carolina, were inventoried by Krombein (1949). In all, 54 species of wasps were listed, including 2 new species. Four wasp families (Pompilidae [spider wasps], Mutillidae [velvet ants], Vespidae [colonial wasps], and Sphecidae [mud-dauber wasps]) were each represented by 11-15 species. Each of two families (Tiphiidae [tiphiid wasps] and Scoliidae [vespoid wasps]) were represented by a single species. Genera of wasps represented by more than one species included *Episyron, Anoplius, Pseudomethoca, Dasymutilla, Timulla, Rygchium, Sternodynerus, Polistes, Tachysphex,* and *Chlorion.*

The ecological significance of wasps in regulating populations of other arthropods is hinted at by their behavior. Spider wasps (Pompilidae) nest in the ground and use their sting to paralyze spiders. Velvet ants (Mutillidae) are often covered by a dense coat of brightly colored (red, orange) hairs. Their larvae are parasitic on

Table 4.2. Insects collected in pitfall traps in maritime forest habitat (mixed oak-hardwood forest) on Cumberland Island, Georgia, summer 1973 (Adapted from Hillestad et al. 1975).

Order Family	Type	No. Individuals
Orthoptera	Grasshoppers, etc.	209
Tettigoniidae	(grasshoppers)	2
Gryllidae	(crickets)	70
Blattodea	Roaches	
Blattidae		137
Hemiptera	True bugs	0[a]
Homoptera	Aphids, scale insects	0[a]
Dermaptera	Earwigs	0[a]
Coleoptera	Beetles, weevils	5,652
Carabidae	(ground beetles)	40
Histeridae	(hister beetles)	43
Silphidae	(carrion beetles)	54
Staphylinidae	(rove beetles)	240
Elateridae	(click beetles)	1
Tenebrionidae	(darkling beetles)	1
Alleculidae	(comb-clawed beetles)	2
Scarabaeidae	(scarabs, june beetles)	5,265
Curculionidae	(weevils)	6
Diptera	True flies	74
Hymenoptera	Ants, wasps, bees	114
Formicidae	(ants)	113
Pompilidae	(spider wasps)	1
Total		6,049

[a] Representatives of these insect orders were not recovered from pitfall traps in the maritime forest habitat but were represented in other forest community types.

cocoons of solitary wasps and bees. Colonial wasps (Vespidae), including paper wasps and yellow-jackets, are known for their powerful sting. In temperate regions the colonies last only one season. Among these social insects, only the queen survives the winter to start a new colony the following spring. Larvae are fed other insects and small animals. The mud-daubers (Sphecidae) are solitary (nonsocial) wasps, although many individuals may build nests near one another, and a few species exhibit rudimentary social organization. Their nests may be in burrows in the ground, in natural cavities in wood, or in the familiar mud structures. Mud daubers feed other insects to their larvae, and some are prey specific (Johnson et al. 1974; Hillestad et al. 1975).

Blood-feeding arthropods

Blood-feeding insects occur abundantly on barrier islands (Johnson et al. 1974; Hillestad et al. 1975). Deer-flies (*Chrysops*) breed in the marsh-forest ecotone. After emergence from the pupal stage, the adults move into more heavily wooded areas. Salt-marsh mosquitos (*Aedes solicitans, Aedes taeniorhynchus,* and *Anopheles crucians*) breed in marshes, but adults often penetrate the maritime forest when seeking a meal. Domestic mosquitos (including *Aedes aegypti* and *Culexpipiens quinquefasciatus*) breed in trash heaps and standing water near human habitation, but can also enter the forest in search of food. Sand flies (*Culicoides*) occur throughout barrier islands. The presence of white-tailed deer (*Odocoileus virginianus*) and feral animals on barrier islands is associated with larger populations of ticks. Common tick species include *Ixodes affinis, I. scapularis, Dermacentor variabilis, Amblyommum americana,* and *Haemaphysalis* sp. (Johnson et al. 1974; Hillestad et al. 1975).

Nuisance insects

The fire ant (*Solenopsis*), an annoying exotic, established in disturbed soils on Cumberland Island, Georgia (Hillestad et al. 1975). Insects associated with damage to forest trees have been reported from a few maritime forest locations, but the incidence of insect damage appears to be no greater than on mainland locations. Hillestad et al. (1975) reported evidence of lightning-damaged slash pines being killed by the coarse writing engraver (*Ips calligraphus*) on Cumberland Island. They also noted slight damage to loblolly pines from the Nantucket pine tip moth (*Rhyacionia frustrana*) and windthrown red cedars damaged by the eastern juniper bark beetle (*Phloeosinus dentatus*). Insect damage to trees of the maritime forest seems temporary (minor defoliation by caterpillars) or focused on trees already damaged by lightning or windthrow.

In 1987, the gypsy moth (*Lymantria dispar*) was first reported from Virginia Beach, Virginia, and the Currituck Banks, North Carolina (Bellis, personal observation). This moth has caused extensive damage to oaks and other hardwoods throughout the Northeast. The susceptibility of live oak and other hardwoods in maritime forest to gypsy moth infestation is unknown, but the potential for significant effects on barrier island vegetation is great. What would happen to maritime forest soils and understory if the dense evergreen oak canopy that protects them from wind erosion and salt damage were to be suddenly removed?

Vertebrate Fauna

The earliest studies of barrier island fauna (Engels 1942, 1952) were directed toward understanding the origin of animal populations. Engels (1942) believed the now-discredited theory that all barrier islands arose from the sea by emergence of offshore sandbars, and, in 1952, assumed that colonization must have occurred over water from the adjacent mainland by chance occurrence or in locations where the barrier islands are nearer the mainland. His "primary aim [was] to ascertain which species have become established on the various islands, and which have been apparently excluded" (1942:273). Although Engels believed the reduced number of animal species on barrier islands resulted primarily from the failure of some species to reach the islands in sufficient numbers to become established, he did allow that "some of the apparent simplicity of the vertebrate fauna almost certainly is due to the lack of diversity of habitat, but this factor alone does not account for all of the absentees" (1952:702, 741).

The explanation of the source of barrier island animal populations has now been shown to be considerably more complex than envisioned by Engels (1942, 1952); however, his effort produced one of the first comparative studies of barrier island and mainland faunas (Engels 1952; Table 4.3). Establishment of the Cape Hatteras National Seashore in 1953 resulted in the need for a biological inventory of lands that came under National Park Service management. Results of this comprehensive survey of vertebrate animal distributions along a major segment of the North Carolina Outer Banks were presented in the form of listings of vertebrate fauna in each of 17 ecological communities (Quay 1959). The faunal list presented under the heading "woods" concentrated on the Buxton Woods maritime forest. This list has been supplemented by results of recent additional censuses of vertebrate animals (Webster 1988; Parnell et al. 1989) in Table 4.4. Several other studies cover the fauna on entire barrier islands such as Sapelo Island, Georgia (Martof 1963); Cumberland Island, Georgia (Hillestad et al. 1975); Bulls Island, South Carolina (Andre 1981); or entire barrier island systems: Georgia (Johnson et al. 1974, Appendix B), and Virginia (Dueser et al. 1979). These more comprehensive faunal lists are similar to the summary list in Table

Table 4.3. Numerical comparison of tetrapod vertebrate fauna of Shackleford Banks, North Carolina, and the immediately adjacent mainland (adapted from Engels 1952).

Taxonomic group	No. of species	
	Shackleford banks	Adjacent mainland
Amphibia	5	32
Reptilia	12	48
Aves	12-16	77
Mammalia	5-7	29
Total	34–40	186

4.4 except for the inclusion of many marine, aquatic, and other animals that are not normal inhabitants of maritime forest habitat.

Lazell (1976) produced a short synthesis describing the dispersal mechanisms and adaptive strategies of vertebrates inhabiting the barrier islands of the Atlantic and Gulf coasts of the United States. It was Lazell's view that, although these barriers are technically islands, they do not conform to island theories of faunal origin. The Atlantic barrier islands are so close to the mainland that overwater or waif dispersal is frequent. The concept of population establishment by pioneer species is probably not applicable to these barrier islands. There is little evidence of species turnover or the existence of an equilibrium between extinction and colonization. Instead, barrier islands from Cape Cod to the Gulf coast share many similar physical and ecological features not encountered on the mainland. Continued survival of a species on a barrier island requires that it be able to contend with occasional drastic modifications of habitat (storms) and periodic extremes in freshwater availability and food supply. Under these circumstances, severe ecological conditions or events are a greater selective factor than the founder effect.

Lazell (1976) also suggested that animal species that have successfully retained populations on barrier islands since island origin have managed to survive there because they were already adapted to the special environments on the barriers. He pointed out that although the barrier islands undergo catastrophic change over geologic time, these island movements are not apparent within the lifetime of an individual animal. Genetic continuity and exchange in a broad population is maintained as island segments are continually separated and then rejoined by geologic forces.

At least along the North Carolina Outer Banks, the process of island fragmentation is not random (Lazell 1976). Inlets migrate to the south or west under the influence of a southerly longshore drift. Animal migration in a southerly direction is made possible as new habitat is created by plant succession north of the inlet. Simultaneously, other populations may be forced to emigrate farther south by erosion of established habitat on the south side of the inlet (Fig. 4.1). Lazell (1976) termed this pattern of progressive dispersal "Giffordian dispersal" in honor of Clay Gifford, long-time chief naturalist at Cape Hatteras National Seashore, who first noted it. The Giffordian pattern of dispersal, in association with a high degree of habitat similarity on various barrier islands, resulted in a ubiquitous assemblage of reptiles and mammals (Table 4.5).

The Buxton Woods, at 3.5" N latitude in the Cape Hatteras National Seashore, is near the area of maximum

Table 4.4. Vertebrates of maritime forests on the Cape Hatteras National Seashore and vicinity, North Carolina (adapted from Quay 1959; Parnell et al. 1989; and Webster 1988). Taxonomy agrees with Banks et al. 1987.

Common name[a]	Scientific name	Common name[a]	Scientific name
Amphibians		Ring-necked pheasant	*Phasianus colchicus*
Salamanders (Caudata)		King rail	*Rallus elegans*
Amphiuma	*Amphiuma means*	Common gallinule	*Gallinula chloropus*
Toads and Frogs (Salienta)		American coot	*Fulica americana*
Fowler's toad	*Bufo woodhousii*	American woodcock	*Scolopax minor*
Green treefrog	*Hyla cinerea*	Common snipe	*Gallinago gallinago*
Squirrel treefrog	*H. squirella*	Spotted sandpiper	*Actitis macularia*
Gray treefrog	*H. versicolor*	Mourning dove*	*Zenaida macroura*
Eastern narrow-mouthed frog	*Gastrophryne carolinensis*	Yellow-billed cuckoo*	*Coccyzus americanus*
Southern leopard frog	*Rana sphenocephala*	Screech owl	*Otus asio*
		Belted kingfisher	*Megaceryle alcyon*
Reptiles		Common flicker*	*Colaptes auratus*
Turtles (Chelonia)		Great crested flycatcher	*Myiarchus crinitus*
Snapping turtle	*Chelydra serpentina*	Common crow	*Corvus brachyrhynchos*
Eastern mud turtle	*Kinosternon subrubrum*	Fish crow	*C. ossifragus*
Spotted turtle	*Clemmys guttata*	Carolina wren*	*Thryothorus ludovicianus*
Yellow-bellied turtle	*Pseudemys scripta*	Gray catbird	*Dumetella carolinensis*
Lizards (Sauria)		Brown thrasher	*Toxostoma rufum*
Ground skink	*Scincella lateralis*	American robin	*Turdus migratorius*
Southeastern five-line		Hermit thrush	*Catharus guttatus*
skink	*Eumeces inexpectatus*	Cedar waxwing	*Bombycilla cedrorum*
Snakes (Serpentes)		White-eyed vireo*	*Vireo griseus*
Brown water snake	*Nerodia taxispilota*	Red-eyed vireo	*V. olivaceus*
Brown snake	*Storeria dekayi*	Prothonotary warbler	*Protonotaria citrea*
Ribbon snake	*Thamnophis sauritus*	Yellow-rumped warbler	*Dendroica coronata*
Black racer	*Coluber constrictor*	Pine warbler	*D. pinus*
Rough green snake	*Opheodrys aestivus*	Prairie warbler	*D. discolor*
Yellow rat snake	*Elaphe obsoleta*	Common yellowthroat*	*Geothlypis trichas*
Eastern kingsnake	*Lampropeltis getulus*	Cardinal	*Cardinalis cardinalis*
Cottonmouth	*Agkistrodon piscivorus*	Rufous-sided towhee*	*Pipilo erythrophthalmus*
Canebrake rattlesnake	*Crotalus horridus*		
Diamondback rattlesnake	*C. adamanteus*	**Mammals**	
		Least shrew	*Cryptotis parva*
Birds		Eastern mole	*Scalopus aquaticus*
Pied-billed grebe	*Podilymbus podiceps*	Eastern cottontail	*Sylvilagus floridanus*
Great blue heron	*Ardea herodias*	Marsh rabbit	*S. palustris*
Green heron	*Butorides virescens*	Silver-haired bat	*Lasionycteris noctivagans*
Little blue heron	*Egretta caerulea*	Red bat	*Lasiurus borealis*
Cattle egret	*Bubulcus ibis*	Gray squirrel	*Sciurus carolinensis*
Common egret	*Casmerodius albus*	White-footed mouse	*Peromyscus leucopus*
Snowy egret	*Egretta thula*	Cotton mouse	*P. gossypinus*
Louisiana heron	*E. tricolor*	Muskrat	*Ondatra zibethicus*
Black-crowned heron	*Nycticorax nycticorax*	Norway rat	*Rattus norvegicus*
Yellow-crowned heron	*N. violaceus*	Marsh rice rat	*Oryzomys palustris*
Wood duck	*Aix sponosa*	House mouse	*Mus musculus*
Ring-necked duck	*Aythya collaris*	Nutria	*Myocastor coypus*
Bufflehead	*Bucephala albeola*	Virginia opossum	*Didelphis virginiana*
Hooded merganser	*Lophodytes cucullatus*	Raccoon	*Procyon lotor*
Turkey vulture	*Cathartes aura*	Mink	*Mustela vison*
Sharp-shinned hawk	*Accipiter striatus*	River otter	*Lutra canadensis*
Cooper's hawk	*A. cooperii*	House cat	*Felis catus = F. domesticus*
Red-shouldered hawk	*Buteo lineatus*	White-tailed deer	*Odocoileus virginianus*
Osprey	*Pandion haliaetus*		

[a] Bird species indicated by an asterisk (*) have been reported as forming breeding populations in maritime forest in South Carolina (Gaddy 1982).

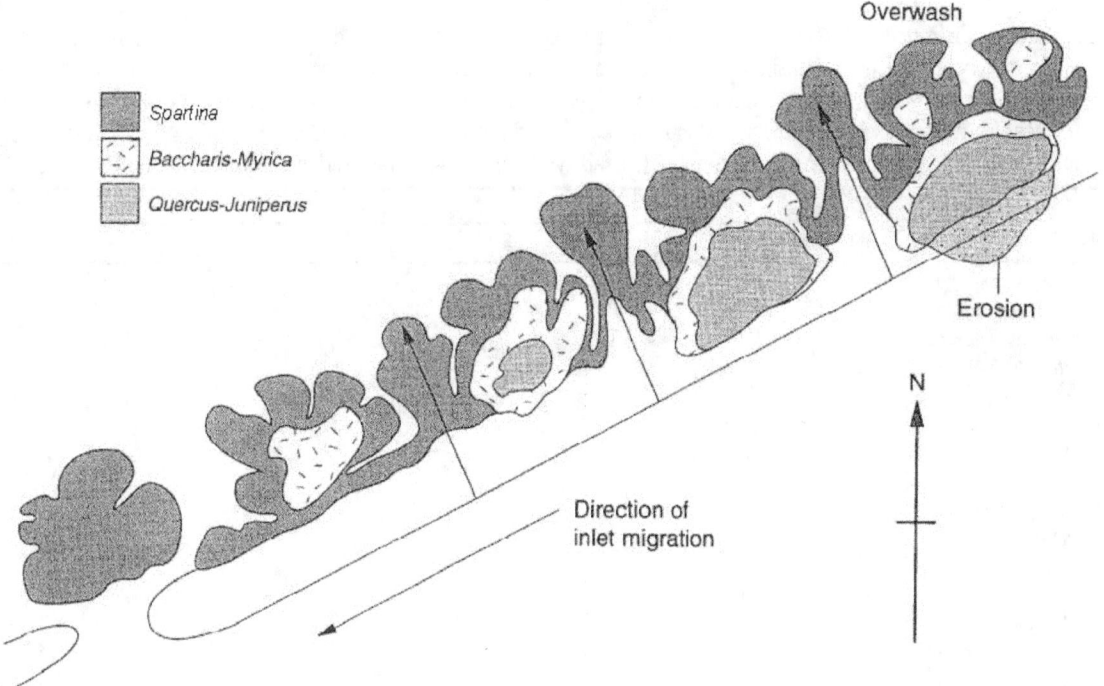

Fig. 4.1. Animal population drift in response to closure of inlets by longshore currents and subsequent succession of old flood-tide deltas to hammocks in North Carolina's inter-capes zone (from Lazell 1976).

plant diversity among Atlantic coast maritime forests (Fig. 3.2). Webster (1988:227) noted that "mammalian diversity in Currituck-Bodie Island is greater than on any other forested barrier island in North Carolina or adjacent coastal states." Webster attributed the maintenance of higher mammalian diversity at Buxton Woods to three factors. First, Hatteras Island periodically has been connected to various mainland locations by island bridges that served as corridors for dispersal from southeastern Virginia and from east-central North Carolina. The island also offers a variety of environments, including freshwater ponds surrounded by maritime forests.

Table 4.5. Ubiquitous reptiles and mammals inhabiting barrier islands on the Atlantic and Gulf of Mexico Coasts (adapted from Lazell 1976).

Common name	Scientific name
Snapping turtle	*Chelydra serpentina*
Diamondback terrapin	*Malaclemys terrapin*
Green water snake	*Nerodia cyclopion* (=*Natrix* sp.)
Black racer	*Coluber constrictor*
Southern hognose snake	*Heterodon platyrhinos*
Native mice	*Peromyscus* spp.
Eastern cottontail	*Sylvilagus* spp.
Raccoon	*Procyon lotor*

Finally, zoogeographers consider the Outer Banks of North Carolina a tension zone of interspecific competition (Lazell 1976), having such pairs as the white-footed mouse (*Peromyscus leucopus*) and cotton mouse (*Peromyscus gossypinus*) and meadow vole (*Microtus pennsylvanicus*) and cotton rat (*Sigmodon hispidus*), which occupy the same niche and remain separated throughout most of the rest of their geographic range. The white-footed mouse and the meadow vole are more common to the north, while the cotton rat and cotton mouse are southern species.

Lists of herpetofauna on several barrier islands between Virginia and Georgia are available. Gibbons and Coker (1978) consolidated these lists in an attempt to elucidate herpetofaunal colonization patterns on Atlantic Coast barrier islands (Table 4.6). An analysis of these data (Table 4.7) confirmed reports by Engels (1942, 1952) and others that the number of species on barrier islands was considerably less than the number of potential colonizers from the nearby mainland (Gibbons and Coker 1978).

Lists of herpetofauna on 10 barrier island locations (Table 4.6) were combined and revealed 108 reptile and amphibian species on the mainland adjacent to two or more of the islands. Of this total, 48 (44%) were not reported from any island. Only seven species (6%) were in their range on all of the islands.

Table 4.6. Occurrence of the nonmarine species[a] of coastal plain reptiles and amphibians on Atlantic Coast barrier islands. (x = present in established populations; o = range does not encompass mainland adjacent to island; -= not established; m = occurs on mainland but not on island (Conant 1975).) All species listed occur on the mainland adjacent to two or more of the barrier islands indicated. Scientific names after Conant (1975). Modified from Gibbons and Coker 1978; Gibbons and Harrison 1981; used with permission of American Midland Naturalist.

Scientific Name	Localities[b]										
	AI	HI	OI	SB	SI	CI	KI	Sal	LCI	CuI	M
Alligator mississippiensis	o	o		x	x	x	x	x	x		
Chelydra serpentina	x	x	x							x	
Sternotherus odoratus											M
Kinosternon baurii	o	o	o	o	o	o	o	o		x	
K. subrubrum	x	x	x	x	x	x	x	x	x	x	
Clemmys guttata	x	x	x								
Terrapene carolina											M
Deirochelys reticularia	o							x			
Chrysemys concinna	o								o	o	M
C. floridana	o										
C. picta	x			o	o		o	o	o	o	
C. scripta		x					x			x	
C. rubriventris	x			o	o		o	o	o	o	
Gopherus polyphemus	o	o	o	o	o		o			c	M
Trionyx ferox	o	o	o	o	o		o			x	
T. spiniferus	o	o	o	o	o				o	o	M
Anolis carolinensis	o			x	x	x	x	x	x	x	
Sceloporus undulatus	x									x	
Leinlopisma laterale		x				x	x	x	x	x	
Eumeces fasciatus										x	
E. laticeps						x	x	x	x	x	
E. inexpectatus	o	x		x	x	x	x			x	
E. egregius	o	o	o	o	o		o				M
Caemidophorus sexlineatus	o	x	x	x	x	x	x	x	x	x	
Ophisaurus ventralis	o	x	x	x	x	x	x	x	x	x	
O. compressus	o	o	o	o	o			x	x	x	
O. attenuatus	o										M
Natrix fasciata and/or *sipedon*[d]	x	x	x	x	x	x	x	x	x	x	
N. erythrogaster											M
N. cyclopion	o	o	o	o	o		o				M
N. taxispilota	o	x									
N. rigida	o										M
Seminatrix pygaea	o										M
Thamnophis sirtalis	x						x	x	x	x	
T. sauritus		x		x			x	x	x	x	
Virginia striatula	o										M
V. valeriae											M
Rhadinaea flavilata	o	o	o	x							
Storeria occipitomaculata											M
S. dekayi		x									

[a] *Malaclemys terrapin* was reported from all of the islands studied but is not considered to be a "nonmarine" species.

[b] Localities, estimated island area (km²) based on topographic maps are:
AI = Assateague Island Va., 82.6/31.9
HI = Hatteras Island N.C., 91.7/35.4
OI = Ocracoke Island N.C., 25.6/9.9
SB = Shackleford Banks N.C., 10.9/4.2
SI = Smith Island N.C., 22.3/8.6
CI = Capers Island S.C., 3.1/1.2
KI = Kiawah Island S.C., 33.2/12.8
SaI = Sapelo Island Ga., 64.2i24.8
LCI = Little Cumberland Island Ga., 12.4/4.8
CuI = Cumberland Island Ga., 86.5/33.4.
M = Mainland

[c] *Gopherus polyphemus* is introduced on Cumberland Island and has not been used in the calculations.

[d] Closely related species with similar ecological requirements.

Table 4.7. Comparative colonization trends of herpetofauna on nine Atlantic Coast barrier islands. Range of percentages takes into account that all species do not have an equal probability of invading each island (From Gibbons and Coker 1978 used with permission of American Midland Naturalist).

	Total species present on mainland	% of possible (mainland species) present per island (Range)			% of species reported from any islands	% of species found on all islands within range
		min.	max.	$\bar{x}$		
Turtles	15	09	50	27	40	07
Lizards	11	22	82	48	18	18
Snakes	37	14	43	30	49	08
All reptiles (includes one crocodilian)	64	18	51	34	41	09
Salamanders	21	0	31	06	71	0
Frogs	23	06	67	32	39	04
All amphibians	44	03	51	21	55	02

A species-by-species case analysis by Gibbons and Coker (1978:219) suggested the following patterns (Fig. 4.2):

Lizards are highly successful island colonizers, whereas salamanders are exceptionally poor. Explanation for the unexpected absence from any barrier islands of certain common mainland species of reptiles and amphibians is inconclusive, although winter drought resulting in higher salinity in freshwater habitats is suggested as an important deterrent to colonization for some species. The amount of woodland habitat, rather than island size per se, is the island feature most highly correlated with numbers of reptiles or amphibian species.

Gibbons and Coker (1978) also concluded that the existing data base lacked sufficient information about phenotypic variability within populations, details of species ecology, and comparative studies on which to base a reasonable understanding of the relative roles of inadequate habitat and barriers to migration in controlling species richness.

The mammalian fauna of 16 sea islands of Georgia were recently compared (Johnson et al. 1974, Table 4.8). Conspicuous terrestrial mammals reported for these islands, in decreasing order of frequency of occurrence, were raccoon (*Procyon lotor*; the only mammal reported for all 16 islands), river otter (*Lutra canadensis*; 13 of 15 reports are based on literature citations unsupported by specimens or recent sightings), marsh rabbit (*Sylvilagus palustris*), white-tailed deer, mink (*Mustela vison*), hispid cotton rat, marsh rice rat (*Oryzomys palustris*),

gray squirrel (*Sciurus carolinensis*), and eastern mole (*Scalopus aquaticus*).

Differences in island fauna are probably more a function of the degree of human presence and habitat modification than of inherent habitat differences among islands. Whether significant faunal differences existed on these and other barrier islands of the Southeast before intensive human intervention will probably never be known because of the lack of historical data. Johnson et al. (1974) did not believe that habitat modification by agriculture or timber harvest had caused the loss of any mammal populations from the islands. Rather, the extirpations that seem to have occurred probably resulted from hunting, deliberate persecution, and disease.

Genetic isolation in the past was apparently sufficient so that taxonomically distinct populations of some mammals have developed on specific barrier islands. Examples include Anastasia Island cotton mouse (*Peromyscus gossypinus anastasae*), St. Simon's Island raccoon (*Procyon lotor litoreus*), and Blackbeard Island deer (*Odocoileus virginiunus nigribarbis*) (Hillestad et al. 1975; Neuhauser 1976). Another mammal, formerly considered to represent a taxonomically distinct island population is Cumberland Island pocket gopher (*Geomys cumberlandius*). This taxon is now regarded as a synonym of G. *pinetis*, a not-uncommon island species (Laerm 1981).

Introduced Fauna

Introduction

Almost all barrier islands support populations of nonnative introduced animals. Domestic animals, including

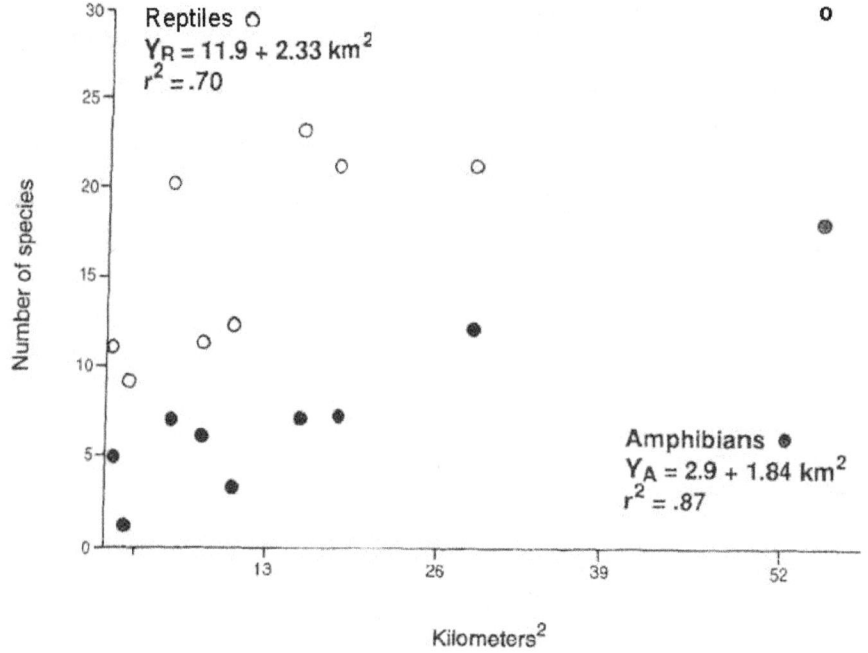

Fig. 4.2. Relationship between amount of woodland habitat (km²) and number of reptile or amphibian species inhabiting nine Atlantic coastal barrier islands. Regression equations are linear and highly significant (from Gibbons and Coker 1978; used with permis-sion of *American Mid-land Naturalist*).

cattle, horses, sheep, goats, and pigs, were brought to the barrier islands early in the colonial period to exploit the extensive grasslands. Cats and dogs, serving humans as helpers or pets, accompanied the livestock. More recently, around the turn of the century, numerous exotic birds and mammals were released on various barrier islands with the intent of providing more diverse hunting opportunities. Still other animals, such as nutria (*Myocastor coypus*), were introduced by wildlife agencies as possible agents for biological control of undesirable vegetation.

Domestic Animals

Livestock was allowed free range on many barrier islands from colonial times until early in the present century. Dependent upon the indigenous environment for shelter and forage, these animals adopted a semiwild mode of existence, and inevitably, feral populations became established. After the Civil War, many barrier islands came under the control of wealthy individuals or organizations and were operated as private hunting reserves. Livestock that survived abandonment became feral, and previously existing feral populations flourished when they were relieved from competition with domestic animals. Although all types of common domestic animals in the coastal region also lived on the barrier islands, only horses and hogs seem to have thrived under reduced management. Wild ponies are most associated with the barrier islands of Virginia and North Carolina, while hogs have been successful farther south.

Horses and hogs have had significant effects on barrier island vegetative cover as well as on other animals (Godfrey and Godfrey 1976; Nelson et al. 1976; Rubenstein 1981). Horses affect the visual quality of the landscape when intensive grazing reduces large areas of salt marsh or grassy dune to close-cropped turf. Hogs are omnivorous and compete with a wide range of native barrier island animals for the same food and habitat resources. Hogs disrupt maritime forest soil as they search for edible roots, subterranean insects, reptiles, and small mammals. Their taste for eggs and fledglings makes them a particular threat to ground-nesting birds such as quail (*Colinus virginianus*) and turkey (*Meleagris gallopavo*), and they have caused serious depredation of sea turtle nests. Feral hogs also affect plant succession on barrier islands. On Cumberland Island, Georgia, hogs consume pennywort (*Hydrocotyle* spp.), one of the pioneer plants in dunes, and their selective feeding on acorns and oak seedlings in preference to pines may result in a change in canopy dominance of the maritime forest (Hillestad et al. 1975).

Although few but the most intrepid hunters decry attempts to exterminate wild hogs, many who support management of barrier islands as natural ecosystems blanch at the thought of removing the free-spirited wild ponies. Public support for maintaining horse populations

Table 4.8. Comparison of occurrence of mammals on 16 islands off the coast of Georgia (Johnson et al. 1974).

Species	Oyster bed	Cock-spur	Tybee	Little Tybee	Wassaw	Ossabaw	St. Catherines	Black beard	Sapelo	Wolf	Little St. Simons	St. Simons	Sea	Jekyll	Little Cumberland	Cumberland
Opossum	O	O	O						S			S	O	S	L*	S
Short-tailed shrew									S							S
Least shrew						S	S	S	S					S		S
Eastern mole						S	S	S	S			S		S	O	S
Southeastern myotis																
Eastern pipistrelle									S						O	S
Big brown bat									S							S
Red bat									O							
Seminole bat									S							S
Yellow bat																S
Cottontail rabbit	S											O	S			
Marsh rabbit		S	O		O	S	S	S	S	S	O	S	S	S	S	S
Gray squirrel		O	L		S	L	S		S	S	O	O		S		S
Fox squirrel						S						O				S
Southern flying squirrel												O				L
Cumberland Is. pocket gopher																S
Marsh rice rat	S	S	S		S	S		S	S			O		S	O	S
Eastern harvest mouse																S
Oldfield mouse																L
Cotton mouse		S	S			S		S	S			S		S	S	S
Hispid cotton rat						S		S	S			L		S	O	
Eastern wood rat																
Black rat	S	S	S			L	S	L	S					S		
Norway rat	L					S	S									
House mouse	S	S	S													S
Nutria					S	S		L*				L				
Goose-backed whale													L	L	S	S
Pygmy sperm whale													L	L	S	
Dwarf sperm whale								L	L							
Atlantic bottle-nosed dolphin					L	S			S						S	S
False killer whale			L							S						
Pilot whale					S	S		S	S		S	L		S	S	
Gray fox					L*				L*			L*				L*
Black bear	L											L*				L*
Raccoon	L		O	O	S	S	S	S	S	S	O	S	O	S	S	S
Mink	L		O	O	L	L	L	L	S	L	O	O		S	O	S
River otter	L		L	L	L	L	L	L	L	L	L	L	L	L	S	L
Bobcat		O*		L		S*			L*		L*	L	L	L*		L*
Manatee						O*					O*	O*	O	O	O*	L
European wild boar					L*	O*					O*	O*		L*	O*	O*
European fallow deer											L		O	O		
Red deer or European elk			L	L							L*					
White-tailed deer	L		L	L	S	S	L	S	S	L	L	L	L	L	L	S

[a] Symbols–S = specimen; L = literature; O = observed; * = exturpated.

but eliminating other feral animals derives, in part, from legends that say the ponies are descendants of fine Arabian stock stranded on the barrier islands when Spanish treasure ships were wrecked off the coast. The legends are supported by neither historical records nor genetic studies (Bellis, personal observation).

Most domesticated animals are not subject to natural mechanisms of population regulation. The number of individuals in a population is thus largely dependent on the available food supply, so that in the absence of human management, such populations can be expected to increase beyond the carrying capacity of the environment. Because migration to better range is seldom an option on a small barrier island, feral populations typically experience cycles in abundance and vigor. A bad year of food production when carrying capacity has already been exceeded can result in drastic losses from to starvation and disease. The survivors may operate with a severely reduced gene pool. Local extirpation may result after several cycles if genetic vigor is not restored by introduction of new individuals.

Several researchers (Godfrey and Godfrey 1976; Nelson et al. 1976; Rubenstein 1981; Turner and Bratton 1987) have offered descriptions of the possible effects of feral horses on barrier island ecology, but experimental studies are extremely limited. Wood (1981) conducted a census from a helicopter and an assessment of the effect on the vegetation of feral ungulates inhabiting Shackleford Banks, North Carolina (Table 4.9). Wood (1981) hypothesized that the effect of feral animals could be estimated by determining their cumulative effect on plant succession and proposed that plant succession becomes retrogressive when exploitation exceeds productivity. Thus, if herbivore consumption exceeds the ecosystem's carrying capacity, then the animals destroy their forage base, which will then destabilize the ecosystem. Wood (1981 :ii) concluded that

> . . . the data gathered [during a 4-year exclosure study] indicated that grazing had not retrogressed succession in recent years although it had been a

Table 4.9. Numbers of feral ungulates on the Shackleford Banks, North Carolina, in late summer 1978-1980 (Wood 1981).

Year	Horses	Cattle	Sheep	Goats
1978	81	64	44[a]	102
1979	91	89	104	121
1980	108	74	144	65[a]

[a] The count of the animals was incomplete because some portion of the herd was hidden and could not be seen from the helicopter in the maritime forest.

serious interrupter of succession and natural plant community dynamics. If the island's vegetation were relieved of grazing pressure, natural processes and rates of processes would likely soon return. The most heavily grazed communities were small in area and the forage resources in these were obviously overused. If the feral herds are allowed to continue increasing they will eventually exceed the ability of these communities to supply them with minimum forage requirements. At some point the forage demand will so greatly exceed supply that substantial herd attrition will begin to occur and may become massive. However, the plant species of the Outer Banks have been naturally selected for exceeding resistance, tenacity, and resilience, and we project that they could survive such a phenomenon and revegetate the island once grazing pressure was greatly lowered or erased.

An additional conclusion from Wood's study (1981) was that the main forces affecting maritime forests have been tree cutting by humans and forest burial by wind-blown sand. Foraging, especially by sheep and goats, on the seedlings and young plants of the mature maritime forest species, such as *Juniperus virginiana* and *Ilex vomitoria*, has slowed encroachment of the forest into new areas. Although the prominent browse line in the maritime forest was suggested as indicative of heavy browsing, the effect of browsing on forest dynamics was considered negligible, because no foraging occurred in the main zone of photosynthesis (canopy) (Wood 1981).

Wood (1981) also reported the food sources of feral ungulates on Shackleford Banks: 87% of the year-round diet of horses and 77% of that of cows was composed of upland grasses and *Spartina*. *Spartina* made up 50% of the horse diet and 32% of the cattle diet. One salt-marsh species, *S. alterniflora*, was considered to represent a substantially more important component of the diet than *S. patens*, which was more abundant in the sand flats. Sheep consumed primarily leaves of woody plants, which were about one-third of their year-round diet. The remaining food sources for sheep were about equal parts of *Spartina* spp., upland grasses, *Juncus* spp., sedges, and forbs. Goats relied even more heavily upon leaves of woody plants, which made up slightly more than half of their year-round diet. The leaves that were such a significant part of the year-round diet of all these feral animals came from the maritime forest or from *Myrica cerifera* thickets, which combined, cover only about 6% of the vegetated area.

That feral horses depend largely on salt-marsh grasses as a major dietary source was substantiated by Turner and Bratton (1987). They reported that feral horses on Cumberland Island, Georgia, spent about 74% of their foraging time in salt-marsh habitat or in the grasslands at the marsh edge. Horses obtained most of their food in grasslands and marshes. However, their selective grazing on oak seeds and seedlings exerted considerable influence on the maritime forest which, by itself, could never support the herd. The horses thus are a source of perturbation that may result in changes in community structure in the maritime forest that favor pines over oaks. By this means, energy originally assimilated in the salt marsh community allows the nonnative horses to effect a floristic change in the maritime forest community.

The particular grazing behavior of horses may also be responsible for their less damaging impact on barrier island vegetation (Turner and Bratton 1987). Horses tend to forage primarily in salt marsh or grasslands, and unlike goats, sheep, and pigs, which often uproot and consume entire grass plants, usually leave the basal meristem intact. Regeneration is rapid and soil erosion minimized.

During the 3 years after removal of most feral ungulates except horses from Shackleford Banks, North Carolina, the feral horse population increased rapidly from 108 to 130 (D.I. Rubenstein, Page A-24, *The* News *and Observer,* Raleigh NC, 2 July 1989). Rubenstein (1981) attributed the population increase to enhanced availability of food following the removal of competitors. He also noted that "the vegetation was [simultaneously] coming back strongly." Rump plumpness (an index of overall health) was declining in the horses, and Rubenstein hypothesized that the weight loss should be interpreted as a sign that the population had reached or slightly surpassed its equilibrium with available food supply. Rubenstein believed that the decline in general physical condition would result in a decline in reproduction and that these conditions would lead to self-regulation in which "the horses, in managing their own numbers, [are] not too detrimental to the island."

Many people believe that most damage to vegetation on barrier islands results from feral animals other than horses. They believe that horses have become naturalized or so much a part of the local culture that they should be allowed to remain, at least until it can be proven they are detrimental (Rubenstein 1989). Such a policy may be popular with the public; however, it should be pointed out that control of feral horse populations, short of death by starvation, does not seem to exist on refuges (Chincoteague, Ocracoke, Shackleford Banks). Refuge managers have periodically had to cull the herds.

One solution to the problem of wild horse population increases and damage to vegetation has been to restrict the herd to a designated area within a pen. Enclosure of the herd, now practiced at Ocracoke, requires more intensive management than for free-ranging animals. Forage must be supplemented with hay, especially during the winter season. The importation of hay from off-island sources and the grazing pressure on existing native grasses by the horses, increase the possibility of accidental introduction of exotic plant species to the barrier islands. Davison (1985) conducted a floristic study at the pony pen on Ocracoke Island; his study revealed a dominance of graminoids and forbs in the pen and a greater density of shrubs outside the pen. Exotic plant species become established in the pen, including bermuda grass (*Cynodon dactylon),* annual buttercup (*Ranunculus sardous*), and several pasture grasses. There was no evidence that these exotic plant species threatened the native flora outside the pen. Plant productivity inside the 52 ha pen was sufficient to support 24-30 ponies in summer and 2– 13 during the winter.

The food preference of cattle and horses is more similar to that of native deer than that of other feral animals such as hogs, goats, and sheep (Hillestad and Speake 1970). Cattle and horses, therefore, compete directly with deer for food and habitat, and the environmental impacts of these two groups are broadly similar. Grazing animals can maintain pasture-like openings in the maritime forest that can be attractive to wild turkeys during the brood-rearing season. Openings in the forest canopy provide the poults with an abundant supply of insects and forage (Hillestad and Speake 1970).

The consensus among biologists about the environmental impact of feral horses seems to be that, although horses compete with native deer for grazing space and are not subject to natural population regulation, they cause less damage to native vegetation than most other species of feral grazers.

Exotic Birds and Mammals

Several exotic birds and mammals have been introduced on various barrier islands. Most of these were introduced by hunters who wanted to increase the diversity of available game. Very few of these introduced species have attained sufficient population size to become naturalized.

Five species of gallinaceous birds were introduced on Jekyll and Sapelo islands, Georgia, around the beginning of this century (Johnson et al. 1974): the guinea fowl (*Numida goleta*), tinamou (*Tinamus robustus),* Central American currasow (*Crux rubra*), ocellated turkey (*Agriocharis ocellata*), and chachalaca (*Ortalis vetula).* These birds are forest dwellers and were expected to become naturalized in the maritime forest. Only the chachalaca on Sapelo Island has survived to the present.

Attempts to introduce big-game animals to the Georgia sea islands have also largely met with failure (Johnston et al. 1974). At various times and on various islands, attempts were made to introduce European wild boar (*Sus scrofa*), fallow deer (*Dama dama*), and red deer (*Cervus elaphus*). Of these, only the fallow deer remain; 400-500 individuals inhabit Little St. Simon's Island and a smaller number inhabit Jekyll Island (Johnson et al. 1974). The wild boar have disappeared; it is thought that they were either extirpated or absorbed genetically into the feral hog populations (Johnson et al. 1974).

Isolation and a mild climate make southern barrier islands ideal locations for breeding of rare and endangered animals. The Bronx Zoo's Wildlife Survival Center operates a breeding program for such animals on St. Catherine's Island, Georgia. This island is currently the home of IS bird, 11 mammal, and 3 tortoise species, mostly natives not of North America. The mammals include Arabian oryx (Oryx *leucorys*), water buck (*Kobus lechee*), slender-horned gazelle (*Gazella* sp.), sable antelope (*Hippotragus niger*), and several lemurs (Cohn 1990).

Faunal Diversity

Native vertebrate animal diversities on four barrier islands in South Carolina were compared by Gaddy and Kohlsaat (1987). They concluded that species richness seemed to be related to island size and habitat diversity (birds), and amount of wetland area (amphibians and reptiles).

Atlantic Coast barrier islands, when compared to the mainland, tend to have less habitat diversity, fewer kinds of freshwater wetlands, and fewer species of plants, amphibians, reptiles, birds, and mammals (Caddy and Kohlsaat 1987). Habitat diversity on barrier islands is largely a function of the geological history of the island. Wide, forested islands with freshwater swale ponds will have a greater variety of habitats than narrow, frequently overwashed islands vegetated only by grasses and scattered shrubs.

CHAPTER 5.

Management of Maritime Forests

Introduction

Maritime forests of the Atlantic Coast have never been a large proportion of the coastal area. Since early in the colonial period, these small, scattered forests have been exploited for their timber and subjected to habitat modification by free-ranging livestock. Native animals were extirpated because of their inability to compete effectively with livestock or with introduced exotic species. On small, isolated islands, hunting pressure alone can eliminate a species or so reduce the numbers that the population succumbs to impaired genetic vigor.

More recently, the realization that barrier islands are migrating slowly landward and that shoreline erosion is a natural and largely uncontrollable geologic phenomenon has focused the attention of oceanside developers on maritime forests because such areas usually represent the most geologically stable portions of an island. In recent decades, much of the available oceanfront property has been developed. The increased human habitation of barrier islands has caused demand for cultural infrastructure, including roads, electrical transmission lines, and water and waste-water systems, to grow exponentially. All along the coast, maritime forests are being dissected into rectangular blocks to provide access and service corridors. Further development means that the remaining forest canopy will be reduced as lots are cleared for construction, parking, and septic systems; to provide an unobstructed view; to reduce habitat for snakes and biting insects; or simply to provide space for a grass lawn. Ultimately, maritime forest could be converted to a rolling sea of mobile homes beneath a canopy of TV antennas or tiered cliffs containing the "summer nests of migratory sunbirds." At present rates of development, most currently unprotected maritime forests will probably be functionally destroyed or physically obliterated by the year 2000 (Bellis, personal observation).

Concern about the effects of loss of maritime forest on the stability of barrier islands is not new. Lewis (1917:18) described conditions on Shackleford Banks, North Carolina:

Before the Civil War... cutting of timber... fires ... grazing by cattle and sheep, and [storms] have broken the protecting wall of vegetation and allowed the sand ... to blow in on the trees ... killing and covering the existing plants ... [W]ithin a few years the forest covering will be obliterated. [This] will probably lead to the [human] abandonment of Shackleford Banks as a permanent place of residence, [and] the drifting sand will fill the narrow sound lying between the bank and the mainland.

Thirty years ago, even before the intensive coastal development of the 1960's and 70's, Bourdeau and Oosting (1959:148–149) wrote that

The maritime forest must have covered extensive areas along the North Carolina coast in the past but fire, burial by wandering dunes, or bulldozing and leveling for real estate development have eliminated all but a few relics which usually are disturbed to some degree. Because the rate of its destruction by man is accelerating and complete elimination of all truly representative stands appears inevitable, it seems desirable to record the results of sociological [quantitative floristic] analyses made of a number of examples ...

Aside from concerns for preserving rare and unusual habitats, there are additional reasons for protecting maritime forests. It seems intuitively obvious to naturalists and environmentalists that maritime forests stabilize otherwise migratory dunes, help protect the barrier island from erosion during storms, and collect and store precipitation in the surface water table. If maritime forests do indeed perform these functions, then they are critical elements in maintaining barrier island stability and suitable conditions for continuing human occupation. Barrier islands that lack maritime forest have seldom been found suitable for permanent human occupation. If maritime forests contribute to barrier island stability, then planners, developers, and land-use managers should consider this function when they decide where and how to build. Documentation in support of the existence of these functional relationships is weak or absent. The presumed functions of maritime forest can be replicated, at least on a temporary basis by engineering (Bellis, personal observation). Beaches can be bulkheaded. Freshwater can be pumped from the mainland or deep underground sources and wastewater can be treated. Building codes can limit building height and proximity to the ocean. Many barrier islands have been urbanized without obvious immediate impact on island stability. Perhaps the apparent success in stabilizing barrier islands is an illusion resulting from the differing time scales of urban development and geologic processes. Development on barrier islands is often attuned to the relatively slower rate of geologic change associated with the mainland (Beflis, personal observation). Building techniques and practices on barrier islands have only recently been modified to take into account the relatively fast pace of geologic change occurring there. Since development and geologic processes are operating on different time scales, it seems inevitable that the cost of engineered solutions to perceived problems with barrier island stability must escalate to a point where they may no longer be economically justifiable.

The human approach to combating shoreline erosion on the beaches has demonstrated the consequence of failure to consider the time scale of geologic processes in barrier island planning(Bellis, personal observation). Along much of the Atlantic shore, the costs of slowing or preventing erosion have risen to the point that they now exceed the value of the structures or property to be protected. North Carolina and the National Park Service have adopted policies of generally allowing nature to take its course along the oceanfront. Artificial hardening of the shoreline to slow erosion is no longer permitted.

Coastal residents are increasingly concerned about the anticipated effect on barrier islands by a projected increase in the rate of sea-level rise, although much uncertainty exists about the speed and magnitude of this change. Because of the incongruency between rate of geological processes and rate of development, it remains doubtful that significant preparation for an impending geological event will be made until planners become convinced that the projections are true or until a sustained period of increased coastal damage from storms has actually occurred (Bellis, personal observation).

The United States Environmental Protection Agency (EPA:EPA 1988) conducted site-specific case studies of expected principal habitat changes under various scenarios of sea-level rise and levels of human attempts to stabilize shorelines. The projected sea-level rise increments used in the study were: baseline (= present day), 2.5 mm/year; low, 9.5 mm/year; and high, 17.0 mm/year. For the Charleston, South Carolina area, the EPA study projected that, without shoreline protection by stabilization, highland (including maritime forest) habitat will decrease from 46.6% of the total

study area (1980) to 41.7% by the year 2075, under the "high" rate. This would represent a loss of 10% of the 1980 highland area. Land that was terrestrial would be transformed into transition-zone or high-marsh habitat. Under the "low" rate, highland area would be reduced to 44.9%.

The Charleston case study illustrated that, although the effect of sea-level rise will have the greatest effect on low marsh (resulting in 40–80% wetland loss, depending on the sea-level rise scenario selected), significant losses could occur in highland habitats as well. The EPA study did not address the possible effects on wetland habitat in maritime forests that may result from an elevated water table or from increased storm and ocean washover activity.

Management of Native Vegetation

Although most anthropogenic modification of barrier island vegetation can be attributed to inadvertent and indirect results of development, some modifications have been intentional. Perhaps the most extensive project has been the construction of sand dunes along the North Carolina coast. Although these dunes were intended to protect roads and small villages from ocean storms, they effectively reduced ocean overwash for several decades (Schroeder et al. 1976). The artificial oceanfront dune system produced a protected leeward zone favorable for development of woody plant species less tolerant of salt aerosol and sand burial than the dune grasses (Fig. 5.1). As a result, woody shrubs have become abundant in this zone. Schroeder et al. (1976) believed

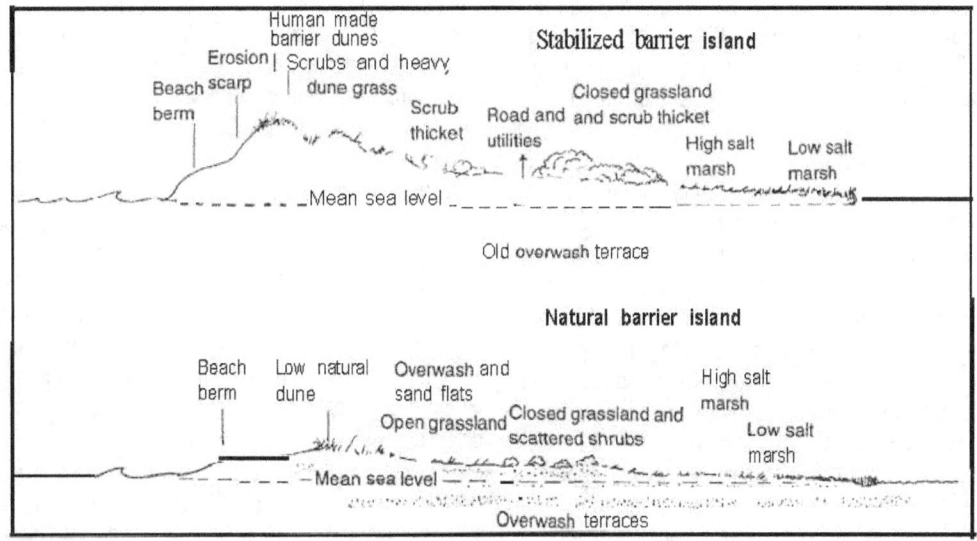

Fig. 5.1. Vegetation cover on a barrier island stabilized by artificial barrier dunes, compared with a natural barrier pattern.

this vegetation phase represented a successional stage in maritime forest development. They cited their concern that this shrubby island-stabilizing plant community would be particularly vulnerable to rapid loss if the artificial dune were destroyed. This prediction proved to be correct, and in fact, extensive segments of artificial dunes are currently being lost to erosion and the process is expected to be hastened soon by a projected increase in sea-level rise (Bellis, personal observation).

Two species of the shrub *Myrica* (waxmyrtle, bayberry) have been among the most successful opportunists on protected sites behind the artificial dune system (Schroeder et al. 1976). *Myrica* contains nitrogen-fixing bacteria in association with its roots and is a rapid colonizer of disturbed soils. *Myrica* has become a nuisance along portions of North Carolina Highway 12 in Cape Hatteras National Seashore and the Pea Island National Wildlife Refuge in North Carolina. The woody, shrublike growth impinged on the road shoulder, blocking drivers' vision and creating a problem for mowing crews. In the wildlife refuge, *Myrica* impedes the easy viewing of waterfowl by bird-watchers and replaces more desirable and less woody sources of waterfowl food (Furbish et al. 1988). Attempts to find nonchemical means for controlling this growth have met with limited success (Furbish et al. 1988).

Maritime Forest Fragmentation

The effects of fragmentation of the maritime forest by urban development on Bogue Banks, North Carolina, were examined by Lopazanski (1987), whose study was designed to determine the minimum area of maritime forest that could maintain vascular-plant diversity (number of species) typical of nonurbanized maritime forest in the region. This researcher concluded that there is no single standard minimum area for the "'maritime forest type." Despite variation between different maritime forest locations on Bogue Banks, the minimal areas determined by this method ranged from 1,000 to 1,400 m^2.

How do these minimum areas compare with existing development practices? On Hatteras Island, North Carolina, most subdivision lots are in the quarter- to half-acre range (about 1,000–2000 m^2) (Bellis, personal observation). Lots must be at least partially cleared to provide access for workers. Vegetation must also be cleared from the building site to provide vehicular access, parking areas, and space for a septic field. Initial site preparation and ground leveling may destroy most or all of the existing vegetative cover on a small lot. Native vegetation that survives the construction phase usually consists of a few shrubs and trees. Subsequent landscaping by the homeowner often results in further loss. Understory is replaced by lawns or by exotic ornamentals. S.P. Bratton, (University of Georgia, Institute of Ecology,

personal communication) noted that the risk of wildfire damage to homes is increased by allowing native shrub vegetation to persist on developed lots. This is a strong reason to discourage homeowners from maintaining existing native vegetation. Bratton further noted, however, that the fire threat is greatly reduced for structures surrounded by mature live oak.

It should be clear from this description that little, if any, maritime forest can survive in subdivisions of the size typically being developed on barrier islands. The quarter-acre or half-acre lot is close to the minimum critical area needed to maintain floristic diversity of the forest before development.

Legislatively supported regulations aimed at minimizing loss of vegetative cover can be justified on the grounds of protecting the common value (i.e., groundwater supply and soil stability); however, the minimum area required to maintain healthy animal populations and communities is unknown. It is highly probable that few populations of larger mammals, snakes, and ground-dwelling animals will survive after their habitat is subdivided (Bellis, personal observation).

Effects of Highway Construction

Development of barrier islands has necessitated extensive construction of roadways (Bellis, personal observation). Trunk corridors extend the length of an island and serve lateral roads and trails running to the beach or toward the mainland side. On many barrier islands, the maritime forest behind an oceanside dune ridge has been the site selected for the trunk road corridor. Such a location permits convenient access by seaside residents and businesses while providing for a measure of protection from storms. The low-growing, dense canopy characteristic of the maritime forest interface with the beach bears the brunt of storm winds and the effects of salt-aerosol. Because a trunk roadway often runs the entire length of a barrier island in or very near the zone of maximum salt impact, opening the canopy for road construction allows greater salt penetration into the maritime forest.

Concern also exists that the immediate damage from clearing the initial highway right-of-way together with the delayed effects of deeper salt-aerosol penetration might eventually result in loss of vegetative cover and stability of the dune system (Bellis, personal observation). Loss of dune stability could hasten loss of beachfront property through erosion or threaten the very road that the dune originally protected.

Experimental studies verified that clearing of highway rights-of-way in maritime forest affects the pattern of salt transport into the forest canopy (Fig. 5.2). A 4-year study of the impact of trunk highway construction

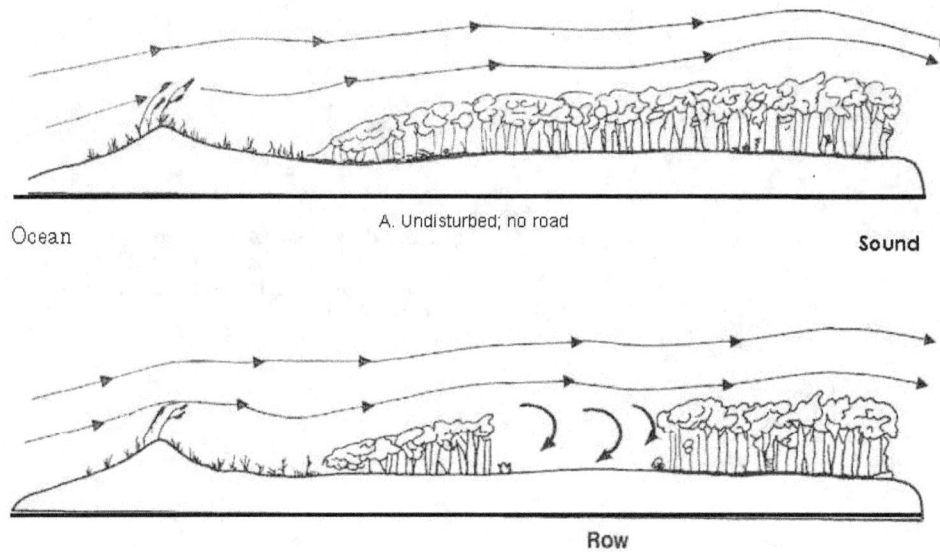

Ocean

A. Undisturbed; no road

Sound

Row

B. Disturbed; with road

Fig. 5.2. Generalized patterns of onshore winds across undisturbed and disturbed barrier island forest (from Seneca and Broome 1981).

on a maritime forest on Topsail Island, North Carolina, was conducted by Eaton (1979) and Seneca and Broome (1981). Important forest canopy species included live oak, redbay, yaupon, waxmyrtle, and red cedar. Yaupon was dominant in all strata, with redbay the primary subdominant in the subcanopy. No significant vegetative change was observed within the forest along the ocean side of the road (in the lee of salt-laden winds) during 4 years. Floristic composition, canopy height, and tree viability remained essentially constant. In contrast, the canopy on the bay side of the road cut was opened to increased salt-aerosol impact and significant dieback was observed. Fifty-seven percent of the original aboveground vegetation was dead after 4 years, with some die-off still occurring. In the most severely affected zone (2.5-3 m from the seaward edge of the exposed forest), the canopy was eliminated. Tree species responded differently to the exposure. Red cedar exhibited the least dieback and redbay the greatest (Figs. 5.3, 5.4, and 5.5). Twenty-seven months after the forest was first exposed, the dieback had ceased and recovery was evident. Although 57% of the original trees were completely defoliated, only 14% appear to have been killed completely; 43% exhibited basal sprouting; bole sprouts, stump sprouts, and sprouts originating from underground stems and roots were well along in forming a new but lower canopy after 4 years (Fig. 5.6).

Results of Seneca and Broome's (1981) study suggested that damage to maritime forest from increased exposure to salt-aerosol impact is concentrated within a few meters of the exposed forest edge and that canopy recovery can occur relatively rapidly. In this study, there was no evidence that dune stability had been compromised by temporary loss of vegetative cover.

From the above results (Seneca and Broome 1981) there is reason for optimism that impacts on maritime forest by trunk roads parallel to the long axis of the barrier island and generally perpendicular to onshore winds may be minimal. There is also increasing concern, however, about the effect of salt aerosols funneled into maritime forest along roads oriented parallel to the direction of onshore winds. Lopazanski et al. (1988) described what they refer to as an "edge effect," in which partial clearing of patches of maritime forests for roads, parking lots, or building sites expose the remaining uncleared fragments of maritime forest to sudden increases in salt-aerosol impact, wind shear, altered drainage, and invasion by opportunistic weeds. Depending upon the severity of microclimatic changes resulting from edge creation, various degrees of mortality can occur among native forest trees and shrubs. In some places along North Carolina Highway 58 on Bogue Banks, the dieback of live oak extends into the center of the maritime forest stand which completely alters the forest's ecology (Lopazanski et al. 1988).

Recreational Impact on the Biota

Residential subdivision and associated development cause significant loss of wildlife habitat. Continuing loss

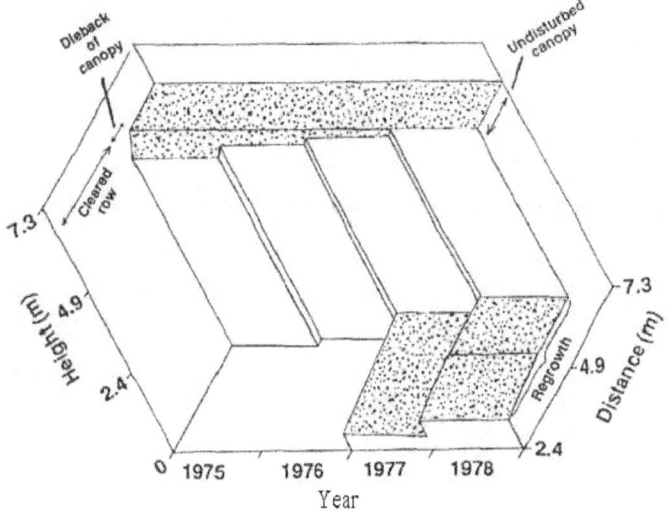

Fig. 5.3. Effect of salt spray on red cedar(*Juniperus silicola*) canopy and sprout regrowth exposed by cutting highway right-of-way (from Seneca and Broome 1981).

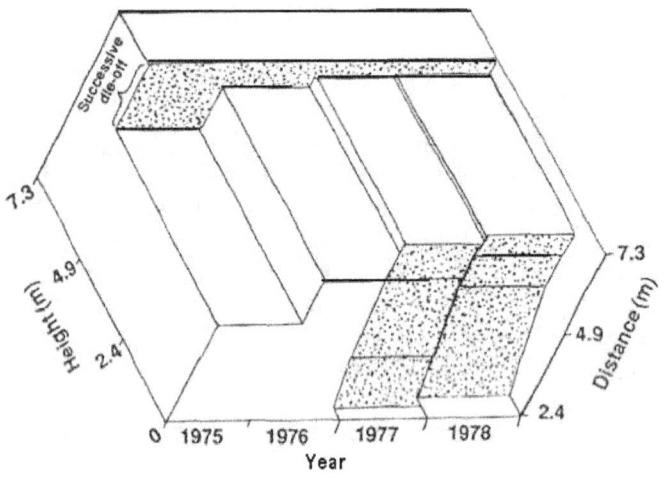

Fig. 5.4. Effect of salt spray on live oak (*Quercus virginiana*) canopy and sprout regrowth exposed by cutting highway right-of-way (from Seneca and Broome 1981).

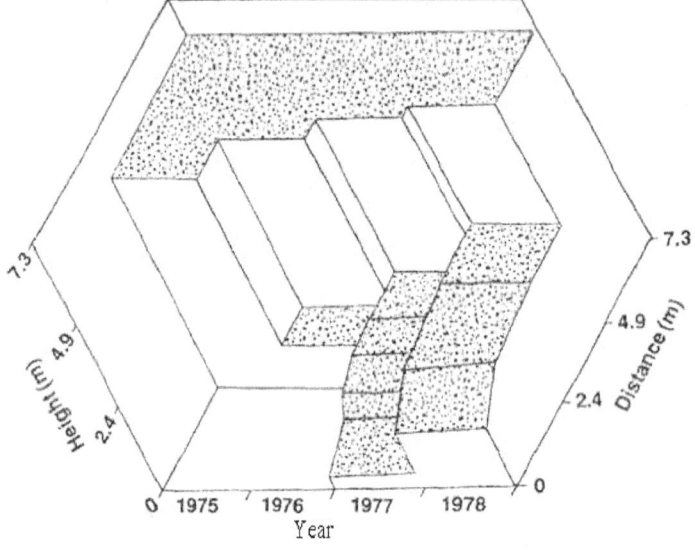

Fig. 5.5. Effect of salt spray on yaupon (*Ilex vomitoria*) and redbay (*Persea borbonia*) *canopy* and sprout regrowth exposed by cutting highway right-of-way (from Seneca and Broome 1981).

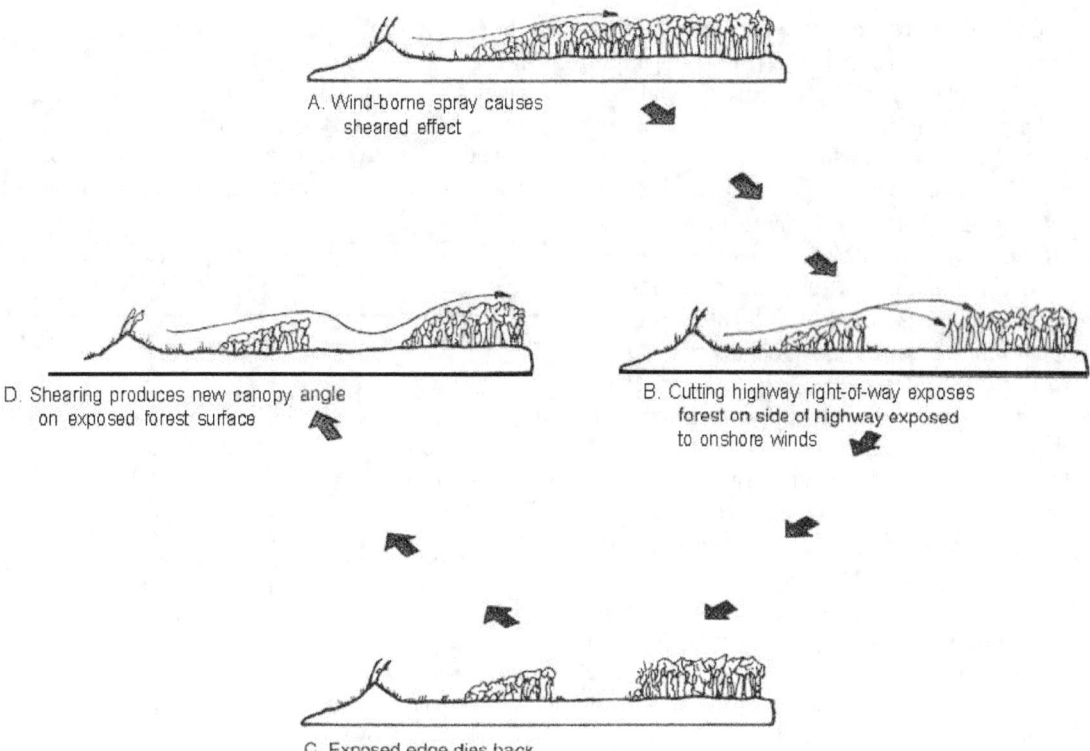

Fig. 5.6. Hypothetical effects of salt spray on maritime vegetation (from Seneca and Broome 1981).

of maritime forest to development will place increasing responsibility on managers of protected forest sites to maintain them in as natural a state as possible. Simultaneously, reduced public access to privately developed barrier islands tends to increase the demand for recreational use of publicly managed sites. Even protected forest preserves typically provide walking trails for visitors and limited roads or tracks for service and management personnel. Other examples of land-disturbing activities that may be required to provide basic services for recreational use of a protected forest include construction of management-staff living quarters, interpretive structures, and picnic or camping facilities; development of water wells and utility lines; and construction of wastewater treatment facilities. Each of these minor development activities contributes to a cumulative effect that increases in magnitude with increasing intensity of use by visitors. The questions for the manager become: How do I detect impending habitat change? How can I measure the degree of habitat modification? How can I avoid or reduce effects before they occur?

Caddy and Kohlsaat (1987) developed quantitative procedures to address the above management considerations. Transects were established perpendicular to various trails and roads within maritime forest habitats on

several barrier islands near Charleston, South Carolina. Sites were selected to provide a range of disturbance conditions. Plant populations were inventoried in each of three vegetation zones across the vegetative cover transition between roadway and forest, designated woodland, wood edge, and road edge. For each zone, they calculated a disturbance index based on an analysis of the proportion of plant species that decreased or increased and the proportion of invaders. Species composition of the road edge and wood edge were different from undisturbed forest. Herbaceous cover was higher along the road edge and wood edge, and woody stem density was greatest in the wood edge. These effects are consistent with the hypothesis that herbaceous cover and woody stem density are initiated largely by loss of the forest canopy because forest clearing opens the area to greater light penetration. Subsequent compaction of the soil by human or vehicles may alter seed germination and seedling success. Sun-tolerant herbaceous plants with wind-blown or animal-dispersed seeds can rapidly invade disturbed roadway sites, where they grow rapidly in a well-lighted valley protected from the wind and salt. Through proliferation of their root and stump sprouts, many barrier island trees and shrubs recover rapidly from destruction of their aboveground portions. These sprouts produce a dense shrub or small-tree zone along either side of the roadway. Catbrier, poison ivy, wild grape, and other vines take advantage of these stems and add their foliage to the dense tangle.

Sun-loving herbaceous plants listed by Gaddy and Kohlsaat (1987) as indicators of disturbance include Elephant's foot *(Elephantopus tomentosus)*, sea oats' relatives *(Chasmanthium* or *Uniola)*, dogfennel *(Eupatorium capillifolium)*, rabbit tobacco or everlasting *(Gnaphalium obtusifolium)*, a goldenrod relative *(Haplopappus divaricatus)*, Venus' looking-glass *(Triodanis perfoliata)*, and poorman's pepper *(Lepidium virginicum)*. Winged sumac *(Rhus copallinum)* and Hercules's club *(Aralia spinosa)* were good indicators of disturbed woodland edge communities. The popular recognition that some plants are good indicators of human trampling is embodied in one of the common names for *Elephantopus tomentosus;* whiteman's footsteps.

The effects of disturbance on maritime forest birds and herpetofauna were also reported by Gaddy and Kohlsaat (1987) (Table 5.1). Although unknown variables other than the degree of habitat disturbance may have affected bird densities along the study transects, some species (vireos, *[Vireo* sp.], indigo bunting *[Passerina cyanea]*, warblers) were generally less abundant at disturbed sites. Other species (common grackle *[Quiscalus quiscula]*, bluejay *[Cyanocitta cristata]*, red-bellied woodpecker *[Melanerpes carolinus]*) may benefit from this type of habitat modification, whereas others (northern cardinal *[Cardinalis cardinalis]*, Carolina wren *[Ihrythorus ludovicianus]*, yellow-billed cuckoo *[Coccyaus americanus]*) may not be greatly affected by it (Table 5.1). Habitat disturbance changes the relative abundance of bird species in a particular site.

Gaddy and Kohlsaat (1987:62) concluded that

. . . visitation on barrier island preserves can be accommodated without seriously compromising their unique features. Footpaths and hiking trails cause little or no change to the structure of the maritime forest vegetation but can affect amphibian and reptile densities. Therefore such plants should be used sparingly. Roads and jeep trails that cause breaks in the forest canopy can lead to the establishment of pioneer vegetation and corresponding changes in composition of the faunal community. More extensive canopy openings, such as those caused by clearings and dikes, can lead to invasion by exotic plants, which can spread into the maritime forest.

Their management recommendations based on the just-stated conclusions were that

Table **5.1.** Densities (pairs per square kilometer) of the most common breeding forest birds (indicated by singing males on territory) along transects through sites with differing disturbance levels on three barrier islands in South Carolina (Modified from Gaddy and Kohlsaat 1987, used with permission of Natural Areas Journal).

Species	Disturbance level		
	Most	Moderate	Least
Common grackle	285	66[a]	101
Bluejay	38	12[a]	7
Red-bellied woodpecker	43	34	27
Blue-gray gnatcatcher	20	14	17
Yellow-bellied cuckoo	14	12	19
Great crested flycatcher	34	15[a]	27
Summer tanager	8	23[a]	7
Cardinal	64	71	75
Carolina wren	82	91	101
White-eyed vireo	5	65[a]	31
Northern parula warbler	19	68	68
Pine warbler	20	30	41
Red-eyed vireo	0	5[a]	18
Painted bunting	16	45	47
Yellow-throated warbler	2	14"	24

[a] Significant difference between moderately disturbed site and least disturbed site (Chi-square test, p = 0.05).

. . . [i]f roads are necessary on the barrier island preserves, great care should be taken in their planning, and two somewhat conflicting points should be kept in mind: (1) roads that run perpendicular to an island's parallel dune ridge system may alter drainage patterns in interdune wetlands, and (2) roads that run parallel to the dune ridges (usually placed on the ridges) may cut off movement of animals between wetlands and ridges, especially reptiles. To be minimally disruptive, roads should be run perpendicular to the ridge system except to bypass major wetlands. A bypass should follow the ridge line, leading away from the deepest part of the wetland. Roads should not be placed where there are major wetlands. To minimize species-area effects, roads should also create as few patches as possible. On most barrier islands the preferred road system would be one that skirts either end of the island; such a system would leave a large undisturbed central area and would minimize disturbance to freshwater wetlands [Fig. 5.7](1987:62).

On islands undergoing beach erosion, the best habitat for nesting least terns and marine turtles may be at either end of the island, which are more likely to be agrading. Roads skirting the center of the island should therefore be terminated short of the beach, and foot traffic should be diverted around those areas. Terminating roads in this manner will also prevent access to the beach and possible disturbance by off-road vehicles (Bellis, personal observation).

Effects of Subdivision Development on the Herpetofauna

Most large, well-developed maritime forests contain interdune bodies of fresh water called swaleponds or maritime swamp forests. Swale ponds seem to owe their origin to rising sea level (Burney and Burney 1984; Bensink and Burton 1975). As sea level rises, the barrier island freshwater lens is raised until it intercepts topographic lows between forest-stabilized dune ridges. Swale ponds may be seasonal or semipermanent, depending on rainfall patterns. Freshwater swale ponds provide habitat for many species that might otherwise be severely limited by lack of a dependable freshwater supply. Swale ponds support species not usually found in maritime forest and the presence of ponds is usually an indication of a richer biotic diversity. Alligators, freshwater turtles, frogs, and water snakes are herpetofauna that require freshwater habitat (Gibbons and Coker 1978). Other frogs,

toads, and salamanders must have access to fresh water to complete their life cycles.

J. W. Gibbons had the opportunity to study the herpetofauna on Kiawah Island, South Carolina, both before (Gibbons and Coker 1978) and after (Gibbons and Harrison 1981) development of a resort community on the island. A pond complex, which before development had harbored a rich herpetofauna, was deepened, enlarged, and cleared of emergent vegetation. Landscape modifications included removal of most understory vegetation and forest litter. Some trees were removed. Buildings and roads were constructed. The pond was stocked with non-native largemouth bass (*Micropterus salmoides*) and sunfish (*Lepomis* sp.). Gibbons observed that although they persisted in the developed areas, the abundance of most species appeared to be considerably reduced. This observation was later verified by Gaddy and Kohlsaat (1987), when they reinterpreted the Gibbons and Harrison (1981) faunal data by using a quantitative measure of plant community disturbance (Table 5.2). Gibbons and Harrison (1981) found that an apparent consequence of these activities was loss of breeding populations of frogs and toads. No frog or toad eggs were found in the pond after its modification by the developers. The absence of eggs was attributed to the frequent use of insecticides in the general area. The absence of reproduction was thought to be due, in part, to the abundance of introduced predators in the pond. Extremely low population densities were

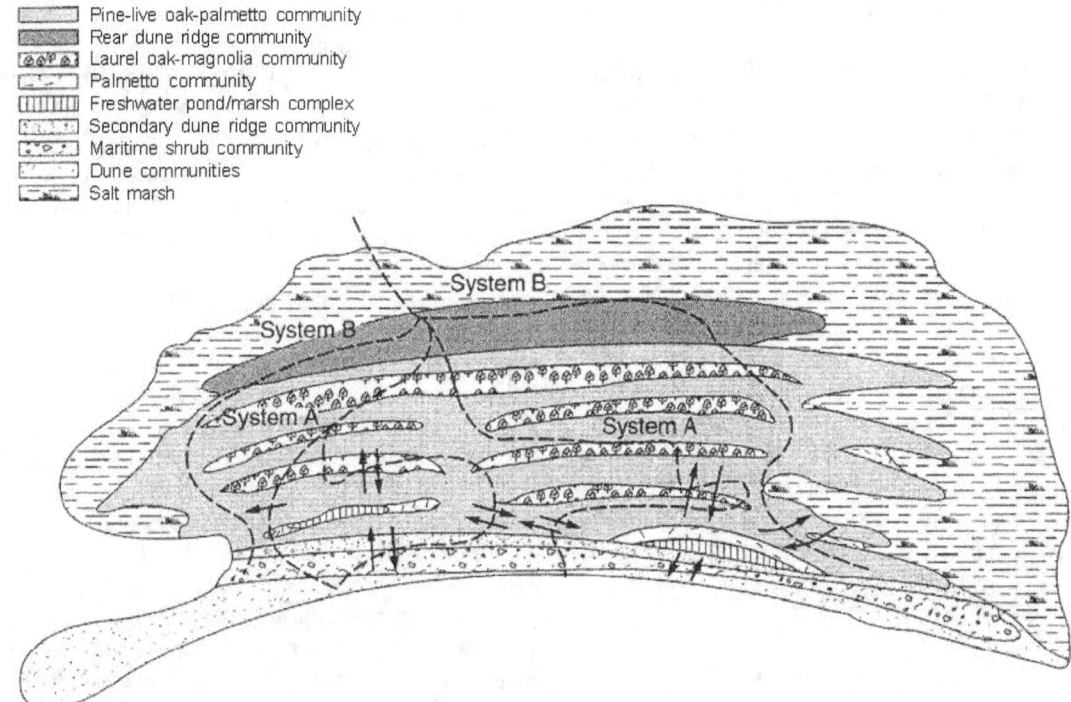

Fig. 5.7. Distribution of plant communities on a hypothetical barrier island, showing design of two road systems (from Gaddy and Kohlsaat 1987; used with permission of *Natural Areas* Journal).

Table 5.2. Summary of reptile and amphibian transect data (excluding turtles and alligators) in maritime forest habitats for three disturbance levels on two barrier islands in South Carolina (modified from Gaddy and Kohlsaat 1987, used with permission of Natural Areas Journal).

Island	Disturbance level	Number of species	Individuals No.	Individuals No./hr.
Kiawah	Most	7	8	1.2
	Moderate	10	75	11.5
	Least	12	200	25.0
Capers	Most	4	19	3.5
	Moderate	7	23	6.6
	Least	7	50	10.0

thought to represent recruitment by dispersal from less developed parts of the island. A former population of slimy salamander (*Plethodon glutinosus*) in a palmetto forest bordering the pond had disappeared, at least in part because of loss of habitat and cover through the removal of organic litter and opening of the area to increased solar drying. Of three species of skinks observed before development, none was in evidence in the later study. Snake populations were lower, probably from the combined results of road kills, conscious efforts to kill venomous species, and reductions in prey food (frogs and toads). Turtles and small alligators (their larger relatives were exiled to ponds in undeveloped portions of the island) persist.

As a result of their before-and-after study of the herpetofauna during the development of Kiawah Island, Gibbons and Harrison (1981) demonstrated that major disruptions of the herpetofauna can result from alteration of the forests and freshwater ponds. Changes in water level or salinity or the removal of vegetative cover and organic litter can impair herpetofaunal populations. Because frogs and other amphibians often constitute a significant portion of the diet of larger animals (snakes, birds, some mammals) in the maritime forest, loss of this food source could result in major trophic disruption.

Terrestrial reptiles and amphibians are most severely impacted by modification of the vegetation (Gibbons and Harrison 1981). Some species are so dependent on organic litter and ground cover that they may be eliminated by landscaping practices designed to and remove undergrowth.

Fire Management

Fire seems to be an important natural feature of maritime forest ecology. Humans have also long used fire to clear land and promote habitat for grazing animals and have rigorously suppressed fire to protect developed property and structures.

Those that manage barrier island and maritime forest areas are finding that they must establish criteria for deciding when to suppress fire and when to use controlled burning as a management tool (Bellis, personal observation). Specific management questions about fire include when and under what conditions fire can be **used** to eliminate stands of exotic vegetation or as a means of manipulating plant succession toward some desired end result; whether overly effective fire suppression results in accumulation of excessive fuel followed by greater incidence of more intense and difficult-to-control fires; and whether maritime forests should be provided with fire breaks.

Bratton (1986a) reviewed the present condition and status of fire management problems in southeastern National Seashores. She emphasized that general, system-wide policies and approaches are probably inappropriate, given the regional differences in fire pattern. She concluded that managers should tailor their fire management programs to individual area needs and natural fire regimes.

Rare Plants and Animals

Barrier islands are often separated from the mainland and from one another. Extensive salt marshes or bodies of open salt water. Depending on the dispersal characteristics of individual species of plants or animals, these habitat conditions may represent barriers to movement and genetic exchange by some species.

The southeastern coastal barrier islands are, however, close enough to the mainland that whole groups of organisms appear to be little affected by these apparent barriers, and most species appear to share a common gene pool with mainland populations.

Microorganisms, including fungi, algae, and protozoa, usually have a cosmopolitan distribution. Spore-bearing ferns may be widely distributed by the wind. Microinvertebrates may be transported from pond to pond by migratory birds. At the other end of the relative size scale, many reptiles, birds, and large mammals have little difficulty traversing salt marshes and mud flats or swimming or flying across moderate expanses of open water.

Animals of intermediate size and those that depend on a freshwater habitat seem most affected by the environmental barriers separating coastal islands. Groups of animals in this category include many amphibians and small mammals. Neuhauser (1976) determined that 6 species and 45 subspecies of mammals in the contiguous United

States are distributed mostly or entirely only on large islands. Among the 45 island subspecies listed by Neuhauser, 32 are small rodents (e.g., shrews, mice, and rats).

Apparently animal populations on some islands have had gene pool reduction and genetic drift to the extent that they are recognized as taxonomically distinct. Examples of taxonomically distinct species or subspecies inhabiting barrier islands of the southeastern United States include the Outer Banks kingsnake (*Lampropeltis getulus sticticeps*), Cumberland Island pocket gopher (*Geomys cumberlundius*), Anastasia Island cotton mouse (*Peromyscus gossypinus anastasae*), St. Simons Island raccoon (*Procyon lotor litoreus*), and Blackbeard Island deer (*Odocoileus virginianus nigribarbis*)(Blaney 1979).

The list of taxonomically distinct barrier island endemic species is short, and even some of these have recently been challenged. Blaney (1979) concluded that the Outer Banks kingsnake (*Lampropeltis getulus sticticeps*) probably represents a relictual intergraded population that has characteristics of *L. g. floridiana* and *L. g. getulus.* A more detailed population study of the Cumberland Island pocket gopher (*Ceomys cumberlandius*) by Laerm (198 1) concluded that this taxon was insufficiently distinct from a coastal population of *G. pinetis* to constitute a separate taxonomic status. The present work of taxonomists studying entire populations of species and species complexes may represent as great a threat to the continued authenticity of island endemic species as development and habitat loss.

It is well documented that the biota of barrier islands is generally less species rich than the biota of the nearby mainland (Engles 1952; Gibbons and Coker 1978; Bellis, personal observation; also see Chapters 3 and 4). It is also apparent that islands with diverse habitats support a greater variety of species than those with more limited habitat alternatives. The greatest biotic diversity on barrier islands of the Southeast seems to occur where wetlands and forests are well developed. Examples of such conditions exist within the Buxton Woods and Nags Head Woods of North Carolina's Outer Banks. This area is also a transition zone between northern and southern biota because it overlaps the northern or southern range limits of many plants and animals (Bellis, personal observation; also see Chapters 3 and 4; Fig. 3.2; Table 4.6). The scientific and aesthetic values of barrier island nature preserves such as that operated by The Nature Conservancy at Nags Head (Atkinson and List 1978) are protection of rare, endangered, or endemic species and protection of a very unusual ecosystem that has limited distribution.

Predatory and other large mammals such as bobcat (*Lynx rufus*), mountain lion (*Felis concolor*), red fox (*Vulpes vulpes*), gray fox (*Urocyon cinereoargenteus*),

and black bear (*Ursus americanus*) have been reported (Bellis, personal observation) from time to time among the fauna of barrier islands, but it is doubtful that many of the islands are large enough to support populations of these species. Most sightings of larger mammals were probably of temporary visitors or disoriented individuals. Residents of the Outer Banks of North Carolina enjoy recounting for visitors the saga of a black bear exiled from his mountain home to the mainland coastal swamps for the purpose of invigorating the local black bear gene pool. Seemingly unhappy with the new accommodations, the bear swam 24 km across the Croatian Sound and emerged from the water, much to the consternation of camping tourists and definitely to the chagrin of National Park Service personnel in the Salvo Campgrounds on Hatteras Island.

Maritime forests do not appear to represent critical habitat for many rare or endangered plant species. An inventory oft-are, threatened, and exotic plants of the Cape Hatteras National Seashore by Gaddy (1985) listed 19 species of native plants reported by Cooper et al. (1977) or Sutter et al. (1983) as species of concern in North Carolina. Three of these plants were dependent on forested habitat, namely the southern twayblade orchid (*Listera australis*), a significantly rare species in North Carolina; the Florida pellitory (*Parietaria floridana*), an endangered peripheral; and the dwarf palmetto (*Sabal minor*), near its northern range limit at Cape Hatteras National Seashore. Two other aquatic plants were restricted to wetland habitat associated with maritime forest: fragrant beakrush (*Rhynchospora odorata*), a threatened peripheral, and a scirpus (*Scirpus etuberculatus*), a rare species in North Carolina.

Apparently no vascular plants in maritime forests of the Southeast are in danger of extinction (Bellis, personal observation). Plant species on various state lists of species of concern are regionally important because they occur near the limits of their range in a particular state, even though the same species may occur abundantly elsewhere. Northward extension of ranges of species exhibiting a southern affinity may be related to the moderating effects of the marine environment on climate extremes.

Maritime forests may be used by several species of endangered or rare birds. Fussell(1978) noted the historic use of maritime forest as nesting sites for bald eagles (*Haliaeetus leucocephalus*) and that an immature bald eagle had been a frequent visitor to a heronry in the forest near Emerald Isle, North Carolina. Peregrine falcons (*Falco peregrinus*), Cooper's hawks (*Accipiter cooperi*), red-shouldered hawks (*Buteo lineatus*), and merlins (*Falco columbarus*) may use maritime forest for resting or feeding during their migrations.

Rare taxa in maritime forests of the Southeast seem to be locally rare rather than globally rare (Bellis, personal observation). Maritime forests do not seem to be essential habitat for nationally threatened species of plants and animals. Absence of an otherwise regionally common species from a barrier island is probably more often a result of unsuitable habitat conditions on the island for that species rather than lack of colonization opportunity.

Current Status of Maritime Forests

Although maritime forests occur on barrier islands along the entire Atlantic Coast of the United States, they seem most extensive and best developed on the sea islands of South Carolina and Georgia. North Carolina produced a comprehensive inventory of its maritime forest resources (Lopazanski et al. 1988). Sufficient information is also available about the vegetative cover of barrier islands in South Carolina and Georgia (Mathews et al. 1980) to estimate the extent of the maritime forests in these states. Because maritime forests dominated by evergreen angiosperm trees occur only rarely north of Bogue Banks, North Carolina, or south of Jacksonville, Florida, it is possible to make a rough estimate of the total remaining maritime forest (Table 5.3).

Inventories by Lopazanski et al. (1988) and Mathews et al. (1980) indicated that within North Carolina, Georgia, and Florida, an estimated 39,000 ha of undeveloped maritime forest remained from an unknown original total before human intervention. Of the remaining undeveloped maritime forest, 25,280 ha (about 65%) are in Georgia. North Carolina has the second longest coastline (about 480 km) and the smallest share of maritime forest

(2,518 ha), about 6.5%. Georgia has a maritime forest density of 160 ha per linear kilometer of ocean shoreline, whereas North Carolina has a density of only 5.3 ha/km. Florida has a longer Atlantic coastline than North Carolina; however, information concerning the extent of maritime forests in that state is insufficient for comparisons.

Assuming that maritime forests owned by conservation organizations and government agencies are protected and that those owned by other entities are unprotected, it seems that about half of the remaining undeveloped maritime forest has some measure of protection. At current rates of development, however, the unprotected half will probably be developed within the next decade.

By the beginning of the 21st century, Georgia is expected to retain the largest area of undeveloped maritime forest, about 16,430 ha or nearly 79% of the currently protected maritime forest (Bellis, personal observation). About 71% of South Carolina's present maritime forests and 55% of North Carolina's could be commercially or residentially developed.

Regulation of Development: A Case History from North Carolina

During summer 1986, residents of Hatteras Island, North Carolina, learned that a 125-lot subdivision and golf course was being proposed for a 260-acre tract within the Buxton Woods Maritime Forest adjacent to Cape Hatteras National Seashore and near the Cape

Table 5.3. Status of maritime forest on the southeastern coast of the United States.[a]

State	Ocean shoreline (km)	Ocean shoreline bordered by maritime forest (km)	Developed forest area (ha)	Undeveloped forest area (ha)	Undeveloped maritime forest open to development (%)
Virginia	225				
North Carolina[b]	484			2,518[a]	55.4
South Carolina[c]	294	163	7,294	11,128	71.1
Georgia[c]	156	137	3,467	25,280	35.0
Florida (east coast, excluding Keys)	692				
Totals	1,851	<-insufficient data->		38,926	161.5

[a] No data available for maritime forests in Virginia and Florida along a combined coastline of 915 km.

[b] Acreage of maritime forest in North Carolina estimated at 4,856 ha (Lopazanski et al. 1988). The estimate of 2,518 ha given is the sum of 24 locations given by Lopananski et al. 1988; omitted was one 2,000-ha location the vegetation of which did not fit the description of maritime forest used in this community profile.

[c] Mathews et al. 1980.

Hatteras Lighthouse. Before the announcement of the proposed development, many visitors to the National Seashore had assumed that most of the maritime forest at Cape Hatteras was in federal ownership and managed by the National Park Service.

A local forest preservation organization, Friends of Hatteras Island, formed to oppose the golf course development and what the organization considered other types of uncontrolled development. At the time there was no zoning ordinance governing development in that part of Dare County.

The North Carolina Chapter of the Sierra Club joined the Friends of Hatteras in nominating about 1,012 ha of the Buxton Woods for classification as a coastal complex natural area of environmental concern (AEC), under provision of the State's Coastal Area Management Act (CAMA; Brower et al. 1980 and Zucchino 1981). Within AEC boundaries, development would require a CAMA permit and would have to conform to development standards intended to minimize the loss of forest canopy, relict dunes, and freshwater wetlands within the forest by encouraging only low-density, low-impact development. Specific provisions of the proposed AEC regulations included minimum lot size of 7,432 m^2 (about 0.8 ha) for single-family dwellings, with a provision that no more than 35% of the total lot area could be cleared, and that all streets follow natural contours and not exceed 12 m in width, including land cleared for shoulders and right-of-way. Other provisions regulated maximum building height, removal of native vegetation, drainage, and minor road crossings. Pilings were recommended as a means of leveling buildings to minimize land disturbance. Additional provisions encouraged cluster construction on large multiunit sites.

The Dare County government reacted negatively to the concept of state-administered regulations and proposed a county ordinance almost identical to the proposed AEC ordinance (Bellis, personal observation). The county proposal was accepted by the state and development within privately owned portions of Buxton Woods is currently regulated by Dare County.

The controversy that developed around the Buxton Woods issue raised sufficient public interest that the North Carolina Department of Environment, Health, and Natural Resources (NCDEHNR) initiated an inventory and assessment of the remaining maritime forests in the state (Lopazanski et al. 1988). Subsequently, a Maritime Forest working group composed of scientists, landscape architects, and land developers was established by the NCDEHNR Division of Coastal Management. The working group was assigned the tasks of defining the term "maritime forest," determining the necessary conditions to maintain maritime forest sites as functioning ecosystems and ranking maritime forest sites by importance for protection. Additional tasks included the development of educational materials for a handbook on development in maritime forests published by the Division of Coastal Management (Zucchino 1990), development of a protection or acquisition plan to protect the identified maritime forest resources, and preparation of a model forest protection ordinance and use standard.

Meanwhile, news that forested portions of barrier islands might soon be subject to greater regulation stimulated some developers to speed up their development plans. Within 18 months, 4 of 24 sites identified by Lopazanski et al. (1988) had been developed to the point where they could no longer be considered naturally functioning ecosystems.

At the time of this writing, no detailed plan for the protection of North Carolina's maritime forests has been presented. Although it has been recognized that protection of maritime forests as functioning natural ecosystems must eventually involve acquisition of tracts large enough to maintain biological diversity, the minimum size of those tracts has not been determined and may vary from area to area. Furthermore, the financial climate for government or private funds for land acquisition is not favorable. Conversely, the pace of urban development in maritime forests has quickened (Bellis, personal observation) to the extent that most currently unprotected maritime forests will probably not exist as naturally functioning ecosystems sometime in the 1990's.

Given this development pressure, North Carolina is again considering designating selected maritime forests as Areas of Environmental Concern (AEC) under the state's Coastal Area Management Act (Bellis, personal observation). Draft designations and use standards have been proposed (Appendix A). While AEC designation does not prevent development, it is an attempt to limit damage to an amount that, in the judgement of knowledgeable persons, can be sustained while still preserving the essential functional values of the ecosystem. The use standards (Appendix A) are presented here as an example of the type and magnitude of development restrictions being considered by one state. This model is presented to give the reader an idea of the values and conditions that should be considered in developing use standards. Citation of the proposed North Carolina standards in this report should not be considered an endorsement of them by either the author or the National Biological Service. These standards were developed for use in North Carolina and seem to represent a functional compromise between development interests and preservation-they allow some development while retaining much of the physical and biological character of a maritime forest. The extent to which these standards actually maintain the natural functioning of maritime forests will become clear over time.

CHAPTER 6.

Research Needs

Introduction

Only a very small portion of the southeastern coastal land area is covered by maritime forests. Many forests are isolated and difficult to reach. Consequently, few long-term or experimental ecological studies have been conducted within this biological community. The information that has been obtained for this report consists mostly of descriptive surveys and inventories of the larger and more conspicuous biota. The following research needs have been compiled by the author over the course of preparing this report and from personal knowledge of previous and current information-gathering activity in the region.

Maritime forests maintain soil stability and provide fresh groundwater sources on barrier islands, although this idea has inadequate scientific documentation. In addition, maritime forests probably provide the habitat and storm refuge required to maintain biological diversity and integrated ecological function on a barrier island.

In the absence of firm documentation of the presumed stabilizing effects of maritime forest, intensive urbanization has taken place in barrier island forests during the last several decades. Thus, there is a pressing need to understand how maritime forests form, develop, and are maintained in a natural setting. Island residents have to know how to balance their need for access and convenience with the continued geological and biological stability of their island home. Future research should address the ecological questions and management concerns listed in the following two sections.

Ecological Questions

- What is the ecological role of the soil microbiota and mycorrhizae in soil formation, soil stabilization, and nutrient cycling?
- What is the ecological role of epiphytic lichens in mineral cycling and moderation of salt toxicity?
- Do barrier island vegetation zones represent stages in succession toward a mature, self-maintaining community or does each zone undergo an independent successional sequence? If both processes occur, which is the dominant process given the present geological regime? Does the landscape determine vegetation cover type or vice versa? What is the role of disturbance in determining the vegetative cover type at any given time or site?
- Did our present barrier island forests and their associated fauna originate from successive colonization events dependent upon over-water or over-marsh transport of initial populations? Or did founders consist of populations gradually and imperfectly separated from genetic exchange with the mainland by rising sea level? Among the nonmigratory fauna inhabiting barrier islands, comparative population studies are needed among species on particular islands and of a single species on several islands and the mainland. More information is needed concerning phenotypic and genotypic variability, competitive exclusion, colonizing ability, density compensation, and size patterns. To what extent have various animal species adapted specifically to maritime environmental conditions?

- What are the ecological interdependencies between barrier island maritime forests and surrounding communities of other types? For instance, what are the net mineral, water, and energy transfers between beach and forest or between forest and salt marsh? How critical is maritime forest refuge in sustaining barrier island populations that spend much of their time in nonforest environments?
- Can maritime forests be reestablished through habitat restoration techniques?
- How will the freshwater table on barrier islands respond to possible relatively rapid increases in the rate of sea-level rise? How might the relative distribution and areal extent of various barrier island communities be affected by an associated increase in the rate of rise of the fresh water table?
- Research needs related specifically to the physical characteristics of interior wetlands of barrier islands that have been identified by Odum et al. (1986) include microtopographic survey and mapping to locate wetland habitat, measurement of surface-water drainage and groundwater transmissivity, modeling of groundwater dynamics, and water-quality studies.

Management Needs

- Many terms have been used to designate the maritime forests of the southeastern United States. Biologists, managers, and agency regulatory authorities should develop a workable definition of the term "maritime forest." Currently, information transfer and management are inhibited by the many of mental images engendered by the term. For some, "maritime forest" means only dwarf sculpted trees along the ocean beach. For others the term brings forth the image of live oak and Spanish moss. It may even be necessary to recognize several types of maritime forest. An initial attempt to produce just such a classification was made by Schafale and Weakley (1990).

- Unprotected maritime forests are being destroyed rapidly. All remaining and historical maritime forests should be inventoried and mapped. Their current status, ownership, and primary uses should be indicated.
- How much drawdown of the barrier island surface fresh water for residential use can be sustained without damaging island ecosystems?
- How much fragmentation of maritime forest can be sustained without sacrificing island biodiversity and natural ecosystem function?
- Does clearing of beachfront vegetation open maritime forest to greater storm and salt impact and thus initiate an increased rate of maritime forest retreat'?
- Should all feral animals be eliminated from maritime forests designated as maritime forest preserves?
- When and under what conditions should managers use prescribed burning to manage maritime forest resources? What level of fire suppression is most compatible with maintenance of maritime forest as a naturally functioning ecological unit?

Acknowledgments

Overall it was a pleasant and intellectually rewarding task to assemble, read, and summarize the contributions made by so many persons during nearly a century of barrier island and maritime forest research.

P. Claxton, Rutgers University, supplied prepublication copies of a review of the scientific literature relevant to the national seashores of the United States. S. Ward, Colorado State University, assembled copies of papers pertinent to maritime forests, abstracted information later used in preparing chapter outlines, and wrote the initial draft of the unit on maritime forest soils.

Various Nature Conservancy and state natural heritage program staff provided updates on current maritime forest research in their states, as follows: (Florida) A. Johnson and J. Wick; (Georgia) R. Bonner; (North Carolina) M. Schafale and K. Skinner; (South Carolina) R. Dunlap and R. Jones; and (Virginia) G. Fenwick. Others who provided reprints, advice, leads to information, and encouragement included B. Beasley, D. Billings, S. Bratton, J. Evans, M. Lopazanski, and R. Shaw. J. Keough, National Biological Service, Southern Science Center, served as project officer of this report.

J. Bellis entered the material into a word processor and edited the original draft; he also wrote the first draft of the units dealing with fire. A. Bellis proofread early drafts as they were completed and L. Mauger redrafted Figs. 3-6 after the originals. Beth Vairin and other staff members of the Technical Support Office of the Southern Science Center provided editorial and graphics support during several stages of manuscript preparation.

Finally, S. Bratton, A. Cole, A. Johnson, W. Laney, J. Nelson, L. Pelej, and R. Shaw reviewed and provided critical comments on the early draft of this manuscript.

References

Andre, J. B. 1981. Habitat use andrelative abundance of the small mammals of a South Carolina barrier island. Brimleyana 5:129–134.

Anonymous. 1938. Forest cover in Cape Hatteras National Seashore area. Research File, Office of the Historian, U.S. Department of the Interior, National Park Service. Washington, D.C.

Art, H. 1971. Atmospheric salts in the functioning of a maritime forest ecosystem. Ph.D. thesis, Yale University. New Haven, Conn. 135 pp.

Art, H., F. H. Bormann, G. K. Voigt, and G. M. Woodwell. 1974. Barrier island forest ecosystem: role of meteorological inputs. Science 184:60–62.

Ashe, W. W. 1906. Report on an examination of certain swamplands belonging to the state. Pages 40-50 in Biennial report of the state geologist, North Carolina Geological Survey, Raleigh.

Atkinson, T. A., and H. E. List. 1978. Basic inventory and natural diversity summary of the NagsHead Woods, Dare County, North Carolina. The Nature Conservancy. 109 pp. Unpublished manuscript.

Au, S. 1969. Vegetation and ecological processes on Shackleford Banks, North Carolina. Ph.D. thesis. Duke University, Durham, N.C. 170 pp.

Au, S. 1974. Vegetation and ecological processes on Shackleford Banks, North Carolina. U.S. National Park Service Scientific Monograph Series 6. 86 pp.

Axelrod, D. 1. 1966. Origin of deciduous and evergreen habits in temperate forests. Evolution 20: I-I 5.

Bagur, J. D. 1978. Barrier islands of the Atlantic and Gulf coasts of the United States: an annotated bibliography. U.S. Fish and Wildlife Service FWS/OBS-77/56. 215 pp.

Banks, R. C., R. W. McDiarmid, and A. L. Gardner. 1987. Checklist of vertebrates of the United States, the U.S. Territories, and Canada. U.S. Fish and Wildlife Service, Resource Publication 166. 79 pp.

Barbour, M. G. 1978. Salt spray as a microenvironmental factor in the distribution of beach plants at Point Reyes, California. Oecologia (Berlin) 32:213–224.

Barbour, M. G., and T. M. DeJong. 1977. Responseof west coast beach taxa to salt spray, seawater, inundation, and soil salinity. Bulletin of the Torrey Botanical Club 104:29–34.

Barrick, W. E. 1973. Salt tolerant plants for Florida landscapes. Proceedings of the Florida State Horticultural Society 91:82–84.

Barry, J. M. 1980. Natural vegetation of South Carolina. University of South Carolina Press, Columbia. 214 pp.

Bascon, W. 1980. Waves and beaches, the dynamics of the ocean surface. Anchor Press, Garden City. 366 pp.

Bellis, V. J. 1980. The vegetative cover on the barrier islands of North Carolina. Veroeffentlichungen des Geobotanischen Institutes der Eidgenoessische Technische Hochschule Stiftung Rubel in Züerich 69: 121-144.

Bellis, V. J. 1988. Microalgae of barrier island freshwaterponds, Nags Head, North Carolina. ASB (Association of Southeastern Biologists) Bulletin 35:164–169.

Bellis, V. J. 1992. Floristic continuity among the maritime forests of the Atlantic coast of the United States. Pages 21-29 in C. A. Cole and F. K. Turner, editors. Barrier island ecology of the mid-Atlantic coast: a symposium. U.S. Department of the interior National Park Service, Atlanta, Ga.

Bellis. V. J., and C. E. Proffitt. 1976. Maritime forests. Pages 22-28 in D. Brower, D. Frankenberg, and F. Parker, editors. Ecological determinants of coastal area management: vol. 2. University of North Carolina Sea Grant Publication UNC-SG-76-05. 392 pp.

Bensink, A. H. A., and H. Burton. 1975. North Stradbroke Island: a place for freshwater invertebrates. Proceedings of the Royal Society of Queensland 86:29–45.

Blaney, R. M. 1979. The status of the outer banks kingsnake, Lampropeltis getulus sticticeps. Brimleyana 1:125–128.

Boc. S. J., and J. Langfelder. 1977. An analysis of beachoverwash along North Carolina's coast. North Carolina State University Center for Marine and Coastal Studies, Report 77-9.

Bond, J. F. 1908. Report on an examination of the sand banks along the North Carolina coast. Pages 42-48 in Biennial Report of the State Geologist, North Carolina Geological Survey, Raleigh.

Boone, J. L. 1988. Small mammal response to fire on Bodie and Hatteras Islands, Cape Hatteras National Seashore, North Carolina. University of Georgia Institute of Ecology. Cooperative Park Studies Unit Technical Report 48. 42 pp.

Bourdeau, P. F., and H. J. Oosting. 19.59. The maritime live oak forest in North Carolina. Ecology 40:148–152.

Boyce, S. G. 1951a. Source of atmospheric salts. Science 113:620–621.

Boyce, S. G. 195 lb. Salt hypertrophy in succulent dune plants. Science 114:544–545.

Boyce, S. G. 1954. The salt spray community. Ecological Monographs 24:29–68.

Bozeman, J. R. 1971. A sociologic and geographic study of the sand ridge vegetation in the coastal plain of Georgia. Ph.D. thesis, University of North Carolina, Chapel Hill. 243 pp.

Bozeman, J. R., and R. M. Fuller. 1975. The vegetation of Cumberland Island. Pages 63-1 17 in H. 0. Hillestad, J. R. Bozeman, A. S, Johnson, C. W. Berisford, and J. I. Richardson, editors. The ecology of Cumberland Island National Seashore, Camden County, Georgia. Georgia Marine Science Center Technical Report Serial 95-5.

Braswell, A. L. 1988. A survey of the amphibians and reptiles of the Nags Head Woods Ecological Preserve. ASB (Association of Southeastern Biologists) Bulletin 35:199–217.

Bratton, S. P. 1985. The vegetation history of Fort Fredcrica, St. Simons, Georgia. Castanea 50: 133-145.

Bratton, S. P. 1986a. Prescribed fiie: is it an option for coastal barrier management? Park Science 6: 1-3.

Bratton, S. P. 1986b. Experimental control of tung trees at Cumberland Island National Seashore. University of Georgia Institute of Ecology. Cooperative Park Studies Unit Technical Report 29. 18 pp.

Bratton, S. P., and S. Bennett, 1987. Vascular plant checklist, Fort Frederica National Monument, St. Simons Island, Georgia. University of Georgia Institute of Ecology. Cooperative Park Studies Unit Technical Report 39.24 pp.

Bratton, S. P., and K. L. Davison. 1985. The disturbance history of Buxton Woods, Cape Hatteras, North Carolina. University of Georgia Institute of Ecology. Cooperative Park Studies Unit Technical Report 16. 36 pp.

Bratton, S. P., and K. L. Davison. 1987. Disturbance and succession in Buxton Woods, Cape Hatteras, North Carolina. Castanea 52:166–179.

Bratton, S. P., and K. Turner. 1986. Final report of the aquatics resources advisory team, Cape Hatteras National Seashore, North Carolina. University of Georgia Institute of Ecology. Cooperative Park Studies Unit Technical Report 24. 13 pp.

Braun, E. L. 1950. Deciduous forests of eastern North America. Blakiston Publishers, Philadelphia. 596 pp.

Brower, D., F. Parker, D. Frankenburg, B. J. Copeland, and R. Alden, 1976. Ecological determinants of coastal area management. 2 vols. University of North Carolina Sea Grant Publication UNC-SC-76-05. 392 pp.

Brower, D., F. Parker, D. Frankenburg, B. J. Copeland, and R. Alden. 1980. Proposed standards for development in maritime forest areas of environmental concern. Center for Urban and Regional Studies. University of North Carolina, Chapel Hill. 22 pp.

Brown, C. A. 1959. Vegetation of the Outer Banks of North Carolina. Louisiana State University, Coastal Studies Series 4. 179pp.

Brown, C. W. 1983. A palynological study of peat layers from Jeanette Sedge, North Carolina Outer Banks. M.A. thesis, Smith College, Northampton, Mass. 56 pp.

Burk, C. J.1961a. A floristic study of the Outer Banks of North Carolina. Ph.D. thesis, University of North Carolina, Chapel Hill. 123 pp.

Burk, C. J. 1961b. A botanical reconnaissance of Portsmouth Island, North Carolina. Journal of the Elisha Mitchell Scientific Society 77:72–74.

Burk, C. J. 1961c. Distribution records and range extensions from the North Carolina Outer Banks. Castanea 26:138–139.

Burk, C. J.1962a. The North Carolina Outer Banks: a floristic interpretation. Journal of the Elisha Mitchell Scientific Society 78:21–28.

Burk, C. J.1962b. An evaluation of three hybrid-containing oak populations on the North Carolina Outer Banks. Journal of the Elisha Mitchell Scientific Society 78: 18-21.

Burk, C. J. 1963. The hybrid nature of Quercus laurifolia. Journal of the Elisha Mitchell Scientific Society 79:159–163.

Burk, C. J. 1966. Dynamics of plant distribution: I. Sabal minor. Advancing Frontiers of Plant Sciences 14:1–4.

Burk, C. J. 1968. A floristic comparison of lower Cape Cod, Massachusetts, and the North Carolina Outer Banks. Rhodora 70:215–227.

Burk, C. J. 1971. Outer Banks revisited. National Parks and Conservation Magazine 45:4–7.

Burk, C. J. 1974. The vegetation of Portsmouth Island, North Carolina: fourteen years of change. ASB (Association of Southeastern Biologists) Bulletin 21:44.

Burk, C. J., H. A. Curran, and T. M. Czemiak. 1981. Dunes and vegetation: natural recovery on a damaged barrier island. Shore and Beach 49:21–25.

Burk, C. J., and S. D. Lauermann. 1975a. Development of vegetation on Portsmouth Island North Carolina: fourteen years of change. Department of Biological Sciences, Smith College, Northampton, Mass. 13 pp. [unpublished report]

Burk, C. J., and S. D. Lauermann. 1975b. Patterns of development in the floras of continental islands of the eastern coast of North America. ASB (Association of Southeastern Biologists) Bulletin 22:44.

Burney, D. A., and L. P. Burney. 1984. A palynological investigation of Nags Head Woods Ecological Preserve, Dare County, North Carolina. A mimeographed report to the Nature Conservancy dated June 15, 1984. Nags Head Woods Ecological Preserve, Nags Head, N.C. 33 pp.

Burney, D. A., and L. P. Burney. 1987. Recent paleoecology of Nags Head Woods on the North Carolina Outer Banks. Bulletin of the Torrey Botanical Club 114:156–168.

Campbell, W. M., and J. M. Dean, editors. 1975. Environmental inventory of Kiawah Island. Environmental Research Center Inc., Columbia, S.C. 692 pp.

Cantral, R. 1988. Wind, waves, and sand. The CAMA Quarterly 1:6–13.

Carico, J. E. 1973. The Nearctic species of the genus *Dolomedes* (Arachnida, Pisauridae). Bulletin of the Museum of Comparative Zoology 144:435–488.

Carter, J. L. 1979. Swimming as a determinant to immigration for small mammals in coastal Virginia. M.S. thesis, Old Dominion University, Norfolk, Va. 58 pp.

Carter, J. L., and J. F. Merritt. 1981. Evaluation of swimming ability as a means of island invasion by small mammals in coastal Virginia. Annals of the Carnegie Museum 50:31-46.

Chamberlain, W. D. 1982. Avian population density in the maritime forest of two South Carolina barrier islands. Birds 36:142–145.

Chamberlain, W. D., and E. B. Chamberlain. 1975. Avifauna of Kiawah Island. Pages AV 1-AV106 in W. M. Campbell, J. M. Dean, and W. D. Chamberlain, editors. Environmental inventory of Kiawah Island. Environmental Research Center, Inc., Columbia, S.C.

Chapman, V. J. 1976. Coastal vegetation 2nd ed. Pergamon Press, Elmsford, N.Y. 292 pp.

Clark, J. R., editor. 1976. Barrier islands and beaches: technical proceedings of the 1976 barrier islands workshop, Annapolis, M.D. The Conservation Foundation, Washington, D.C. 149 pp.

Clark, J. R., and R. Turner. 1976. Barrier islands: a threatened fragile resource. Conservation Foundation letter. 12 pp.

Clayton, J. L. 1972. Salt spray and mineral cycling in two California coastal ecosystems. Ecology 53:74–81.

Coates, D. R., editor. 1973. Coastal geomorphology: proceedings of the 3rd annual geomorphology symposia series. State University of New York, Binghamton. 404 pp.

Cobb, C. 1906. Where the wind does the work. Journal of the Elisha Mitchell Scientific Society 22:80–85.

Cockfield, B. A., J. B. Tormey, and D. M. Forsythe. 1980. Barrier island maritime forest. American Birds 34:29.

Cohn, J. P. 1990. An island for conservation. BioScience 40:342–345.

Coker, W. C. 1905. Observations on the flora of the Isle of Palms, South Carolina. Torreya 5:135–145.

Coker, W. C. 1918. A visit to Smith Island. Journal of the Elisha Mitchell Scientific Society 34:150–153.

Colwell, P. B. 1983. Mammals of coastal islands of southeastern North Carolina. M.S. thesis, University of North Carolina, Wilmington. 78 pp.

Conant, R. 1975. Field guide to reptiles and amphibians. Houghton-Mifflin, Boston. 429 pp.

Cooper, A. W., and S. Satterwaite. 1964. Smith Island and the Cape Fear Peninsula: a comprehensive report on an outstanding natural area. Wildlife Preserves, Inc. with North Carolina Academy of Science, Raleigh. 80 pp.

Cooper, J. E., S. S. Robinson, and J. B. Funderburg, editors. 1977. Endangered and threatened plants and animals of North Carolina. North Carolina State Museum of Natural History, Raleigh. 444 pp.

Cooper, S. 1986. Birds found in the Buxton Woods, Cape Hatteras National Seashore during May and June 1986. The Nature Conservancy. [unpublished preliminary report]

Cooper, S. 1988. Breeding birds of Nags Head Woods, Dare County, North Carolina. ASB (Association of Southeastern Biologists) Bulletin 35:218–222.

Cowardin, L. M., V. Carter, F. C. Golet, and E. T. LaRoe. 1979. Classification of wetlands and deepwater habitats of the United States. U.S. Fish and Wildlife Service FWS/OBS-79/31. 103 pp.

Crandell, H. C. 1962. Geology and groundwater resources of Plum Island, Suffolk County, New York. U.S. Geological Survey Water Supply Paper 1539-X. 35 pp.

Cry, G. W. 1967. Effects of tropical cyclone rainfall on the distribution of rainfall over the eastern and southern United States. U.S. Environmental Science Services Administration Professional Paper 1, Asheville, N.C. 67 pp.

Curtis, C. R., T. L. Laurer, and B. A. Francis. 1977. Foliar sodium and chloride in trees: seasonal variations. Environmental Pollution 14:69–80.

Davison, K. L. 1983. Cumberland Island fire effects study. Park Science 4:20–22.

Davison, K. L. 1984. Vegetation response and regrowth after fire on Cumberland Island National Seashore, Georgia. U.S. Department of the Interior, National Park Services, Research/Resource Management Report SER-69. 121 pp.

Davison, K. L. 1985. The vegetation and carrying capacity of the Ocracoke Pony Pen, Cape Hatteras National Seashore. University of Georgia institute of Ecology. Cooperative Park Studies Unit Technical Report 13. 21 pp.

Davison, K. L. 1986. Vegetation responses to fire on Cape Hatteras National Seashore, North Carolina. University of

Georgia Institute of Ecology. Cooperative Park Studies Unit Technical Report 25.26 pp.

Davison, K. L. 1988a. Vascular vegetation of selected Nags Head Woods ponds. ASB (Association of Southeastern Biologists) Bulletin 35:170–180.

Davison, K. L. 1988b. Vegetation map and cover analysis, Buxton Woods, North Carolina. University of Georgia Institute of Ecology. Cooperative Park Studies Unit map. 1 pp.

Davison, K., and S. P. Bratton. 1986. The vegetation history of Canaveral National Seashore, Florida. University of Georgia Institute of Ecology. Cooperative Park Studies Unit Technical Report 22.75 pp.

Davison, K. L., and S. P. Bratton. 1987. A survey of the vegetation and fuels of Buxton Woods, Cape Hatteras National Seashore, North Carolina. University of Georgia Institute of Ecology. Cooperative Park Studies Unit Technical Report 40. 45 pp.

Davison, K. L., S. P. Bratton, and L. Graham. 1987. Vascular plant species checklist, Bodie Island, Cape Hatteras National Seashore, North Carolina. University of Georgia Institute of Ecology. Cooperative Park Studies Unit Technical Report 33. 30 pp.

Dolan, R. 1973. Barrier islands: natural and controlled. Pages 263-278 in D. R. Coates, editor. Coastal geomorphology. State University of New York, Binghamton. 404 pp.

Dolan, R. 1976. Barrier beachfronts. Pages 76-85 in Barrier islands and beaches. The Conservation Foundation, New York.

Dolan, R., P. J. Godfrey, and W. E. Odum. 1973. Man's impact on the barrier islands of North Carolina. American Scientist 61:153–162.

Doutt, J. K. 1941. Wind pruning and salt spray as a factor in ecology. Ecology 22: 195-196.

Ducser, R. D., W. C. Brown, G. S. Hogue, C. McCaffrey, S. A. McCuskey, and G. S. Hennessey. 1979. Mammals of the Virginia barrier islands. Journal of Mammology 60:425–429.

Dunbar, G. S. 1958. Historical geography of the North Carolina Outer Banks. Louisiana State University Coastal Studies Series 3, Louisiana State University Press, Baton Rouge. 234 pp.

Dunbar, G. S. 1960. The Hatteras Indians of North Carolina. Ethnohistory 7:410–418.

Dunbar, G. S., and F. Kniffen. 1956. Geographical history of the Carolina Banks. Louisiana State University Coastal Studies Technical Report 8A. 249 pp.

Duncan, W. H. 195.5. Woody vegetation of Sapelo Island, Georgia. ASB (Association of Southeastern Biologists) Bulletin 2:5. [abstract]

Duncan, W. H. 1982. The vascular vegetation of Sapelo Island, Georgia. Georgia Department of Natural Resources, Atlanta.

Dunham, R. J., and P. H. Nye. 1974. The influence of soil water content on the uptake of ions by roots: II. Chloride uptake and concentration gradients in soils. Journal of Applied Ecology 11:581–596.

Eaton, T. E. 1979. Natural and artificially altered patterns of salt spray across a forested barrier island. Atmospheric Environment 13:705–709.

Edwards, R. S., and S. M. Claxton. 1964. The distribution of airborne salt of marine origin in the Aberystwyth area. Journal of Applied Ecology 1:253–263.

Emery, K. O., and L. E. Garrison. 1967. Sea levels 7,000 to 20,000 years ago. Science 157:684–687.

Engels, W. L. 1942. Vertebrate fauna of North Carolina coastal islands: a study in the dynamics of animal distribution. American Midland Naturalist 28:273–304.

Engels, W. L. 1952. Vertebrate fauna of North Carolina coastal islands: II. Shackleford Banks. American Midland Naturalist 47:702–742.

Etherington, J. R. 1967. Studies of nutrient cycling and productivity in oligotrophic ecosystems: I. Soil potassium and wind-blown saltspray in a New South Wales dune grassland. Journal of Ecology 55:743–752.

Etkins, R., and E. S. Epstein. 1982. The rise of global mean sea level as an indication of climate change. Science 215:287–289.

Everts, C. H. 1985. Sea level rise effects on shoreline position. Journal of Waterway, Port, Coastal and Ocean Engineers 3:985–999.

Fisher, J. J. 1962. Geomorphic expression of former inlets along the Outer Banks of North Carolina. M.A. thesis, University of North Carolina, Chapel Hill. 120 pp.

Fisher, J. J. 1967a. Origin of barrier island chain shorelines, middle Atlantic States. Geological Society of America Special Paper 115:66–67.

Fisher, J. J. 1967b. Developmental pattern of relict beach ridges, Outer Banks chain, North Carolina. Ph.D. thesis, University of North Carolina, Chapel Hill. 250 pp.

Fisher, J. J. 1968. Barrier island formation: discussion. Geological Society of America Bulletin 79: 1421-1426.

Fisher, J. J. 1972. Bathymetric projected profiles and the origin of barrier islands - Johnson's shoreline of emergence, revisited. Pages 161-l 79 in D. B. Coates, editor. Coastal geomorphology. State University of New York, Binghamton. 404 pp.

Floyd, E. O. 1979. Groundwater movement in the vicinity of Fresh Pond at Nags Head and Kill Devil Hills, Dare County, North Carolina. Hydrologist's report for Moore, Gardner, and Associates, Inc., Consulting Engineers, Cary, N.C. 8 pp. [unpublished report]

Francisco, W., L. T. Jenkins, Jr., M. McWilliams, and J. Rathman. 1970. Wassaw Island study. University of Georgia, Environmental Design Services 1, Athens. 129 pp.

Funderburg, J. B., and D. S. Lee. 1978. Preliminary list of the vertebrate fauna of Nags Head Woods, Dare County, North Carolina. North Carolina State Museum of Natural History, Raleigh.

Furbish, C. E., S. P. Bratton, and K. L. Turner. 1988. An assessment of cutting and salting control methods on small Myrica shrubs at Cape Hatteras National Seashore. University of Georgia Institute of Ecology. Cooperative Park Studies Unit Technical Report 45. 18 pp.

Fussell, J. O. 1974. Breeding bird census: mixed maritime and swamp forest. American Birds 28: 1004-1005.

Fussell, J. O. 1974a. Brief summary of vegetational distribution of Roosevelt Natural Area. 6 pp. [unpublished manuscript]

Fussell, J. O. 1974b. Natural communities of the Roosevelt Natural Area. 14 pp. [unpublished manuscript]

Fussell, J. O. 1974c. Mixed maritime and swamp forest (bird census). American Birds 28: 1004–1005.

Fussell, J. O. 1978. Rogue Banks, North Carolina: a description of vegetative communities and annotated lists of amphibians, reptiles, birds, mammals, and endangered and threatened species. A report from the Office of Marine Affairs, North Carolina Department of Administration to the U.S. Fish and Wildlife Service. 115 pp.

Gaddy, L. L. 1981. Observations on some maritime forest spiders of four South Carolina Barrier Islands. Brimleyana 6:159–162.

Gaddy, L. L., editor. 1982. Man's impact on the vegetation, avifauna, and herpetofauna of South Carolina's barrier islands: a habitat approach to carrying capacity. A study completion report to the South Carolina Wildlife and Marine Research Department, Division of Wildlife and Freshwater Fisheries. Columbia. 167 pp.

Gaddy, L. L. 1985. Rare, endangered, threatened, and exotic plants of the Cape Hatteras National Seashore. University of Georgia Institute of Technology. Cooperative Park Studies Unit Technical Report 18. 32 pp.

Gaddy, L. L., and T. L. Kohlsaat. 1987. Recreational impact on the vegetation, avifauna, and herpetofauna of four South Carolina barrier islands. Natural Areas Journal 7:55–64.

Gaddy, L. L., and D. A. Raynor. 1980. Rare or overlooked?: recent plant collections from South Carolina. Castanea 45:181–184.

Gibbons, J. W., and J. W. Coker. 1978. Herpetofaunal colonization patterns of Atlantic Coast barrier islands. American Midland Naturalist 99:219–233.

Gibbons, J. W., and J. R. Harrison. 1981. Reptiles and amphibians of Kiawah and Capers Island, South Carolina. Brimleyana 5:145–162.

Gifford, C. L. 1971. Fire history of the Cape Hatteras National Seashore and environments. U.S. Department of the Interior, National Park Service, Cape Hatteras National Seashore, Manteo, N.C. [unpublished report]

Gifford, S. M., and P. A. Opler. 1983. Natural history of seven hairstreaks in coastal North Carolina. Journal of Lepidopterist's Society 37:97–105.

Godfrey, P. J. 1972. Ecology of barrier islands influenced by man. Proceedings of the American Association for the Advancement of Science, 139th meeting, Washington, D.C. 19 pp.

Godfrey, P. J. 1976a. Comparative ecology of east coast barrier islands: hydrology, soil, vegetation. Pages 5-34 in J. C. Clark, editor. Barrier islands and beaches. The Conservation Foundation, Washington, D.C. 149 pp.

Godfrey, P. J. 1976b. Barrier beaches of the east coast. Oceanus 19:27–40.

Godfrey, P. J. 1976c. Vegetation maps and ecological descriptions of Cape Lookout and Cape Hatteras National Seashores (draft proposal). U.S. Department of the Interior, National Park Service, Cape Lookout National Seashore, Beaufort, N.C. 7 pp. [unpublished report]

Godfrey, P. J. 1980. Oceanic overwash and its ecological implications on the Outer Banks of North Carolina. U.S. Department of the Interior, National Park Service, Denver Service Center, Colo. 42 pp.

Godfrey, P. J., and M. M. Godfrey. 1973. Comparison of ecological and geomorphic interactions between altered and unaltered barrier island systems in North Carolina. Pages 239-258 in D. R. Coates, editor. Coastal geomorphology. State University of New York. Binghamton. 404 pp.

Godfrey, P. J., and M. M. Godfrey. 1976. Barrier island ecology of Cape Lookout National Seashore and vicinity North Carolina. U.S. National Park Service Scientific Monograph Series 9. 160 pp.

Green, E. L. 1939. Report on the wildlife and park museum at Cape Hatteras State Park, Buxton, North Carolina. Archives of Cape Hatteras National Seashore, Manteo, N.C. 8 pp. [unpublished report]

Greller, A. M. 1977. A classification of mature forests on Long Island, New York, USA. Bulletin of the Torrey Botanical Club 104:376–382.

Greller, A. M. 1980. Correlation of some climate statistics with distribution of broadleaved forest zones in Florida, USA. Bulletin of the Torrey Botanical Club 107: 189-2 19.

Haines, E. B. 1976. Nitrogen content and acidity of rain on the Georgia coast. Water Resources Bulletin 12: 1223-1231.

Harper, R. M. 1911. The relation of climax vegetation to islands and peninsulas. Bulletin of the Torrey Botanical Club 38:515–525.

Harris, E. B. 1984. White-tailed deer census, Buxton Woods, Cape Hatteras National Seashare. Available at the Archives of Cape Hatteras National Seashore, Manteo, N.C. [unpublished report]

Harris, R. L., G. F. Levy, and J. E. Perry. 1983. Re-evaluation of vegetational characteristics at the Coastal Engineering Research Center, Miscellaneous Report 83-4, Field Research Facility, Duck, N.C. U.S. Army Corps of Engineering, Coastal Engineering Research Center, Fort Belvoir, Va. 127 pp.

Harvill, A. M. 1967. The vegetation of Assateague Island, Virginia. Castanca 32: 105–108.

Hayes, M. O. 1979. Barrier island morphology as a function of tidal and wave regime. Pages 1-28 in S. P. Leatherman, editor. Barrier islands. Academic Press, New York. 325 pp.

Higgins, E. A. T., R. D. Rappleye, and R. G. Brown. 1971. The flora and ecology of Assateague Island. Contribution 4398 of the Maryland Agricultural Experiment Station, Department of Botany, Bulletin A-l 72.

Hill, S. R. 1986. An annotated checklist of the vascular flora of Assateague Island (Maryland and Virginia). Castanea 51:265–305.

Hillestad, H. O., J. R. Bozeman, A. S. Johnson, C. W. Berisford, and J. L. Richardson. 1975. The ecology of the Cumberland Island National Seashore, Camden County, Georgia. University of Georgia Marine Science Center. Technical Report Serial 75-5. 299 pp.

Hillestad, H. O., and D. W. Speake. 1970. Activities of wild turkey hens and poults as influenced by habitat. Proceedings of the Annual Conference of the Southeastern Association of Game and Fish Commissioners 24:244–25 1.

Hooper, M. 1975. Hunting on Hatteras Island in the early 1900's. Seachest 3:47–51.

Hosier, P. E. 1973. The effects of oceanic overwash on the vegetation of Core and Shackleford Banks, North Carolina. Unpublished Ph.D. thesis, Duke University, Durham, N.C. 230 pp.

Hosier, P. E. 1975. Dunes and marsh vegetation. Pages D 1-D96 *in* W. M. Campbell, J. M. Dean, and W. D. Chamberlain, editors. Environmental inventory of Kiawah Island. Environmental Research Center, Inc. Columbia, S.C.

Hosier, P. E., and W. J. Cleary. 1977. Cyclic geomorphic patterns of washover on a barrier island in southeastern North Carolina. Environmental Geology 2:23–3 1.

Hosier, P. E., and W. J. Cleary. 1978. Geomorphic and vegetational recovery patterns following washovers in southeastern North Carolina. Geological Society of American Abstracts—Southeastern Section 27th Annual Meeting 10: 17.

Hosier, P. E., and T. E. Eaton. 1980. The impact of vehicles on dunes and grassland vegetation on a southeastern North Carolina barrier beach. Journal of Applied Ecology 17:173–182.

Hoyt, J. H. 1967. Barrier island formation. Geological Society of America Bulletin 78: 112.5-1 136.

Hoyt, J. H. 1968. Barrier island formation (reply). Geological Society of America Bulletin 79:947.

Hoyt, J. H., and V. J. Henry, Jr. 197 1. Origin of capes and shoals along the southeastern coast of the United States. Geological Society of America Bulletin 82:59–66.

Hunt, K. W. 1947. The Charleston woody flora. American Midland Naturalist 37:670–756.

Jackson, C. G., Jr., and M. M. Jackson. 1970. Herpetofauna of Dauphin Island, Alabama. Quarterly Journal of the Florida Academy of Sciences 33:281–287.

Jarrett, J. T. 1983. Changes of some North Carolina barrier islands since the mid-19th century. Coastal Zone 83:641-661.

Johnson, A. 1900. Notes on the flora of the banks and sounds at Beaufort, North Carolina. Botanical Gazette 30:405–410.

Johnson, A. F. 1977. A survey of the strand and dune vegetation along the Pacific and southern Gulf coasts of Baja California, Mexico. Journal of Biogeography 7:83–99.

Johnson, A. F., and M. G. Barbour. 1990. Dunes and maritime forests. Pages 429-480 *in* R. L. Myers and J. J. Ewel, editors. Ecosystems of Florida. University Press of Florida, Gainesville. 765 pp.

Johnson, A. S., H. 0. Hillestad, S. F. Shanholtzer, and G. F. Shanholtzer. 1974. An ecological survey of the coastal region of Georgia. U.S. National Park Service Scientific Monograph Series 3. Washington, D.C. 233 pp.

Kearney, T. H. 1900. The plant covering of Okracoke Island: a study in the ecology of the North Carolina strand vegetation. Contributions from the U.S. National Herbarium 5:261–319.

Kerley, L. L. 1962. The vegetation of a coastal island--Shackleford Bank. Honors essay, Botanical Department, University of North Carolina, Chapel Hill. 45 pp.

Kling, G. W. 1986. The physiochemistry of some dune ponds on the Outer Banks, North Carolina. Hydrobiologia 134:3–10.

Koske, R. E., and W. R. Polson. 1984. Are VA mycorrhizae required for sand dune stabilization? Bioscience 34:420–424.

Kraft, J. C., E. A. Allen, D. F. Belknap, C. J. John, and E. M. Maurmeyer. 1979. Process and morphologic evolution of an estuarine and coastal barrier system. Pages 149-183 in S. P. Leatherman, editor. Barrier islands. Academic Press, New York.

Krombein, K. V. 1949. An annotated list of wasps from Nags Head and the Kill Devil Hills. Journal of the Elisha Mitchell Scientific Society 65:262–272.

Kurz, H. 1940. The reaction of magnolia, scrub live oak, slash pine, palmetto, and other plants to dune activity on the western Florida coast. Proceedings of the Florida Academy of Sciences 4: 195–203.

Kurz, H. 1942. Florida dunes and scrub, vegetation and geology. Florida Geological Survey Geological Bulletin 23:1–145.

Kurz, H., and K. Wagner. 1957. Tidal marshes of the Gulf and Atlantic coasts of northern Florida and Charleston, South Carolina. Florida State University Studies 24. Tallahassee. 168 pp.

Laerm, J. 1981. Systematic status of the Cumberland Island pocket gopher, Geomys *cumberlandius*. Brimleyana 6:141–151.

Laessle, A. M. 1958. The origin and successional relationship of sandhill vegetation and sand-pine scrub. Ecological Monographs 28:361–386.

Laessle, A. M., and C. D. Monk. 1961. Some live oak forests of northeastern Florida. Quarterly Journal of the Florida Academy of Sciences 24:39–55.

Lazell, J. D. 1976. Deployment, dispersal, and adaptive strategies of land vertebrates on Atlantic and Gulf barrier islands. Pages 415-419 *in* R. M. Linn, editor. Proceedings of the first conference on science research in the national parks. National Park Service. Transactions and Proceedings Series 5, Vol. 1, U.S. Department of the Interior, Washington, D.C. 682 pp.

Lazell, J. D., and J. A. Musick. 1973. The kingsnake, *Lampropeltis getulus sticticeps*, and the ecology of the Outer Banks of North Carolina. Copeia 1973:497–503.

Lazell, J. D., and J. A. Musick. 1981. Status of the Outer Banks kingsnake—*Lampropeltis getulus sticticeps*. Herpetological Review 12:7.

Leatherman, S. P. 1976. Assateague Island: A case study of barrier island dynamics. Pages 769-775 *in* R. M. Linn, editor. Proceedings of the first conference on national parks. No. 5, Vol. 2. U.S. Department of the Interior, Washington, D.C. 642 pp.

Leatherman, S. P., ed. 1979. Barrier islands: from the Gulf of St. Lawrence to the Gulf of Mexico: Proceedings of a coastal research program. Academic Press, New York. 325 pp.

Lee, D. S. 1972. List of the amphibians and reptiles of Assateague Island. Bulletin of the Maryland Herpetological Society 8:90–95.

Levy, G. F. 1976. Vegetative study at the Duck Field Research Facility, Duck, North Carolina. U.S. Army Corps of Engineers, Coastal Engineering Research Center, Miscellaneous Report 76-6. Fort Belvoir, Va. 80 pp.

Lewis, 1. F. 1917. The vegetation of Shackleford Bank. North Carolina Geologic and Economic Survey, Economic Paper 46. Raleigh. 32 pp.

Lewis, T. H. 1946. Reptiles and amphibians of Smith Island, N.C. American Midland Naturalist 36:682-684.

Liddle, J. J., and K. G. Moore. 1974. The microclimate of sand dune tracks: the relative contribution of vegetation removal and soil compression. Journal of Applied Ecology 11:1057-1068.

List, J. T., and H. E. List. 1988. Environmental parameters of Nags Head Woods preserve ponds. ASB (Association of the Southeastern Biologists) Bulletin 35: 156-163.

Lloyd, F. E., and S. M. Tracy. 1901. The insular flora of Mississippi and Louisiana. Bulletin of the Torrey Botanical Club 28:61-101.

Lopazanski, M. J. 1987. The effects of forest fragmentation on the maritime forest of Bogue Banks, North Carolina. Project report submitted to the School of Forestry and Environmental Studies, Duke University, Durham, N.C. 60 pp.

Lopazanski, M. J., J. P. Evans, and R. E. Shaw. 1988. An assessment of the maritime forest resources of the North Carolina coast. A final report submitted to the North Carolina Department of Natural Resources and Community Development, Division of Coastal Management. Raleigh, N.C. 108 pp.

Mackaness, F. P. 1942. Bryophytes of the Live Oak Forest. Louisiana Academy of Sciences Proceedings 6:48-49.

MacPherson, T. F. 1988. Benthic macroinvertebrates of selected ponds in the Nags Head Woods Ecological Preserve. ASB (Association of the Southeastern Biologists) Bulletin 35:181-188.

Maggs, J., and C. J. Pearson. 1977. Litter fall and litter decay in coastal scrub at Sydney, Australia. Oecologia (Berlin) 31:239-250.

Marmer, H. A. 1951. Sea level changes along the coast. Shore and Beach 19:22-23.

Martin, W. E. 1959. The vegetation of Island Beach State Park, New Jersey. Ecological Monographs 29: 1-46.

Martof, B. S. 1963. Some observations of the herpetofauna of Sapelo Island, Georgia. Herpetologica 19:70-72.

Martof, B. S., W. M. Palmer, J. R. Bailey, and J. R. Harrison. 1980. Amphibians and reptiles of the Carolinas and Virginia. University of North Carolina Press, Chapel Hill. 264 pp.

Mathews, T. D., F. W. Stapor, C. R. Richter. J. V. Miglarese, M. D. McKenzie, and L. A. Barclay, editors. 1980. Ecological characterization of the Sea Island coastal region of South Carolina and Georgia, vol. 1: physical features of the characterization area. U.S. Fish and Wildlife Service, FWS/OBS-79/40. 120 pp.

Mayes, C. H., and H. E. List. 1988. A symposium on interdunal ponds in maritime forests: Nags Head Woods Ecological Preserve. ASB (Association of the Southeastern Biologists) Bulletin 35:145-148.

McCaffrey, C. A. 1975. Major vegetative communities of the Virginia Barrier Islands: Metomkin Island through Smith Island inclusive. The Nature Conservancy, Washington, D.C. 192 pp.

McCormick, J., and M. F. Buell. 1968. The plains: pygmy forests of the New Jersey pine barrens, a review and annotated bibliography. New Jersey Academy of Sciences Bulletin 13:20-34.

McKenzie, M. D., J. V. Miglarese. B. S. Anderson, and L. A. Barclay, editors. 1980. Ecological characterization of the Sea Island coastal region of South Carolina and Georgia, vol 2: socioeconomic features of the characterization area. Marine Research Division of the South Carolina Wildlife and Marine Research Department, Charleston. 120 pp.

McPherson. G. R. 1988. Boundary dynamics on Cumberland Island National Seashore. University of Georgia Institute of Ecology. Cooperative Park Studies Unit Technical Report 49. 112 pp.

Mehlhop, P.. and J. F. Lynch. 1978. Population characteristics of Peromyscus leucopus introduced to islands inhabited by Microtus pennsylvanicus. Oikos 31: 17-26.

Miller. T. L., N. D. Noneman, D. J. Brower, and L. M. Vorgetts. 1980. Proposed standards for development in maritime forest areas of environmental concern. Center for Urban and Regional Studies, University of North Carolina, Chapel Hill. 22 pp.

Milliman, J. D., and K. 0. Emery. 1968. Sea levels during the past 35,000 years. Science 162:1121-1123.

Missimer, T. M. 1976. Hydrology. Pages 165-194 in J. Clark. editor. The Sanibel report. Conservation Foundation, New York.

Monk, C. D. 1966a. The ecological significance of evergreenness. Ecology 47:504-505.

Monk, C. D. 1966b. Successional and environmental relationships of the forest vegetation of north central Florida. American Midland Naturalist 79:441-457.

Moslow, T. F., and S. D. Heron. Jr. 1979. Quaternary evolution of Core Banks, North Carolina: Cape Lookout to New Drum Inlet. Pages 211-236 in S. I? Leatherman, editor. Barrier islands from the Gulf of St. Lawrence to the Gulf of Mexico: proceedings of a coastal research symposium, Academic Press, New York.

Moslow, T. F., and S. D. Heron, Jr. 1986. Cape Lookout depostional systems. Pages 399-413 in D. A. Textoris, editor. Southeastern United States. Society of Economic Palentologists and Mineralogists guidebooks. Raleigh, N.C.

Moss, A. E. 1940. Effect on trees of wind-driven salt water. Journal of Forestry 38:421-425.

Myers, R. L., and J. J. Ewel. editors. 1990. Ecosystems of Florida. University Presses of Florida, Gainesville. 765 pp.

Nelson, J. B. 1986. The natural communities of South Carolina. South Carolina Wildlife and Marine Resource Department. 55 pp.

Nelson, K. 1975. Goodbye, wild Kiawah. National Parks and Conservation Magazine 49: 17-21.

Nelson, W. G., D. I. Rubenstein. M. A. Nelson, and J. A. Commito. 1976. A preliminary analysis of grazing impact on the vegetation of Shackleford Banks. Duke University Marine Laboratory, Beaufort, N.C. 13 pp. [file report1

Neuhauser, H. N. 1976. Wildlife resources of barrier islands. Pages 35-42 in J. R. Clark, editor. Barrier islands and beaches. The Conservation Foundation, Washington, D.C.

Odum, W. E., and J. W. Harvey. 1988. Barrier island interdunal freshwater wetlands. ASB (Association of Southeastern Biologists) Bulletin 35: 149–155.

Odum, W. E., J. Harvey, L. Rozas, and R. Chambers. 1986. The functional assessment of selected wetlands of Chincoteague Island, Virginia. U.S. Fish and Wildlife Service, National Wetlands Research Center Open File Report 86-7. Washington, D.C. 127 pp.

Oertel, G. F., and M. Larsen. 1976. Developmental sequences in Georgia coastal dunes and distribution of dune plants. Bulletin of the Georgia Academy of Sciences 34:35–48.

Olson, J. J. 1958a. Lake Michigan dune development: I. Wind velocity profiles. Journal of Geology 66:254–263.

Olson, J. J. 1958b. Lake Michigan dune development: II. Plants as agents and tools in geomorphology. Journal of Geology 66:345–351.

Olson, J. J. 1958c. Rates of succession and soil changes on southern Lake Michigan sand dunes. Botanical Gazette 119:125–170.

Oosting, H. J. 1945. Tolerance to salt spray of plants of coastal dunes. Ecology 26:85–89.

Oosting, H. J. 1954. Ecological processes and vegetation of the maritime strand in the southeastern United States. Botanical Review 20:226–262.

Oosting, H. J. 1956. The study of plant communities. 2nd ed. W.H. Freeman, San Francisco. 440 pp.

Oosting, H. J., and W. D. Billings. 1942. Factors affecting vegetation zonation on coastal dunes. Ecology 23:131–142.

Otte, L. J., D. K. S. Atkinson, and T. A. Atkinson. 1984. Ecological inventory of a portion of the Nags Head Woods, Dare County, North Carolina. Unpublished report to the North Carolina Nature Conservancy. 58 pp.

Otte, L. J., D. K. S. Atkinson, and T. A. Atkinson. 1985. Ecological inventory of The Nature Conservancy portion of the Nags Head Woods, Dare County, N.C. Unpublished report to the North Carolina Nature Conservancy. 105 pp.

Otvos, E. G. 1970. Development and migration of barrier islands, northern Gulf of Mexico. Geological Society of America Bulletin 81:241–246.

Otvos, E. G. 1976. Barrier island studies, Mississippi-Alabama Gulf coast. Pages 781-785 in R. M. Linn, editor. Proceedings of the first conference on science research in the national parks. National Park Service. Transactions and Proceedings Serial 5, vol. 2.

Ovington, J. D., ed. 1983. Ecosystems of the World 10: temperate broad-leaved evergreen forests. Elsevier Publishers. 241 pp.

Palmer, W. N. A. Undated. List of amphibians and reptiles collected at Cape Lookout National Seashore. North Carolina State Museum, Raleigh. 4 pp.

Papperman, S., and M. Benedict. 1973. A vegetation study of the aspect of dominance on Shackleford Banks. Duke University Marine Laboratory, Beaufort, N.C. 18 pp.

Paradiso, J. L., and C. O. Handley, Jr. 1965. Checklist of mammals of Assateague Island. Chesapeake Science 6: 167–171.

Parnell, J. F., W. D. Webster, and T. L. Quay. 1989. An evaluation of changes in the avian and mammalian faunas of the Cape Hatteras National Seashore 1956-1989. Final project report (submitted July 1989) to the National Park Service. 102 pp.

Patrick, R., and C. Reimer. 1966. The diatoms of the United States: vol. 1. National Academy of Sciences, Philadelphia, Pa. 688 pp.

Payette, S., and L. Filion. 1975. Ecology of the northern limits of the maritime forests. Hudson Bay New-Quebec, Canada. Natnraliste Canadien (Quebec) 102:783–802.

Pelton, M. R. 1975. The mammals of Kiawah Island. Pages Ml-M45 in W. M. Campbell and J. M. Dean, editors. Environmental inventory of Kiawah Island. Environmental Research Center, Inc. Columbia, S.C.

Penfound, W. T., and J. A. Howard. 1940. A phytosociological study of an evergreen oak forest in the vicinity of New Orleans, Louisiana. American Midland Naturalist 23: 165–174.

Penfound, W. T., and M. E. O'Neill. 1934. The vegetation of Cat Island, Mississippi. Ecology 15: 1-16.

Peterson, M. C. 1977. Plants regarded as rare or endangered in our area of the Outer Banks. U.S. Department of the Interior, National Park Service, Cape Hatteras National Seashore, Manteo, N.C. [unpublished report]

Pierce, J. W., and D. J. Colquhoun. 1970. Holocene evolution of a portion of the North Carolina coast. Geological Society of America Bulletin 81:3697–3714.

Pierce, J. W., and D. J. Colquhoun. 1971. Holocene evolution of a portion of the North Carolina coast (reply). Geological Society of America Bulletin 82:2371–72.

Pilkey, O. H., Jr., W. J. Neal, and O. H. Pilkey, Sr. 1978. From Currituck to Calabash: living with North Carolina's barrier islands. North Carolina Scientific and Technological Research Center, Research Triangle Park. 228 pp.

Pinchot, G., and W. W. Ashe. 1897. Timber trees and forests of North Carolina. North Carolina Geological Survey Bulletin 6, Raleigh. 227 pp.

Poer, L. D. Jr. 1967. A herpetological survey the Isle of Palms, a South Carolina coastal island. M.S. thesis, University of South Carolina, Columbia. 43 pp.

Porter, C. W. 1938. Forest cover of Cape Hatteras seashore area in historic times. U.S. Department of the Interior, National Park Service, Southeast Regional Office, Atlanta. 91 pp.

Porter, J. H., and R. D. Dueser. 1982. Niche overlap and competition in an insular small mammal fauna: a test of the niche overlap hypothesis. Oikos 39:228–236.

Poumelle, G. H., and B. A. Barrington. 1953. Notes on mammals of Anastasia Island, St. Johns County, Florida. Journal of Mammalogy 34:133–135.

Pratt, J. H. 1908. Investigations of the North Carolina geological and economic survey relating to forestry problems along the North Carolina Banks. Journal of the Elisha Mitchell Scientific Society 24: 125-138.

Price, J. 1926. A description of Ocracoke Inlet. Reprint of a paper originally published in 1795 by F.X. Martin, New Bern, N.C. North Carolina Historical Review 3:624–633.

Proffitt, C. E. 1977. Atmospheric inputs and flux of chloride, calcium and magnesium in a maritime forest on Bogue Bank, North Carolina. M.A. thesis, East Carolina University, Greenville, N.C. 123 pp.

Quay, T. C. 1959. The birds, mammals. reptiles, and amphibians of the Cape Hatteras National Seashore Recreational Area. Unpublished report to the U.S. Department of the Interior, National Park Service. Department of zoology, North Carolina State University, Raleigh. 88 pp.

Radford, A. E.. H. E. Ahlies, and C. R. Bell. 1968. Manual of the vascular flora of the Carolinas. University of North Carolina Press, Chapel Hill. 1183 pp.

Rayner, D. A. 1974. An analysis of maritime closed dune vegetation in South Carolina. M.S. thesis, University of South Carolina, Columbia. 128 pp.

Rayner, D. A., and W. T. Batson. 1976. Maritime closed dunes vegetation in South Carolina. Castanea 41:58–70.

Rebertus, R. A. 1979. Factors affecting establishment of woody vegetation on the Outer Banks of North Carolina with special reference to Japanese Black Pine (*Pinus thunbergii* Parl.) and soil chemical properties. M.S. thesis, Department of Forestry, North Carolina State University, Raleigh. 129 pp.

Redfield, A. C. 1967. Postglacial change in sea level in the western Atlantic Ocean. Science 157:687.

Richmond, E. A. 1962. The flora and fauna of Hog Island, Mississippi. Gulf Research Reports 1:59–106.

Riggs, S. R. 1976. Barrier islands as natural storm dependent systems. Pages 58-75 *in* J. R. Clark, editor. Barrier islands and beaches. The Conservation Foundation, Washington, D.C.

Robertson, W. B., and E. L. Tyson. 1950. Herpetological notes from eastern North Carolina. Journal of the Elisha Mitchell Scientific Society 66: 130– 147.

Rubenstein. D.I. 1981. Behavioral ecology of island feral horses. Equine Veterinary Journal 13:27–34.

Ruffner, J. A., and F. E. Blair, editors. 1977. The weather almanac, 2nd ed. Gale Research Company, Detroit. 728 pp.

Sandifer, P. A., J. V. Miglarese, D. R. Calder, J. J. Manzie, and L. A. Barclay, editors. 1980. Ecological characterization of the Sea Island coastal region of South Carolina and Georgia, vol. 3. Biological features of the characterization area. Marine Resources Division, South Carolina Wildlife and Marine Resources Department. Charleston. 1SO pp.

Schafale, M. P., and A. S. Weakley. 1990. Classification of the natural communities of North Carolina. North Carolina Natural Heritage Program, Division of Parks and Recreation. North Carolina Department of Environmental, Health, and Natural Resources. Raleigh. 325 pp.

Schlesinger, W. H., and B. F. Chabot. 1977. The use of water and minerals by evergreen and deciduous shrubs in Okeefenokee Swamp. Botanical Gazette 138:490–497.

Scholl, D. W., and M. Stuiver. 1967. Recent submergence of southern Florida: acomparison with adjacent coasts and other eustatic data. Geological Society of America Bulletin 78:437.

Schroeder, P. M., R. Dolan, and B. P. Hayden. 1976. Vegetation changes associated with barrier-dune construction on the Outer Banks on North Carolina. Environmental Management 1:105–114.

Schwartz, F. J. 1970. Fishes and changing ecology of Mullet Pond, a barrier beach island pond on Shackleford Banks, North Carolina. Journal of the Elisha Mitchell Scientific Society 86:3 1-34.

Schwartz, F. J. 1983. Fishes and ecology of freshwater ponds located on North Carolina's Outer Banks from the Virginia-North Carolina state line, 36" 33'N to Ocracoke Inlet, 1983, with comments on geological origins and fate of the area. Institute of Marine Science Special Publication, Morehead City, N.C. 69 pp.

Schwartz, F. J. 1987. Foraging distances by **marine** birds utilizing spoil islands in the estuarine Cape Fear River, North Carolina. Journal of the Elisha Mitchell Scientific Society 103:56–62.

Schwartz, F. J. 1988. Pre- and post-drought fish surveys of selected ponds located in the Nags Head Woods, Nags Head, North Carolina. ASB (Association of Southeastern Biologists) Bulletin 35:189–198.

Schwartz. M. L. 1971. The multiple causality of barrier islands. Journal of Geology 79:91–94. Reprinted 1973. Pages 393–395 in M. L. Schwartz. editor. Barrier islands. Dowden. Hutchinson, and Ross, Stroudsburg, Pa. 45 I pp.

Seneca, E. D., and S. W. Broome. 1981. The effect of highway construction on maritime vegetation in North Carolina. A research report submitted to the North Carolina Department of Transportation, Division of Highways, Raleigh. 73 pp.

Settle, S. 1937. Timber survey-Hatteras Woods. Dated 9-3-37. Archives of Cape Hatteras National Seashore, Manteo. N.C. 28 pp. [typed carbon]

Sharitz, R. R. 1975. Forest communities of Kiawah Island. Pages F1-F39 in W. M. Campbell, J. M. Dean, and W. D. Chamberlain, editors. Environmental inventory of Kiawah Island. Enviromental Research Center Inc., Columbia, S.C.

Shure, D. J. 1970. Ecological relationships of small mammals in a New Jersey beach habitat. Journal of Mammalogy 51:267–278.

Shure, D. J. 1971. Tidal flooding dynamics: its influence on small mammals in barrier beach marshes. American Midland Naturalist 85:36–43.

Simon, D. M. 1986. Fire **effects in coastal habitats of** east central **Florida. University of Georgia Institute of Ecology.** Cooperative **Park Studies Unit Technical Report 27. 140 pp.**

Snow, A., and P. J. Godfrey. 1978. The vegetation of Cape Lookout National Seashore. National Park Service Cooperative **Research Unit, University of** Massachusettes **Cooperative Park** Studies **Unit Report 4** I. Amherst. Mass. 34 pp.

Snow, B. C. 1955. Effects of hurricanes on North Carolina beaches. Shore and Beach 23: 14–17.

Somes, H. A, **Jr., and T. R. Ashbaugh. 1973. Vegetation of St. Catherine's Island, Ga. J. McCormick and Associates. Devon.** Pa. Prepared **for American Museum of Natural History,** New **York. 47 pp.**

Soots, R. F., and J. F. Parnell. **1975. Ecological succession** of breeding birds in relation **to plant succession on dredge** islands in **North Carolina. University of North Carolina** Sea Grant **Program UNC-SC-75-27. Raleigh.** 91 pp.

Spence, L 1985. **Our dwindling maritime forests. Wildlife in North Carolina 49: 17-2** I.

Stalter, R.1971. **The summer and fall flora of Huntington** Beach State **Park, Georgetown County, South Carolina.** Castanea 36:167–174.

Stalter, **R. 1972. The flora of** Outer Otter Island, Colleton County. South Carolina. Castanea 37:298–300.

Stalter, R. 1973. The flora of Turtle Island, Jasper County, South Carolina. Castanea 38:35–37.

Stalter, R. 1974a. A floristic study of South Carolina's barrier islands. ASB (Association of Southeastern Biologists) Bulletin 21:86. [abstract]

Stalter, R. 1974b. The evergreen maritime forest of South Carolina's barrier islands. American Journal of Botany 54:66. [abstract]

Stalter, R. 1974c. A synecological study of the evergreen maritime forest of three South Carolina barrier islands. ASB (Association of Southeastern Biologists) Bulletin 21:86. [abstract]

Stalter, R. 1976. The major plant communities of the Fire Island National Seashore. pages 177-181 in R. M. Linn, editor. Proceedings of the first conference on science research in the national parks. National Park Service. Transactions and Proceedings Serial 5, vol. 2.

Stalter, R. 1979. Some ecological observations on an Ilex forest, Sandy Hook, New Jersey. Castanea 44:202–207.

Stalter, R. 1984. The flora of Bulls Island, Charleston County, South Carolina. Bartonia 50:27–30.

Stalter, R., and S. C. Dial. 1984. Hammock vegetation of Little Talbot Island State Park, Florida. Bulletin of the Torrey Botanical Club 111:494–497.

Stalter, R., S. C. Dial, and A. Laessle. 1981. Some ecological observations of the arborescent vegetation in Highlands Hammock State Park, Florida. Castanea 46:30–35.

Stembridge, J. E. 1978. Vegetated coastal dunes: growth detection from aerial infrared photography. Remote Sensing of Environment 7:73–76.

Stratton, D. A., S. P. Bratton, and D. M. Simon. 1984. An inventory of forest fire fuels at Cumberland Island National Seashore, Georgia. University of Georgia Institute of Ecology. Cooperative Park Services Unit Technical Report 6. 33 pp.

Stroh, T. 1982. A study of the shrub and vegetation patterns on Bodie Island, North Carolina from 1932-1982. U.S. Department of the Interior, National Park Service, Cape Hatteras National Seashore, Manteo, N.C. 12 pp. [unpublished report]

Susman, K. R., and S. D. Heron, Jr. 1979. Evolution of a barrier island, Shackleford Banks, Carteret County, North Carolina. Geological Society of America Bulletin 90:205–215.

Sutter, R., L. Mansberg, and J. Moore. 1983. Endangered, threatened, and rare plant species of North Carolina: a revised list. ASB (Association of Southeastern Biologists) Bulletin 30:147–157.

Swank, W. T., and G.S. Henderson. 1976. Atmospheric input of some cations and anions to forest ecosystems in North Carolina and Tennessee. Water Resources Research 12:541–546.

Sweet, H. C., J. E. Poppfeton, H. G. Shuey, and T. O. Peeples. 1980. Vegetation of central Florida's east coast: the distribution of six vegetational complexes of Merritt Island and Cape Canaveral Peninsula. Remote Sensing of Environment 9:93–108.

Swift, D. J. P. 1975. Barrier island genesis: evidence from the central Atlantic shelf, eastern USA. Sedimentary Geology 14:1–43.

Tatham, W. 1807. Survey of the coast of North Carolina from Cape Hatteras to Cape Fear, 1806. U.S. Department of the Interior, National Park Service, Cape Lookout National Seashore, Beaufort, N.C. 56 pp. [unpublished report]

Tippins, V. K., and J. B. Nevins. 1972. The geological evolution of a barrier island: Shackleford Banks, North Carolina. Honors thesis, Smith College, Northampton, Mass. JO2 pp.

Titus, J. G., editor. 1988. Greenhouse effect, sea level rise and coastal wetlands. U.S. Environmental Protection Agency. EPA-230-05-86-013. Washington, D.C. 152 pp.

Tormey, J. B., B. A. Cockfield, and D. M. Forsythe. 1980. Barrier island golf course subdivision. American Birds 34:40.

Touliatos, P., and E. Roth. 1971. Hurricanes and trees: ten lessons from Camille. Journal of Forestry 69:285–289.

Travis, R. W., and P. J. Godfrey. 1976. Interactions of plant communities and oceanic overwash on the manipulated barrier islands of Cape Hatteras National Seashore, North Carolina. Pages 777-780 in R. M. Linn, editor. Proceedings of the first conference on science research in the National Park Service. Transactions and Proceedings Serial 5, vol. 2.

Troutman, C. H. 1980a. A comparison of two soils with respect to their associated flora. U.S. Department of the Interior, National Park Service, Cape Lookout National Seashore, Beaufort, NC. 8 pp. [unpublished report]

Troutman, C. H. 1980b. Memorandum to Phil Brneck, chief ranger: vegetation transects. U.S. Department of the Interior, National Park Service, Cape Lookout National Seashore, Beaufort, N.C. 2 pp. [unpublished memorandum]

Troutman, C. H. 1981. Cape Lookout National Seashore: description, history, and management. Department of Botany, North Carolina State University, Raleigh. 9 pp. [unpublished paper]

Turner, K. 1985. Fire history summary, Cape Hatteras National Seashore. Archives of Cape Hatteras National Seashore, Manteo, N.C. 17 pp. [unpublished manuscript]

Turner, M. G., and S. P. Bratton. 1987. Fire, grazing, and the landscape heterogeneity of a Georgia barrier island. Pages 85–101 in M. G. Turner, editor. Landscape heterogeneity and disturbance: ecological series 64, Springer-Verlag, New York. 239 pp.

Turner, S. 1984. The fire history of Cumberland island National Seashore 1900-1983. University of Georgia Institute of Ecology. Cooperative Park Studies Unit Technical Report 7. 113 pp.

Turner, S., and S. P. Bratton. 1987. The recent fire history of Cumberland Island, Georgia. Castanea 52:300–303.

Tyndall, R. W., and G. F. Levy. 1978. Plant distribution and succession within interdunal depressions on a Virginia barrier dune system. Journal of the Elisha Mitchell Scientific Society 94:1–15.

U.S. Army Corps of Engineers. 1962. The storm and the Outer Banks of North Carolina. Shore and Beach 30:5–6.

U.S. Department of Commerce, National Oceanic and Atmospheric Administration. 1974. Climates of the States, vol. 1: Eastern States. Water Information Center Inc., Point Washington, N.Y. 480 pp.

U.S. Department of the Interior, Fish and Wildlife Service. 1980. Endangered and threatened wildlife and plants: review of plant taxa for listing as endangered or threatened species. Federal Register 45:82480–82569.

US. Department of the Interior. National Park Service. 1978. Enviromental assessment: Cape Lookout National Seashore. U.S. Department of the Interior, National Park Service, Denver Service Center, Colo. 134 pp.

U.S. Department of the Interior, National Park Service. 1983. Cape Lookout National Seashore: resources management plan and enviromental assessment. U.S. Department of the Interior, National Park Service, Denver Service Center, Colo. 177 pp.

U.S. Department of the Interior, National Park Service 1984. Enviromental assessment for wilderness suitability study and proposal. Cape Lookout National Seashore, North Carolina, U.S. Department of the Interior, National Park Service, Denver Service Center, Colo. 44 pp.

U.S. Department of the Interior, Heritage, Conservation, and Recreation Service. 1978. Report of barrier islands working group. Washington, D.C. 80 pp.

Van der Valk, A. G. 1974a. Environmental factors controlling the distribution of forbs on coastal foredunes in Cape Hatteras National Seashore. Canadian Journal of Botany 52:1057-1073.

Van der Valk, A. G. 1974b. Mineral cycling in coastal foredune plant communities in Cape Hatteras National Seashore. Ecology 55: 1349-1358.

Voges, K. 1978. Status of certain animals in Cape Lookout National Seashore based on a review of "Endangered and threatened plants and animals of North Carolina". [unpublished report]

Wagoner, G. S. 1975. Eastern deciduous forest, southeastern evergreen and oak-pine region. Vol. 1. U.S. Department of the Interior, National Park Service. National Historical Theme Studies 1. 206 pp.

Ward, R. C. 1975. Principles of hydrology. McGraw-Hill Ltd., Maidenhead, Berkshire, England. 367 pp.

Warner, L. 1976. The status of the barrier islands of the southeastern coast. A summary of the barrier island inventory. The Open Space Institute. New York. 43 pp. [unpublished]

Warner, L., and D. Strass. 1976. Inventory of the barrier islands of the southeastern coast. Open Space Institute and Natural Resources Defense Council, New York. 300 pp.

Weakley, A. S., and M. P. Schafale. 1987. Buxton Woods Natural Area. Community profile conducted by the North Carolina Natural Heritage Program, Division of Parks and Recreation. North Carolina Department of Natural Resources and Community Development, Raleigh, N.C. 10 pp.

Webster, W. D. (Undated manuscript). The mammals of Buxton Woods, Cape Hatteras National Seashore Recreation Area. 14 pp.

Webster, W. D. 1987. The effects of introduced and feral animals on the native mammalian fauna of Shackleford Banks, North Carolina. Cape Lookout National Seashore. 14 pp.

Webster, W. D. 1988. The mammals of Nags Head Woods Ecological Preserve and surrounding area. ASB (Association of Southeastern Biologists) Bulletin 35:223-229.

Welby, C. W. 1970. Observations on the origin of the North Carolina Outer Banks, results from a geophysical study. Geological Society of America Abstracts 2:248.

Wells. B. W. 1928. Plant communities of the coastal plain of North Carolina and their successional relations. Ecology 9:230-242.

Wells, B. W. 1939. A new forest climax: the salt spray climax of Smith Island, North Carolina. Bulletin of the Torrey Botany Club 66:629-634.

Wells, B. W. 1942. Ecological problems of the southeastern United States coastal plain. Botanical Review 8:533-561.

Wells, B. W., and I. V. Shunk. 1937. Seaside shrubs: wind forms vs. spray forms. Science 85:499.

Wells, B. W., and I. V. Shunk. 1938. Salt spray: an important factor in coastal ecology. Bulletin of the Torrey Botanical Club 65:485-492.

Wells. G. S. 1954. The forest that blew away, American Forests 60:14-16, 51-52.

Westman. W. E. 1975. Edaphic climax pattern of the pygmy forest region of California. Ecological Monographs 45: 109-135.

Westman, W. E.. and R. H. Whittaker. 1975. Biomass and primary productivity of the pygmy forest region of California. Journal of Ecology 63:493-520.

Wharton, C. H. 1978. The natural environments of Georgia. Georgia Department of Natural Resources, Office of Planning Resources and Geology and Water Resources, Atlanta. 227 pp.

Whittecar. G. R., and J. Salyer. 1986a. Hydrology of the Nags Head Woods area, Kill Devil Hills and Nags Head. North Carolina. The Nature Conservancy, Arlington, Va. 14 pp.

Whittecar. G. R., and J. Salyer. 1986b. Hydrology of the Nags Head Woods Area, Kill Devil Hills, and Nags Head. NC. The Nature Conservancy, Nags Head Wmds Ecological Preserve, Kill Devil Hills, N.C. 71 pp.

Williamson. R. B.. and E. M. Black. 1981. High temperature of forest tires under pines as a selective advantage over oaks. Nature 293:643-644.

Wilson, A. T. 1959. Surface of the ocean as a source of air-borne nitrogenous material and other plant nutrients. Nature 184:99-101.

Wilson, W. F. 1960. Subsurface stratigraphy and structure in part of coastal plain of North Carolina. Journal of the Elisha Mitchell Scientific Society 76:186.

Winner, M. D., Jr. 1975. Groundwater resources of the Cape Hatteras National Seashore, North Carolina. U.S. Geological Survey Atlas HA-540, Reston, Va. 2 maps.

Winner, M. D., Jr. 1979. Freshwater availability on an offshore barrier island. U.S. Geological Survey Professional Paper 1150, U.S. Geological Survey. 117 pp.

Wolfe, C. B. 1984. List of bolete basidiomycetes collected in the Nags Head Woods Nature Preserve. 2 pp. (unpublished letter1

Wood, G. W. 1981. Assessment of the impact of feral ungulates on the vegetation of Shackleford Banks, Cape Lookout National Seashore. The Belle W. Baruch Forest Science Institute, Clemson University, Clemson, S.C. 35 pp.

Wood, G. W., and M. A. Murphy. 1979. Preliminary assessment of the impact of feral ungulates on Shackleford Bank, Cape Lookout National Seashore. In proceedings of the Second Conference on Science Research in the National Parks, San Francisco.

Wood, U. J. 1981. Live oaking: southern timber for tall ships. Northeast University Press, Boston. 206 pp.

Worthington, J. S. 1972. An evaluation of environmental impact: Little Cumberland Island, Georgia. M.S. thesis, University of Massachusettes, Amherst. 161 pp.

Wright, J. S. 1973. A pileated woodpecker at Bodie Island, North Carolina. The Chat 37:106–107.

Wu, J. 1981. Evidence of sea spray produced by bursting bubbles. Science 212:324–326.

Zeichner, L. L. 1987. The historic landscape of Dungeness, Cumberland Island National Seashore, Georgia, University of Georgia Institute of Ecology. Cooperative Park Studies Unit Technical Report 35. 126 pp.

Zeigler, J. M. 1973. Origin of the sea islands of the southeastern United States, with comments. Pages 92-107 *in* J. B. Coates, editor. Barrier islands. Dowden, Hutchinson, and Ross, Stroudsburg, Pa. 404 pp.

Zingmark, R. G. 1975. The phytoplankton of Kiawah Island. Pages Pl-P38 in W. M. Campbell, J. M. Dean, and W. D. Chamberlain, editors. Environmental inventory of Kiawah Island. Environmental Research Center Inc., Columbia, S.C.

Zucchino, L. R. 1981. Development planning for barrier island maritime forests. Carolina Planning 6: 14-21.

Zucchino, L. R. 1990. A guide to protecting maritime forests through planning and design. North Carolina Department of Environment, Health, and Natural Resources, Division of Coastal Management. 24 pp.

Zweifel, R. G., and C. J. Cole, 1974. An annotated checklist of the amphibians and reptiles of St. Catherine's Island, Georgia. American Museum of Natural History, New York. 32 pp.

Appendix A. Draft Use Standards for Maritime Forest AEC (July 1989). North Carolina Coastal Resources Commission.

[This text from a North Carolina statute is offered as an example of use standards that attempt to protect the natural features of maritime forests on barrier islands.]

.0506 COASTAL COMPLEX NATURAL AREAS

(d) Designation. The Coastal Resources Commission hereby designates the maritime forests identified in Section (e) of this Rule as coastal complex natural areas of environmental concern. Maritime forests are those woodlands that have developed under the influence of salt spray on barrier islands and estuarine shorelines. They are different from inland forests because of their adaptations to the high winds, salt spray, and sandy soils characteristic of the coastal environment. Some of the important functions attributed to maritime forests include island stabilization, soil production, water and nutrient conservation, and storm protection. Their aesthetic, recreational, and habitat values are also significant. Because these systems are located on the more protected and alluring sections of coastal barriers, they are generally under intense development pressures. Unmanaged development practices, such as the uncontrolled clearing of forest vegetation, leveling of relict dunes and protective frontal dunes, alteration of wetlands, and drawdown of the water table, can result in the loss of resources that are critical to the long-term health and integrity of the maritime forest system. Scientists believe that this natural system can be maintained only by concentrating, or "clustering", development and setting aside as large an area of contiguous undeveloped land as possible.

The Commission also recognizes that there exist other maritime forests which have similar characteristics and functions to those identified in Section (e) of this Rule, but which receive adequate, legally binding protection from some other means or combination of means, such as public ownership, local zoning ordinance, or conservation easement. Those areas are identified in Section (f) of this Rule. The maritime forests in Sections (e) and (f) of this Rule will be reviewed by DCM at least every three years to determine whether they should be placed in Section (e) or (f). The Commission may add or move forest areas to either section at any time, following proper rulemaking notice and procedures as provided in North Carolina General Statute 150B.

(e) Maritime Forest AEC's. Maritime Forest AEC's include the following sites. The boundaries for these areas shall be depicted on individual site maps approved by the CRC and on file with the Division of Coastal Management. [Specific maritime forests sites to be listed.]

(f) Other Maritime Forests. Identified maritime forests which are not designated as Maritime Forest AEC's include the following sites. The boundaries for these areas shall be depicted on individual site maps approved by the CRC and on file with the Division of Coastal Management.

(1) Nags Head Woods (The Nature Conservancy-managed lands)
(2) Buxton Woods (State and Federal lands)
(3) Shackleford Island
(4) Theodore Roosevelt Natural Area
(5) Bear Island (Hammocks Beach State Park)
(6) Bluff Island

(g) Use Standards. Development in maritime forest AEC's shall be consistent with the use standards set out in the following paragraphs of this Rule:

(1) Permanent structures shall be permitted as follows: On individual lots platted of record on or before _____ 1989, development and associated clearing shall not exceed 35% of the total lot area. Development on all other tracts of land shall be clustered in such a way that the maximum amount of contiguous land area remains undisturbed, and development and associated clearing does not exceed 20% of the total land area.

(2) Soil-disturbing activities and site alteration shall not exceed the minimum necessary to provide for the location of the principal use structure, accessory use improvements, driveway access, and utility service improvements. Trees and understory vegetation shall not be removed except as necessary for the construction of the principal use structure, accessory use, parking area, driveway access, and septic system. Planting of grassed lawns and other nuisance plant species that are exotic to the maritime forest setting is prohibited.

(3) Roof lines shall conform to the natural profile of the forest canopy as much as possible.

(4) Right-of-way widths shall not exceed 45 feet, including land cleared for shoulders and drainage, and shall follow the land insofar as possible. Curb and drainage systems shall not be installed.

(5) Wetlands and ponds shall not be dredged, filled, or otherwise altered from their natural state, except as authorized by the U.S. Army Corps of Engineers as "minor road crossings" for property access. No impervious surfaces shall be located within 20 feet of any pond or wetland. No ground absorption wastewater treatment system shall be located within 50 feet of any pond or wetland.

(6) The artificial lowering of the water table through use of ditches, wells, or any other means for purposes not associated with domestic or commercial uses of fresh water is prohibited.

Appendix B. Checklist of Vertebrates Inhabiting the Barrier Islands of Georgia (Johnson et al. 1974).[a] Taxonomic reference is Banks et al. 1987.

Amphibians and Reptiles[b]

Order Caudata

Family Salamandridae

Notophthalmus viridescens - eastern newt

Family Amphiumidae

Amphiuma means - two-toed amphiuma

Order Anura

Family Pelobatidae

Scaphiopus holbrookii - eastern spadefoot toad

Family Bufonidae

Bufo quercicus - oak toad
B. *terrestris* - southern toad

Family Hylidae

Hyla cinerea - green treefrog
H. *femoralis* - pine woods treefrog
H. *squirella* - squirrel treefrog
Limnaoedus ocularis - grass frog
Pseudacris nigrita - southern chorus frog

Family Microhylidae

Gastrophryne carolinensis - eastern narrow-mouthed toad

Family Ranidae

Rana grylio - pig frog
R. *sphenocephala* - southern leopard frog

Order Testudines

Family Kinosternidae

Kinosternon subrubrum - mud turtle

Family Chelydridae

Chelydra serpentina - snapping turtle

Family Emydidae

Terrapene Carolina - eastern box turtle
Malaclemys terrapin - diamondback terrapin
Pseudemys scripta - yellow-bellied turtle

Deirochelys reticularia - chicken turtle

Family Testudinidae

Gopherus polyphemus - gopher tortoise

Family Chelonlidae

Caretta caretta - loggerhead sea turtle
Lepidochelys kempii - Ridley turtle
Chelonia mydas - green turtle

Order Squamata

Family Iguanidae

Anolis carolinensis - green anole
Sceloporus undulatus - fence lizard

Family Teiidae

Cnemidophorus sexlineatus - six-line racerunner

Family Scincidae

Scinecella lateralis - ground skink
Eumeces fasciatus - five-lined skink
E. *laticeps* - broad-headed skink
E. *inexpectatus* - southeastern five-lined skink

Family Anguidae

Ophisaurus ventralis - eastern glass lizard
0. *compressus* - island glass lizard

Suborder Serpentes

Family Colubridae

Nerodia fasciata - banded water snake
Thamnophis sirtalis - garter snake
T. *sauritus* - ribbon snake
Coluber constrictor - black racer
Masticophis flagellum - coachwhip
Opheodrys aestivus - rough green snake
Elaphe obsoleta quadrivittata - greenish rat snake
E. *guttata* - corn snake
Cemophora coccinea - scarlet snake
Lampropeltis getulus - kingsnake

Family Viperidae

Agkistrodon piscivorus - cottonmouth
Crotalus adamanteus - diamondback rattlesnake

---

[a] Condensation of listing given in Johnson et al. 1974.
[b] Modified from compilation by H. O. Hillestad.

Order Crocodilia

Family Alligatoridae

Alligator mississippiensis - alligator

Birds of Forests, Clearings, Freshwater Marshes, and Ponds[c]

Order Podicipediformes

Family Podicipedidae

Podilymbus podiceps - pied-billed grebe

Order Pelecaniformes

Family Anhingidae

Anhinga anhinga - anhinga

Order Ciconiiformes

Family Ardeidae

Butorides striatus - green-backed heron
Egretta caerulea - little blue heron
Bubulcus ibis - cattle egret
Casmerodius albus - great egret
Egretta thula - snowy egret
Egretta tricolor - tricolored heron
Nycticorax nyticorax - black-crowned night heron
Nycticorax violaceus - yellow-crowned night heron
Ixobrychus exilis - least bittern
Botaurus lentiginosus - American bittern

Family Threskiornithidae

Plegadis falcinellus - glossy ibis
Eudocimus albus - white ibis

Family Ciconiidae

Mycteria americana - wood stork

Order Anseriformes

Family **Anatidae**

Branta canadensis - Canada goose
Chen caerulescens - snow goose
Anas platyrhynchos - mallard
A. rubripes - American black duck
A. fulvigula - mottled duck
A. strepera - gadwall
A. acuta - Northern pintail

A. crecca - green-winged teal
A. discors - blue-winged teal
A. clypeata - shoveler
A. americana - American widgeon
Aix sponsa - wood duck
Aythya collaris - ring-necked duck
A. affinis - lesser scaup
Oxyura jamaicensis - ruddy duck
Mergus merganser - common merganser
M. serrator - red-breasted merganser

Order Falconiformes

Family Catbartidae

Cathartes aura - turkey vulture
Coragyps atratus - black vulture

Family Accipitridae

Elanoides forficatus - swallow-tailed kite
Zctinia mississippiensis - Mississippi kite
Accipiter striatus - sharp-shinned hawk
A. cooperii - Cooper's hawk
Buteo jamaicensis - red-tailed hawk
B. lineatus - red-shouldered hawk
B. platypterus - broad-winged hawk
B. lagopus - rough-legged hawk
Aquila chrysaetos - golden eagle
Haliaeetus leucocephalus - bald eagle
Circus cyaneus - marsh hawk

Subfamily Pandioninae

Pandion haliaetus - osprey

Family Falconidae

Falco peregrinus - peregrine falcon
F. columbarius - pigeon hawk
F. sparverius - sparrow hawk

Order Galliformes

Family Cracidae

Ortalis vetula - chachalaca

Family Phasianidae

Subfamily Meleagrididae

Meleagris gallopavo - turkey

Subfamily Odontophorinae

Colinus virginianus - bobwhite

---

[c]**Modified** from compilation by G. F. **Shanholtzer**; names with (*)
indicate that the species is known to nest on Georgia barrier islands.

Order Gruiformes

Family Rallidae

Rallus elegans - king rail
R. *limicola* - Virginia rail
Porzana carolina - sora
Cotumicops noveboracensis - yellow rail
Porphyrula martinica - purple gallinule
Gallinula chloropus - common moorhen
Fulica americana - American coot

Family Aramidae

Aramus guarauna - limpkin

Family Gruidae

Grus americana - whooping crane

Order Charadriiformes

Family Charadriidae

Charadrius vociferus - killdeer

Family Recurvirostridae

Recurvirostra americana - American avocet
Himantopus mexicanus - black-necked stilt

Family Scolopacidae

Subfamily Scolopacinae

Scolopax minor - American woodcock
Gallinago gallinago - common snipe
Bartramia longicauda - upland plover
Tringa solitaria - solitary sandpiper
T. *melanoleuca* - greater yellowlegs
T. *flavipes* - lesser yellowlegs
Calidris melanotos - pectoral sandpiper
Limnodromus scolopaceus - long-billed dowitcher
Calidris himantopus - stilt sandpiper
Tryngites subruficollis - buff-breasted sandpiper

Subfamily Phalaropodinae

Phalaropus tricolor - Wilson's phalarope

Order Columbiformes

Family Columbidae

Columba livia - rock dove
Zenaida asiatica - white-winged dove
Z. *macroura* - mourning dove
Columbina passerina - ground dove

Order Cuculiformes

Family Cuculidae

Coccyzus americanus - yellow-billed cuckoo
C. *erythropthalmus* - black-billed cuckoo

Order Strigiformes

Family Tytonidae

Tyto alba - barn owl

Family Strigidae

Otus asio - screech owl
Bubo virginianus - Great horned owl
Nyctea scandiaca - snowy owl
Athene cunicularia - burrowing owl
Strix varia - barred owl
Asio otus - long-eared owl
A. *flammeus* - short-eared owl
Aegolius acadicus - saw-whet owl

Order Caprimulgiformes

Family Caprimulgidae

Caprimulgus carolinensis - Chuck-will's_widow
C. *vociferus* - whip-poor-will
Chordeiles minor - common nighthawk

Order Apodiformes

Family Apodidae

Chaetura pelagica - chimney swift

Family Trochilidae

Archilochus colubris - ruby-throated hummingbird

Order Coraciiformes

Family Alcedinidae

Ceryle alcyon - belted kingfisher

Order Piciformes

Family Picidae

Colaptes auratus - yellow-shafted flicker
Dryocopus pileatus - pileated woodpecker
Centurus carolinus - red-bellied woodpecker
Melanerpes erythrocephalus - red-headed
    woodpecker
Sphyrapicus varius - yellow-bellied sapsucker
Picoides villosus - hairy woodpecker
P. pubescens - downy woodpecker
P. *borealis* - red-cockaded woodpecker
Campephilus principalis - ivory-billed woodpecker

Order Passeriformes

Family Tyrannidae

Subfamily Fluvicolinae
Sayornis phoebe - eastern phoebe
Empidonax flaviventris - yellow-bellied flycatcher
*E. virescens - Acadian flycatcher
Contopus virens - eastern wood peewee
Pyrocephalus rubinus - vermilion flycatcher

Subfamily Tyranninae

*Tyrannus tyrannus - eastern kingbird
*T. dominicensis - gray kingbird
T. verticalis - western kingbird
T. forficatus - scissor-tailed flycatcher
*Myiarchus crinitus - great crested flycatcher

Family Hirundinidae

Tachycineta bicolor - tree swallow
Riparia riparia - bank swallow
*Stelgidopteryx ruficollis - rough-winged swallow
*Hirundo rustica - barn swallow
Hirundo pyrrhonota - cliff swallow
*Progne subis - purple martin

Family Corvidae

*Cyanocitta cristata - blue jay
*Corvus brachyrhynchos - common crow
*C. ossifragus - fish crow

Family Paridae

*Parus carolinensis - Carolina chickadee

Family Sittidae

Sitta carolinensis - white-breasted nuthatch
S. canadensis - red-breasted nuthatch
*S. pusilla - brown-headed nuthatch

Family Troglodytidae

Troglodytes aedon - house wren
T. troglodytes - winter wren
Thryomanes bewickii - Bewick's wren
*Thryothorus ludovicianus - Carolina wren
*Cistothorus palustris - long-billed marsh wren
C. platensis - short-billed marsh wren

Family Certhiidae

Certhia americana - brown creeper

Family Mimidae

*Mimus polyglottos - mockingbird
*Dumetella carolinensis - catbird
*Toxostoma rufum - brown thrasher

Family Muscicapidae

Subfamily Sylviinae

*Polioptila caerulea - blue-gray gnatcatcher
Regulus satrapa - golden-crowned kinglet
R. calendula - ruby-crowned kinglet

Subfamily Turdinae

*Turdus migratorius - robin
*Hylocichla mustelina - wood thrush
Catharus guttatus - hermit thrush
C. ustulatus - Swainson's thrush
C. minimus - gray-cheeked thrush
C. fuscescens - veery
*Sialia sialis - eastern bluebird

Family Motacillidae

Anthus spinoletta - water pipit
A. spragueii - Sprague's pipit

Family Bombycillidae

Bombycilla cedrorum - cedar waxwing

Family Laniidae

*Lanius ludovicianus - loggerhead shrike

Family Sturnidae

*Sturnus vulgaris - starling

Family Vireonidae

*Vireo griseus - white-eyed vireo
*V. flavifrons - yellow-throated vireo
V. solitarius - solitary vireo
*V. olivuceus - red-eyed vireo
V. philadelphicus - Philadelpha vireo

Family Emberizidae

Subfamily Parulinae

Mniotiltu varia - black-and-white warbler
*Protonotaria citrea - prothonotary warbler
Limnothlypis swainsonii - Swainson's warbler
Helmitheros vermivorus - worm-eating warbler
Vermivora chrysoptera - golden-winged warbler
V. pinus - blue-winged warbler
V. bachmanii - Bachman's warbler
V. peregrina - Tennessee warbler
V. celata - orange-crowned warbler
*Parula americana - pamla warbler
Dendroica petechia - yellow warbler
D. magnolia - magnolia warbler
D. tigrim - Cape May warbler
D. caerulescens - black-throated blue warbler
D. coronata - Myrtle warbler

D. virens - black-throated green warbler
D. fusca - Blackbumian warbler
*D. dominica - yellow-throated warbler
D. pensylvanica - chestnut-sided warbler
D. striata - blackpoll warbler
*D. pinus - pine warbler
D. kirtlandii - Kirtland's warbler
D. discolor - prairie warbler
D. palmarum - palm warbler
Seiurus aurocapillus - ovenbird
S. noveboracensis - northern waterthrush
S. motacilla - Louisiana waterthrush
Oporornis formosus - Kentucky warbler
O. agilis - Connecticut warbler
*Geothlypis trichas - yellowthroat
*Icteria virens - yellow-breasted chat
* Wilsonia citrina - hooded warbler
W. canadensis - Canada warbler
Setophaga ruticilla - American redstart

Subfamily Thraupinae

Piranga olivacea - scarlet tanager
*P. rubra - summer tanager

Subfamily Cardinalinae

*Cardinalis cardinalis - cardinal
*Guiraca caerulea - blue grosbeak
*Passerina cyanea - indigo bunting
*P. ciris - painted bunting

Subfamily Emberizinae

*Pipilo erythrophthalmus - rufous-sided towhee
Calamospiza melanocorys - lark bunting
Passerculus sandwichensis - Savannah sparrow
Ammodramus savannarum - grasshopper sparrow
A. caudacutus - LeConte's sparrow
A. henslowii - Henslow's sparrow
Pooecetes gramineus - vesper sparrow
Chondestes grammacus - lark sparrow
*Aimophila aestivalis - Bachman's sparrow
Junco hyemalis - dark-eyed junco
Spizella passerina - chipping sparrow
*S. pusilla - field sparrow
Zonotrichia leucophrys - white-crowned sparrow
Z. albicollis - white-throated sparrow
Passerella iliaca - fox sparrow
Melospiza lincolnii - Lincoln's sparrow
M. georgiana - swamp sparrow
M. melodia - song sparrow
Calcarius lapponicus - Lapland longspur
Plectrophenux nivalis - snow bunting

Subfamily Icterhae

Dolichonyx oryzivorus - bobolink

*Sturnella magna - eastern meadowlark
S. neglecta - western meadowlark
Xanthocephalus xanthocephalus - yellow-headed blackbird
*Agelaius phoeniceus - redwinged blackbird
*Icterus spurius - orchard oriole
I. galbula - Baltimore oriole
Euphagus carolinus - rusty blackbird
*Quiscalus mexicanus - boat-tailed grackle
*Q. quiscula - common grackle
Molothrus ater - brown-headed cowbird

Family Passeridae

*Passer domesticus - house sparrow

Family Fringillidae

Subfamily Carduelinae

Coccothraustes vespertinus - evening grosbeak
Carpodacus purpureus - purple finch
Carduelis pinus - pine siskin
C. tristis - American goldfinch
Loxia curvirostra - red crossbill

Mammals[d]

Order Marsupialia

Family Didelphidae

Didelphis virginiana - opossum

Order Insectivora

Family Sorlcidae

Blarina brevicauda - short-tailed shrew
Cryptotis parva - least shrew

Family Talpidae

Scalopus aquaticus - eastern mole

Order Chiroptera

Family Vespertilionidae

Myotis austroriparius - southeastern myotis
Pipistrellus subflavus - eastern pipistrille
Eptesicus fuscus - big brown bat
Lasiurus borealis - red bat
L. seminolus - Seminole bat
L. intermedius - yellow bat

---

[d] Modified from compilation by H. N. Neuhouser and W. W. Baker.

Order Rodentia

Family Sciuridae

Sciurus carolinensis - gray squirrel
S. niger Linnaeus - fox squirrel
Glaucomys volans - southern flying squirrel

Family Geomyidae

Geomys cumberlandius - Cumberland Island pocker gopher

Family Muridae

Subfamily Sigmodontinae

Oryzomys palustris - marsh rice rat
Reithrodontomys humulis - eastern harvest mouse
Peromyscus polionotus - oldfield mouse
P. gossypinus - cotton mouse
Sigmodon hispidus - hispid cotton rat
Neotoma floridana - eastern wood rat

Subfamily Murinae

Rattus rattus - black rat
R. norvegicus - Norway rat
Mus *musculus* - house mouse

Family Mycastoridae

Myocastor coypus - nutria

Order Carnivora

Family Canidae

Urocyon cinereoargenteus - gray fox

Family Ursidae

Ursus americanus - black bear

Family Procyonidae

Procyon lotor - raccoon

Family Mustelidae

Subfamily Mustelinae

Mustela vison - mink

Subfamily Lutrinae

Lutra canadensis - river otter

Family Felidae

Lynx *rufus* - bobcat

Order Artiodactyla

Family Suidae

Sus *scrofu* - European wild boar

Family Cervidae

Dama dama - European fallow deer
Cetvus *elaphus* - red deer or European elk
Odocoileus virginianus - white-tailed deer
0. virginianus   virginianus
Alces alces - moose

Order Lagomorpha

Family Leporidae

Sylvilagus floridanus - cottontail rabbit
S. palustris - marsh rabbit

A list of current *Biological Reports* follows.

7. A Model of the Productivity of the Northern Pintail, by John D. Carlson, Jr., William R. Clark, and Erwin E. Klaas. 1993.20 pp.

a. Guidelines for the Development of Community-level Habitat Evaluation Models, by Richard L. Schroeder and Sandra L. Haire. 1993. 8 pp.

9. Thermal Stratification of Dilute Lakes-Evaluation of Regulatory Processes and Biological Effects Before and After Base Addition: Effects on Brook Trout Habitat and Growth, by Carl L. Schofield, Dan Josephson, Chris Keleher, and Steven P. Gloss. 1993.36 pp.

10. Zinc Hazards to Fishes, Wildlife, and Invertebrates: A Synoptic Review, by Ronald Eisler. 1993. 106 pp.

11. In-water Electrical Measurements for Evaluating Electrofishing Systems, by A. Lawrence Kolz. 1993.24 pp.

12. Ecology of Red Maple Swamps in the Glaciated Northeast: A Community Profile, by Francis C. Golet, Aram J. K. Calhoun, William R. DeRagon, Dennis J. Lowry, and Arthur J. Gold. 1993. 151 pp.

13. Proceedings of the Symposium on the Management of Prairie Dog Complexes for the Reintroduction of the Black-footed Ferret, edited by John L. Oldemeyer, Dean E. Biggins, Brian J. Miller and Ronald Crete. 1993. 96 pp.

14. Evaluation of Habitat Suitability Index Models for Riverine Life Stages of American Shad, with Proposed Models for Premigratory Juveniles, by Robert M. Ross, Thomas W. H. Backman, and Randy M. Bennett. 1993.26 pp.

15. In Situ Toxicity Testing with Locally Collected *Daphnia*, by Elaine Snyder-Conn. 1993.14 pp.

16. Proceedings of the Eighth American Woodcock Symposium, by Jerry R. Longcore and Greg F. Sepik. 1993. 139 pp.

17. Qualitative and Quantitative Bacteriological Studies on a Fluidized Sand Biofilter Used in a Semiclosed Trout Culture System, by G. Bullock, J. Hankins, J. Heinen, C. Starliper, and J. Teska. 1993.15 pp.

18. Habitat Suitability Index Model for Brook Trout in Streams of the Southern Blue Ridge Province: Surrogate Variables, Model Evaluation, and Suggested Improvements, by Christopher J. Schmitt, A. Dennis Lemly, and Parley V. Winger. 1993.43 pp.

19. Proceedings of the Symposium on Restoration Planning for the Rivers of the Mississippi River Ecosystem, edited by Larry W. Hesse, Clair B. Stalnaker, Norman G. Benson, and James R. Zuboy. 1994.502 pp.

20. Famphur Hazards to Fish, Wildlife, and Invertebrates: A Synoptic Review, by Ronald Eisler. 1994.23 pp.

21. Relations Between Habitat Variability and Population Dynamics of Bass in the Huron River, Michigan, by Ken D. Bovee, Tammy J. Newcomb, and Thomas G. Coon. 1994.63 pp.

22. Recreational-boating Disturbances of Natural Communities and Wildlife: An Annotated Bibliography, by Darryl York. 1994.30 pp.

23. Acrolein Hazards to Fish, Wildlife, and invertebrates: A Synoptic Review, by Ronald Eisler. 1994.29 pp.

24. Instream Flows to Assist the Recovery of Endangered Fishes of the Upper Colorado River Basin, by Jack A. Stanford. 1994.47 pp.

25. Rainbow Smelt-Larval Lake Herring Interactions: Competitors or Casual Acquaintances? by James H. Selgeby, Wayne R. MacCallum, and Michael H. Hoff. 1994.9 pp.

26. Radiation Hazards to Fish, Wildlife, and Invertebrates: A Synoptic Review, by Ronald Eisler.1994.124 pp.

27. Sodium Monofluoroacetate (1080) Hazards to Fish, Wildlife, and Invertebrates: A Synoptic Review, by Ronald Eisler. 1995.47 pp.

28. Endangered Ecosystems of the United States: A Preliminary Assessment of Loss and Degradation, by Reed F. Noss, Edward T. LaRoe III, and J. Michael Scott. 1995. 60 pp.

29. The Instream Flow Incremental Methodology-A Primer for IFIM, by Clair Stalnaker, Berton L. Lamb, Jim Henriksen, Ken Bovee, and John Bartholow. 1995.45 pp.